The Manual of
Museum Management

The Manual of Museum Management

Gail Dexter Lord and Barry Lord

SECOND EDITION

A Division of
ROWMAN & LITTLEFIELD PUBLISHERS, INC.
Lanham • New York • Toronto • Plymouth, UK

AltaMira Press
A division of Rowman & Littlefield Publishers, Inc.
A wholly owned subsidiary of The Rowman & Littlefield Publishing Group, Inc.
4501 Forbes Boulevard, Suite 200
Lanham, MD 20706
www.altamirapress.com

Estover Road
Plymouth PL6 7PY
United Kingdom

British Library Cataloguing in Publication Information Available

Library of Congress Cataloging-in-Publication Data

Lord, Gail Dexter, 1946–
    The manual of museum management / Gail Dexter Lord and Barry Lord. —
2nd ed.
        p. cm.
    Includes index.
    ISBN-13: 978-0-7591-1197-4 (cloth : alk. paper)
    ISBN-10: 0-7591-1197-9 (cloth : alk. paper)
    ISBN-13: 978-0-7591-1198-1 (pbk. : alk. paper)
    ISBN-10: 0-7591-1198-7 (pbk. : alk. paper)
    [etc.]
    1. Museums—Planning—Handbooks, manuals, etc. 2. Museums—
Management—Handbooks, manuals, etc. I. Lord, Barry. II. Title.
    AM121.L66 2008
    069'.5—dc22   2008048229

Printed in the United States of America

♾™ The paper used in this publication meets the minimum requirements of
American National Standard for Information Sciences—Permanence of Paper for
Printed Library Materials, ANSI/NISO Z39.48–1992.

Contents

List of Case Studies

List of Figures

List of Tables

profit global health service based in Boston, Paris, and Pretoria, funded by the Bill and Melinda Gates Foundation. David has received numerous awards for his work and lives in Boston and Paris with his wife, Aurelie, and three sons.

Eleanor Goldhar, Laura Miller, Ashley Prymas, and **Francesca Merlino** constitute the Solomon R. Guggenheim Foundation external affairs marketing team. Eleanor Goldhar is deputy director for external affairs, a communications and marketing executive with experience in museums, cultural and performing arts agencies, and commercial theater in Canada, the United States, and Great Britain, and is responsible at the Foundation for branding and global communications initiatives of the Guggenheim museum network. Laura Miller, an MBA from Columbia University, is the Foundation's marketing director, with over twenty years of marketing and business development experience in for-profit and nonprofit museum environments, also serving as an adjunct professor at New York University's Steinhardt School, where she co-teaches a course on marketing the arts, and as a member of the National Arts Marketing Program Steering Committee. Ashley Prymas, with a master's in arts administration from New York University, is the Foundation's marketing manager and in that capacity directs the strategic marketing for a number of Guggenheim programs, including the First Fridays series and online marketing. Marketing associate Francesca Merlino, a graduate of Fordham University's College of Business Administration, where she consulted with the International Service Learning program connecting students with small third-world businesses using fair trade and microfinancing, develops co-op promotions, e-mail campaigns, and social networking initiatives for the Foundation.

Willis E. (Buzz) Hartshorn was appointed director of the International Center for Photography in New York in 1994, having joined the ICP in 1982, where he served in previous positions as traveling exhibitions coordinator, director of exhibitions, and deputy director for programs. A graduate of the University of Rochester with a master of fine arts degree in photographic studies from the Visual Studies Workshop in that city, he began his career there and as a curatorial assistant at the International Museum of Photography at George Eastman House in Rochester. Having received two National Endowment for the Arts photography fellowships, he has exhibited his own photographs widely since 1973 and has curated major exhibitions for the ICP on such subjects as Czech modernism and the photographs of Man Ray. He has taught at all levels of the ICP education program for over a decade, has served on the board of the Museum Association of New York, and is an active member of the Association of Art Museum Directors.

Amy Kaufman is the U.S. director for Lord Cultural Resources, providing consulting and management services throughout the United States from her New York office. A graduate of Tulane University in New Orleans, she initially managed a commercial gallery in that city before undertaking graduate work at New York University. Amy was director of visitor services for the Solomon R. Guggenheim Museum in New York at the time she describes in her case study. Before returning to New York, during her first several years with Lord Cultural Resources, she supervised the planning, creation, and management of Constitution Hill, the historic site in the former jail in Johannesburg, South Africa, that had counted both Mahatma Gandhi and Nelson Mandela among its prisoners. In recent years she has actively planned audience development and operations for institutions ranging from art museums to heritage sites to botanical gardens.

Barry Lord is cofounder and copresident of Lord Cultural Resources, the world's largest company specialized in the planning and management of cultural institutions. Born in Hamilton, Ontario, he graduated from McMaster University there, and went on to graduate work at Harvard University, by which time he had started his museum career as a summer assistant at the National Gallery of Canada in Ottawa. After taking the National Gallery's Museum Training Course, Barry served as assistant curator at the Vancouver Art Gallery and as curator of art at the New Brunswick Museum in Saint John before becoming editor of *artscanada*, the nation's leading art magazine. Barry subsequently returned to the National Gallery as head of education services and later served the National Museums Corporation in Ottawa as assistant director of the Museum Assistance Programs. Having taught art history at several Canadian universities, Barry has more recently lectured and led seminars on museum planning and management at universities and museums around the world. He and his wife, Gail, founded Lord Cultural Resources in 1981, and he has subsequently led hundreds of museum planning projects throughout North America, Europe, Asia, and Australia. A well-known art historian and critic and author of *The History of Painting in Canada* (1974), he is best known today as coauthor and editor with Gail of *Planning Our Museums/La Planification de Musées* (1983) and of the series of museum manuals that includes the present volume, *The Manual of Museum Management*, second edition, the first edition of which was published in 1997, as well as *The Manual of Museum Planning* (1st ed., 1991, 2nd ed. 1999), *The Manual of Museum Exhibitions* (2002), and *The Manual of Museum Learning* (2007).

Gail Dexter Lord is cofounder and copresident with her husband, Barry, of Lord Cultural Resources. A graduate in history from the University of

Toronto, Gail was an art critic for the *Toronto Star*, and taught art history at Ryerson University in that city. In 1983 Gail and Barry edited *Planning Our Museums* (National Museums of Canada), which was the world's first book on the subject of museum planning. Since then she has established an outstanding reputation not only as one of the world's leading museum planners, but also as one of the leading thinkers about museums and culture. Having lectured in cultural management at the University of Victoria and in many other venues, she is now invited to speak at major museum conferences around the world. Gail directed hundreds of planning and management projects for museums both large and small in North America, Europe, and Asia. In 1989 she and Barry were coauthors with John Nicks of *The Cost of Collecting*. One of a number of new museums she has helped to bring into existence is the Museum of the African Diaspora in San Francisco, which is the subject of Janera Solomon's case study in this book. Gail also led the Lord Cultural Resources contribution to the much larger National Museum of African American History and Culture, planned as part of the Smithsonian Institution for the National Mall in Washington, D.C. Having written and edited the museum manual series with Barry, in 2007 Gail joined Kate Markert as coauthor of *The Manual of Strategic Planning for Museums*. With Barry, she is coauthor of both the first edition of this book (1997) and this second edition.

David Loye is a certified general accountant (CGA) who joined the Canadian Museum of Civilization in Gatineau, Quebec, in 1990. During his time with the museum, David has occupied the position of chief of financial planning, followed by an appointment as the corporation's first chief financial officer. In 2007 he accepted the position of chief operating officer of the corporation. Prior to joining the museum, he held various financial management positions within the government of Canada.

Kate Markert is the associate director of the Walters Art Museum in Baltimore, where she oversees the finance, development, operations, and marketing divisions of the museum. She works closely with the board to ensure the efficiency and effectiveness of its governance structure and process. Kate was director of the Wadsworth Atheneum Museum of Art in Hartford, Connecticut from 2000 to 2003, and deputy director and acting director of the Cleveland Museum of Art from 1995 to 2000. She has a master of arts in art history and a master of business administration. In 2007 Kate was coauthor with Gail Dexter Lord of *The Manual of Strategic Planning for Museums*. As associate director at the Walters, she has been directly involved in the transition to free admission that she describes in her case study.

Janera Solomon serves as principal of j.a.solomon & partners in Pittsburgh. She has been actively involved in cultural development in that city and in Philadelphia, where she served as director of a major annual arts festival. Coming from a family rooted in the Caribbean steel drums tradition, Janera has a strong musical background. At the time she describes in her case study, Janera was working with Lord Cultural Resources on the planning of the Museum of the African Diaspora in San Francisco. An expert facilitator (as the case study shows), Janera works with her clients to reach consensus and develop innovative programs that effectively meet the collective's mission, vision and objectives.

Peter Wilson is an associate consultant of Lord Cultural Resources in the United Kingdom. After a museum career of more than three decades at Tate he became, in 2005, the project director for the Royal Shakespeare Company's transformation of their theaters at Stratford-on-Avon and now undertakes occasional museum consultancy by arrangement with the RSC. Peter has an MA in natural sciences from Cambridge University and a diploma in conservation, for which he trained at Tate, the Courtauld Institute, and under Garry Thompson at the National Gallery Scientific Department in London. His long career at Tate began in the Conservation Department in 1972 and embraced Collections Management and Operational Management. He was their director of projects and estates from 1990 to 2005, acting as formal client for a series of construction projects, including the Clore Gallery of the Turner Collection (1987), Tate St. Ives (1993), Tate's Collections Centre (1992 onward), Tate Liverpool Phase 2 (1998), Tate Modern (2000), Tate Britain Centenary Development (2001), and the Hyman Kreitman Research Centre for Tate's Library & Archive (2004).

- Spread of museums: The idea of the museum, combining the preservation of national or local heritage with the opportunity to participate in the global culture of loan exhibitions, has been taken up even more widely than ever before, most recently among the Gulf Emirates but also throughout East, South, and Southeast Asia.
- Valorizing global brands: Museum managers at major institutions especially have come to recognize that their international reputation as a source of cultural capital means that they have, in effect, global "brands" that can be effectively utilized both at home and abroad.
- The importance of leadership: Over the past decade or more there has been a growing awareness that management (which may be termed "doing the thing right") is effective only if the museum also has strong leadership ("doing the right thing"). Although this distinction was observed in the first edition, it has become progressively more important in the intervening years.
- Civil society institutions: Most subtly, but also most profoundly, the status of museums in society has been altered by the continuing success of the museum as a public institution. As civil society institutions, museums derive funding from multiple sources, public and private, and are accountable to an ever-broader public for effective management of the art, science, or heritage resources they preserve and display.

In the preface to the original edition in 1997, we wrote: "In the past few decades especially, the pace of change in philosophy, in technology, in funding and in public expectations has required those responsible for museums to adapt rapidly and continuously, while attempting to hold fast the museum's fundamental objectives." How much truer that is today, as the foregoing list of significant changes in the environment of museum management attests.

Despite these changes—and at the same time, because of them—the fundamental issues of museum management remain the challenges that all those concerned with these institutions must master. Indeed, maintaining museum management fundamentals while responding to the new conditions has become critical. This second edition of the *Manual of Museum Management* therefore acknowledges the effects of these changes throughout the content of this volume, but in doing so preserves the classic organization of the first edition in the way that the issues are presented:

- We begin in chapter 1 with the question "Why?" Why do we need museum management, and what is its appropriate role?
- We then turn in chapter 2 to the people who animate museums and the structure of museum organization (the "Who" of museum management).

- Finally, in chapter 3, we examine the tools available to museum leadership—the "How" of museum management.

This second edition of the *Manual of Museum Management*, like the first, is for all those involved or interested in the challenge of managing and leading museums in the twenty-first century:

- those inside museums—museum management and staff, trustees, volunteers, and committee members;
- those outside museums but concerned with them, such as academic administrators, government and foundation staff, personnel at other agencies responsible for museums or the funding for them, exhibition designers, security companies, and other museum service providers;
- and, perhaps most important, teachers and their students in museum studies and related programs in universities and colleges around the world who will manage the museums of the near future.

A special effort was made in the first edition, and has been redoubled in this one, to ensure that the text is as useful to one-person museums as it is to those working in major institutions around the world.

Particularly important in a book of this kind are the case studies, which in some instances illustrate a point, but often go beyond the main body of the text to advance the argument in creative and exciting directions that are currently being opened up. Accordingly, this second edition has all new case studies that illuminate the world of museum management as it appears around the end of the first decade of the twenty-first century and point toward possibilities for at least the half-century ahead. Taken together, these new case studies alone show the need for a new edition of this now classic text. As before, we hope that this completely revised edition, and the new case studies in it, will help to guide the way to still better museums.

Acknowledgments

Originally issued by The Stationery Office in London, the *Manual of Museum Management* has subsequently been published in the United States by AltaMira Press as part of the series of manuals on museum practice written and edited by Gail and Barry Lord. Although the text of some of the other manuals is composed of contributions from a range of authors, both the first and this second edition of the *Manual of Museum Management* have been written, except for the case studies, entirely by Gail and Barry.

Their text had its origins in a certificate course on museum organization and management that the authors had prepared many years ago for the Ontario Museums Association. The course and its text travelled with the Lords and evolved through seminars, courses, and presentations they made to museum professionals—including Museums Association seminars in London, the museum training program at the *Niederoesterreichisches Landesakademie* in Austria, the Cultural Resources Management program at the University of Victoria in Canada, museum training seminars at the Urban Training School in Hong Kong, a course for Southeast Asian museum professionals at the Singapore Philatelic Museum (which Lord Cultural Resources had planned), and an intensive three-day seminar on museum management in Belgrade. The authors extend their appreciation to the many students and colleagues whose questions, challenges, and insights continually stimulated the development of the course and eventually the content of this manual over the years.

Still more than the first, this second edition also reflects the Lords' continuing international experience in the management of museums large and small in their role as consultants to museum professionals and trustees in over forty countries around the world. Grateful acknowledgment is therefore due to their clients and colleagues for their creativity, resourcefulness, and professionalism, which it is hoped this volume sufficiently reflects.

Special thanks are due to the authors of the case studies, all of which are new to this edition. They focus the general points made in the text on best contemporary practice, and in many ways they bring the book to life and point it in the direction of current developments. These authors, who are described in the list of contributors, have all taken time from their own busy professional careers to compose lively and cogent adjuncts to this new edition. Thanks are also due to the photographers for the illustrations in the case studies, which

Figure 1.1. The Purpose of Management

FACILITATE
DECISIONS

This understanding of the purpose of museum management implies the first, very simple but effective means of *evaluation* of museum management:

> *1. Is the museum's management facilitating decisions that lead to the achievement of its mission, mandate, goals and objectives for all of its functions?*

If so, management is doing its job. If not, changes are needed. And, since life is almost always a matter of degree, the quality of management may be evaluated by the *extent* to which it facilitates decisions that lead to the achievement of the museum's mission, mandate, goals and objectives in fulfillment of the museum's functions.

1.2 FOUNDATION STATEMENTS

Museums are not the buildings that house them, nor even the collections they protect—important as these are. Museums are complex cultural institutions uniquely concerned both with collecting and preserving the material cultural heritage and at the same time *communicating its meaning*—whether that meaning arises from works of art, archaeological and historical artifacts, or scientific specimens. The social and even political dimensions of the communication of meaning result in an institution that combines those aspects with the "hardware" functions of housing and caring for a collection.

The purpose of a particular museum is expressed in terms of its:

- mission;
- mandate;
- goals; and
- objectives.

Collectively, these are called foundation statements. *Mission: The mission statement of a cultural institution is an objective, brief, and hopefully inspiring assertion of its raison d'etre, or relevance.* It should answer the question, "Why should people care about this museum?" The mission statement directs our sights toward the long-range reason for the museum's existence. It is the foundation of all policy development. An example might be:

> *"The mission of the County Museum is to preserve and communicate to residents and visitors the history and creative spirit of those who have lived here from the beginning of human habitation."*

> *Mandate: The mandate of a cultural institution is the range of material culture for which it assumes responsibility.* This may be stated in terms of:

- an academic discipline;
- geographical range;
- chronological range;
- specialization; and
- the relationships of the mandate to other institutions concerned with the same subject.

An example of a mandate statement, which distinguishes our exemplar county museum from another institution, might be:

> *"The mandate of the County Museum is the archaeology, history, and fine and decorative art of the inhabitants of what is now our county from the first human occupation of the area to the present day; the natural history of the county is the mandate of the University Museum, and will therefore be included in County Museum exhibits only to the extent necessary to support the human history displays."*

The mandate statement not only locates the museum's mission in the objective world of public responsibilities, but also lays the foundation for the museum's relations with other institutions—governmental, educational, and private sector—as well as with other museums.

Goals: The terms *goals* and *objectives* are often used inversely—some see objectives as broader and goals as more specific, whereas others, as we do in this book, see goals as broader, while objectives are more particular to a given time period or budget. If the opposite usage of words is employed, the effect is the same.

In our usage, therefore, *the goals of a museum may be defined as the long-range qualitative levels of collection development, collection care, and visitor service toward which the institution is striving.* They may be articulated for a given period of the museum's development in a strategic plan or in a master plan. Achieving them may take years.

Objectives: By contrast, in our usage *a museum's objectives may be described as short-range, quantified expressions of particular steps on the way to the longer-range goals.* Such objectives are placed on a timetable or schedule for fulfillment, and they are usually specific to a one-year or two-year planning period. They may be articulated as part of a one-year plan of action or as part of a budget exercise. Again, if the opposite usage is preferred, with objectives as the longer-range qualitative levels and goals as the shorter-range quantified targets, the effect is the same—both apply the mission and mandate to specific museum functions.

Functions: In defining its mission, mandate, objectives, and goals, it is important for a museum to focus these on museum functions. There are six main museum functions that taken together define what is unique about museums. Three are related to the museum's assets, the other three to its activities (see table 1.1).

A seventh function, pulling the other six together (although not unique to museums), is *administration.* The relationship of all seven may be seen as a triangle, with the functions affecting assets grouped to one side, those representing activities along the other, and administration endeavouring to reconcile these two dimensions (see figure 1.2).

Please note that the fact that administration is an overarching, coordinating function does *not* imply that it is superior to or controlling the other functions. The downward-pointing triangle in figure 1.2 is intended to indicate not a decline, but a forward motion in realizing the museum's functions more fully as the institution develops. The triangle is an appropriate image for museum functions because (a) it is an inherently strong structural form, and (b) it points to or suggests movement in a particular direction.

Yet at the same time, the inherent divergence of the two functions—assets-based and activity-related—is made clear. As many have observed, the best way to achieve the assets functions—collecting, documenting, and preserving the collections—would be to keep the museum's collections in a dark, locked room, whereas the most effective way to realize the activities functions of research, display, and interpretation would be to make them as publicly accessible as possible. *There is an inherent tension of contradiction between the two main groups of museum functions.*

Table 1.1. Museum Functions

Assets	Activities
Collecting	Research
Documentation	Display
Preservation	Interpretation

Figure 1.2. The Triangle of Museum Functions

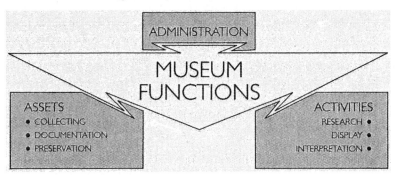

The key role of administration in transforming this divergence into a creative rather than disabling tension is also indicated by the triangle diagram. That role is described in section 1.3, with this triangle diagram returning to our composite management diagram to take its rightful place at the conclusion of the chapter.

1.3 THE ROLES OF MANAGEMENT IN MUSEUMS

In order for museum management to facilitate the achievement of mission, mandate, goals, and objectives, it must be adept at playing not one but five roles:

- to *inspire* with a sense of the museum's *mission*;
- to *communicate* the museum's *mandate*;
- to *lead* toward the museum's *goals*;
- to *control* the attainment of *objectives*; and
- to *evaluate* the fulfillment of museum *functions* in *outcomes*.

We can all identify with the fact that most managers cannot perform all five roles equally well. Yet understanding each of these roles in museum terms can help museum managers build on their strengths and identify and strengthen those roles in which they may be weak. The diagram we are developing in this chapter illustrates how these roles are mutually supportive.

1.3.1 To Inspire with a Sense of Mission

A former director of the Corning Museum of Glass once told us, "My mission is to get people excited about glass." And because he was himself excited about glass, he was able to do so very well. A good museum manager has a clear sense of the museum's mission and inspires others to join in the fulfillment of that mission. This sense of mission is a well of creativity from which the manager derives original solutions to problems, redirects struggling staff toward the essential objectives, or sets challenges that lead the museum on to greater accomplishments. The manager's comprehension of the mission must be so infectious that people who meet him or her (from staff and volunteers to donors, visitors, and the general public) want to get involved. The manager (or director) must believe in the mission: it must matter emotionally, as well as intellectually, to him or her.

This role of management suggests a second criterion for the evaluation of museum management:

> *2. Does management inspire staff, volunteers, supporters, visitors, and others with a sense of the museum's mission?*

If inspiration is not forthcoming, it may be a weakness of management, or it may be that the mission is out of date or has become irrelevant or less significant in the twenty-first century. If this is the case, management should set about to work with the museum's governing body to review and revise the mission statement. It is surprising how frequently trustees meeting to discuss the museum's mission discover divergent views despite their prior confidence that everyone shares a common sense of purpose. Generally, major revisions to the mission statement are undertaken only as part of a strategic planning process, as described in chapter 3, and as detailed in *The Manual of Strategic Planning for Museums* by Gail Lord and Kate Markert (2007).

Getting the mission right may take time, but it is essential to the long-range direction of the institution because the mission is the core around which *policies* should be formed. Without a fully understood and relevant mission, policies remain an empty form. However, when they are supportive of an agreed-upon mission, policies can more effectively be directed toward a common end.

1.3.2 To Communicate the Mandate

A museum manager must understand the mandate of the institution and be able to communicate it to others, both within the museum and beyond its walls. He or she must be aware of the extent and limitations of that mandate and also of its relationship with the mandates of other institutions. By exercising the mandate consciously, the manager (or director) and the museum may be said to be "communicating" the mandate clearly to visitors, funders, and the museum's own governing body and staff.

Figure 1.3. The Roles of Management: Mission and Policies

If a museum is not fulfilling its mandate, and if that mandate is of real interest and concern to others, then another institution—a new museum or an existing museum or related institution—may compete for or fulfill that mandate. Usually it is not a question of a complete replacement, but of a gradual encroachment from other institutions expanding their field of activity. If, for example, a museum of Asian art is not very active in exhibiting or collecting contemporary Asian art, then a museum of contemporary art in the same city may expand into that field, and effectively usurp the Asian art museum's mandate, leading to competition for collections and exhibitions. "Use it or lose it" applies to mandate.

On the other hand, lack of clarity about the museum's mandate can also lead the institution to distractions that interfere with the accomplishment of the museum's purposes. It may, for example, be tempting for the County History Museum to offer an exhibition on dinosaurs because of their popularity, even though there were never any such creatures in what is now that county. This exhibition might be admissible as part of a temporary program of "Opening a Window on the World," but if such exhibitions become a major activity, absorbing the energies of staff while the permanent collection of archaeological and historical artifacts is neglected, then the museum is losing sight of its mandate.

Figure 1.4. The Role of Management: Communicating the Mandate

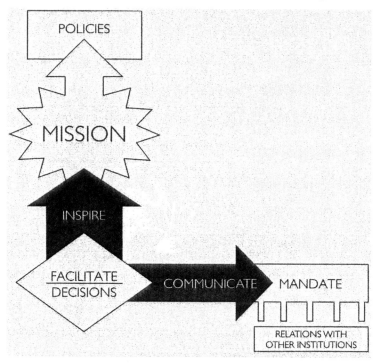

A third criterion of effective museum management could therefore be phrased as follows:

3. Are both the extent and the limitations of the museum's mandate understood? Are they being fully exercised and clearly communicated both within the museum and outside? Do the museum's relations with other institutions—governmental, educational, and private sector, as well as other museums—reflect a clear and complete understanding of this mandate?

1.3.3 To Lead toward Goals

Management and leadership are related, but are not identical. It is often said that management is about "doing it right," while leadership is "doing the right thing." A leader is constantly aware of the institution's goals and, therefore, is able to guide others toward their achievement.

For example, once it has been decided that one of the goals of the museum's documentation program is the conversion of all of its records to an electronic form with an image of every object, it will require leadership as well as good management to steer toward that goal and to dedicate the necessary staff and resources to its achievement despite the many other demands on time, funds, and facilities. It will also require leadership to balance the dedication to that goal with the requirements of a temporary exhibition program that also needs attention from the same registrar who is responsible for the documentation conversion project. Or consider the leadership needed to achieve the management goal of diversifying the museum's staff over a period of many years.

Long-range institutional goals should be identified in plans such as strategic plans or master plans that link those goals to the museum's mission (and therefore to its policies) and mandate.

Leadership is the fourth criterion for good management:

4. Is management effectively leading the museum toward long-range goals articulated in plans that are consistent with the museum's mission, policies, and mandate?

As noted in the preface to this edition, the importance of strong leadership has become increasingly apparent in the museum field in recent years. Partly because of the popular success of museums, partly for the opposite reason of the decrease in public funding for museums in many jurisdictions, leadership is needed more than ever to balance the myriad demands on institutions, and to keep them on the path to fulfilling their missions, mandates, goals, and

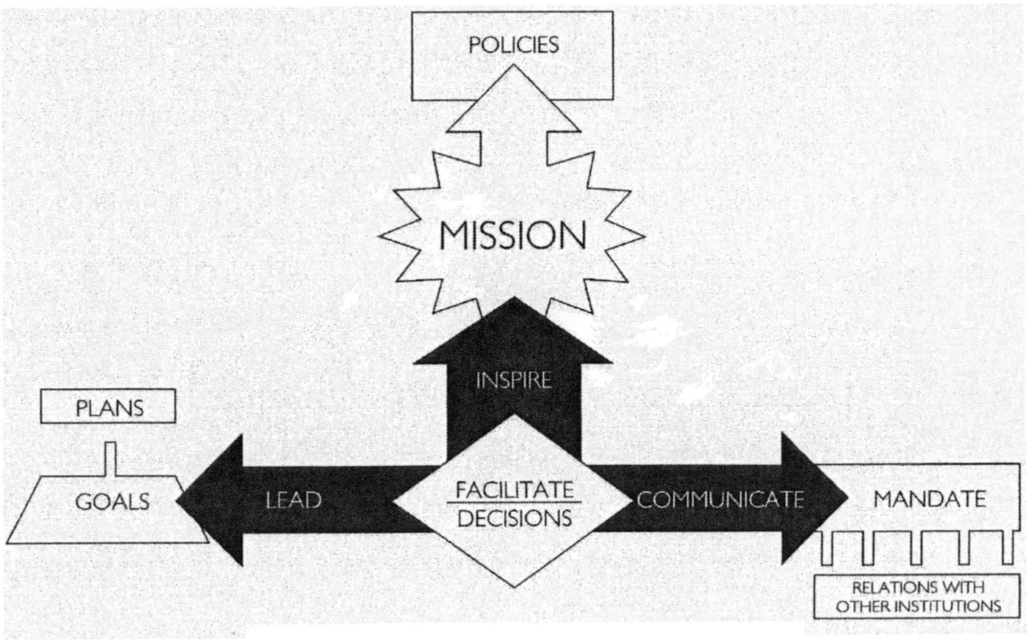

Figure 1.5. The Role of Management: Leading Toward Goals

objectives. However intangible, inspired leadership is an indispensable factor in the successful management of museums more than ever today.

1.3.4 To Control the Attainment of Objectives

To achieve the broad institutional goals articulated in the museum's plans, management must break them down into short-range, measurable objectives that, taken together, will lead to the qualitative change that is expressed in the goals. Management is then responsible for assigning resources needed to achieve these objectives and to make sure they are accomplished on schedule and on budget.

Monitoring the *budget* (a plan with costs and revenues attached) and the *schedule* (a plan with a calendar attached)—ensuring that resources of time and money are utilized in accordance with the allocations—is one of the key functions of management. This is essentially the *control* function of management.

This controlling role of management suggests a fifth evaluation criterion:

5. Are long-range goals being translated into short-range measurable objectives? Is the attainment of annual objectives controlled by the monitoring of the budget and other resource allocation plans? Is this attainment on schedule?

Figure 1.6. The Role of Management: Control to Achieve Objectives

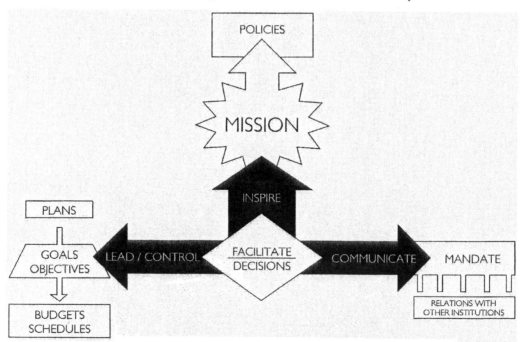

1.3.5 To Evaluate the Fulfillment and Impact of Museum Functions

The achievement of a museum's mission, the accomplishment of its mandate, and even the attainment of short-term objectives en route to long-range goals are valuable to the museum only if all of these are related to the specific functions of a museum—the six functions ranged along the two diverging sides of the triangle in figure 1.2. An important role of management, therefore, is to evaluate the fulfillment of these functions. How well is the museum collecting, documenting, and preserving its collection (its assets)? And how well is it studying, displaying, and interpreting that collection to the public (its activities)? This management role, which is not merely a passive recording but an active evaluative intervention, may be referred to as *administration*.

The evaluation of the six specifically museological functions of collecting, documentation, preservation, research, display, and interpretation or education, and the evaluation of administration itself, should be made in terms of both *effectiveness* and *efficiency*:

- *Effectiveness* measures the extent to which the museum's efforts achieve the intended result, which should have been quantified as far as possible in the work plan for that function.
- *Efficiency* measures that effect in relation to the effort required—in person-hours, in money, in space (which is often at a premium in museums), or in the use of facilities or equipment. The term "*cost-effectiveness*" is sometimes used to describe efficiency measured in financial terms; "person-effectiveness" and "space-effectiveness" would be equally useful concepts, but all three are really measures of efficiency.

Accurate and sensitive evaluation of the fulfillment of museological functions is a sixth measure of the success of museum management:

> 6. Is management actively evaluating both the effectiveness and the efficiency of the museum's fulfillment of its functions, and utilizing these evaluations to facilitate their fulfillment?

In recent years, as museums have become more aligned as "civil society" institutions with diverse funding sources throughout the community, funders, and donors both public and private are challenging the idea that museums should be evaluated only in terms of their fulfillment of their own professional functions. There is a strong trend to evaluate museums in terms of the *outcomes* they achieve for society as a whole. In the United Kingdom this has been seen as evaluation according to such criteria as "social inclusion," while in the United States there has been a move to evaluate museum programs and collections in terms of the diversity they represent or serve. In either case the focus is on evaluation by societal *outcomes*, which have been advanced by some philanthropic foundations as well as by governments.

Figure 1.7 has been built from all the figures discussed in this chapter. It illustrates the five roles of management in relation to museum functions and policies. And at the very heart of the diagram is the reminder that the purpose of management is to make it easier (for it will never be easy!) for people who work and volunteer in museums to do their jobs—which is the subject of chapter 2.

Figure 1.7. Summary of Museum Management

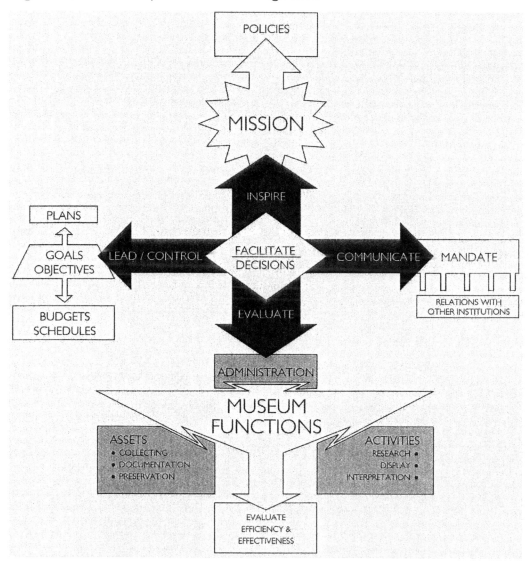

WHO
The Structure of Museum Organization

Museums are governed, managed, and operated by people: they are inherently social institutions in which people work together to achieve and sustain the mission, mandate, goals, and objectives. Who these people are and how they work together are the subjects of this chapter. We consider first the alternate modes of museum governance and then the three fundamental roles that people perform in the governance, management, and operation of museums:

- trustees (2.2);
- staff (2.3); and
- volunteers (2.4).

We then end this chapter (section 2.5) with a twenty-first-century update on the changing roles of all three groups in the civil society institutions that museums are becoming.

2.1   MODES OF GOVERNANCE

The governing body of a museum assumes the ultimate legal and financial responsibility for it. Despite the wide variety of circumstances in which museums around the world have been established, there are only four principal modes of governance:

- line departments (2.1.1);
- arm's-length institutions (2.1.2);
- nonprofit or charitable organizations (2.1.3); and
- private ownership (2.1.4).

Those involved in establishing a new museum should carefully consider which mode of governance will best meet the long-term needs of the institution. And those responsible for existing museums should also review governance issues, because what was a suitable form of governance fifty years ago may no longer be appropriate. In the early twenty-first century societal trends toward decentralization and privatization are sometimes reflected in the tendency to change the governance of museums that were once part of government agencies or public authorities to the nonprofit or charitable sector. More broadly, museums are now very often conceived as "civil society" institutions with mixed public and private funding, but with accountability both fiscal and moral to the public at large. The process of reviewing and possibly changing a museum's governance is called *institutional planning*.

This section outlines the characteristics, advantages, and disadvantages of each of the four modes of governance and concludes with table 2.1, which summarizes all four.

2.1.1 Line Departments

National, state, provincial, county, and local authority museums and galleries are often part of the cultural departments of the relevant level of government. This is equally true of specialized museums in their respective departments: a postal museum, for example, may be part of a national postal or telecommunications service; a geology museum may be part of a university's geology department; and an automotive museum may be established within the public relations department of a car manufacturer. These are all examples of *line department museums*.

Line department museums form part of a government, university, or corporation department. Their employees are civil servants if the museum is a government line department, or employees of the university or corporation that operates the museum. The director of a government line department museum may be appointed by the departmental administration or may be recruited through the civil service process; directors of university or corporate line department museums, and of some government museums, may be engaged in the same way as other departmental administrators. In any case, the governance of the line department museum is integrated with that of the larger body.

Line department museums are funded primarily through allocations from the budget of the governing organization. This is usually not grant-aid, but a line item in the department budget. Some line department museums are therefore free of charge, while others charge admission and raise additional revenue in other ways, but all have a central allocation from their governing body to sustain them. The collection and the buildings of line department museums are often owned by the parent body.

Many government line department museums around the world share a common problem in the disposition of their earned revenues, which typically go to a central government finance department and do not benefit the institution directly. As a result, many of these museums have little incentive to provide retail or food services of good quality, and their shops and cafes sometimes reflect this. Amending this accounting principle so that line department museums can keep their earnings has resulted in vast improvements in food services, retailing, and service in many national museums.

Since they are part of a larger departmental body, most line department museums do not have a membership organization. Some have recruited "friends" groups both as a means of retaining earned income and of obtaining financial support. Volunteers are also often more difficult to recruit in a line department museum because of the perception that everything is being done by paid staff.

If a line department museum has a board, it will be an *advisory board* without governing authority. This advisory group (sometimes called a *visiting committee*) typically reports to the political authority, in the case of government line department museums, or to the university or corporation president in other instances. Members of such boards or committees are usually said to represent the public or academic interest in the museum, although some may also be appointed to represent concerned interest groups. In some instances the advisory board or visiting committee may advise the department administration or the president of the university or corporation on the selection of the director. But in any case the trustees are advisory only, having neither decision-making authority nor that responsibility.

Many governments—national, state, provincial, county, or municipal—operate museum systems in which several museums are grouped together to form a *museum service*. These associations of multiple museums are cost-effective for their administrations due to the centralization of at least some functions. The constituent museums may share their governing authority's accounting, personnel, maintenance, security, or other services, adding only the curatorial and programming staff that are unique to each museum. Many museum services have found it cost-effective to centralize conservation and documentation functions for all participating institutions, and in some cases to erect or renovate nonpublic collection stores and laboratories in one central location. The disadvantages of such services for the participating museums can be loss of independence and difficulty in maintaining a distinct identity and public image, which may affect fundraising, but if well-managed they can be both efficient and effective in providing a wide range of museum experiences for residents and visitors throughout the jurisdiction of the presiding government.

2.1.2 Arm's-Length Institutions

Although many levels of government, universities, and corporations are content to operate their museums as line departments, some have discovered advantages to establishing (or reestablishing) them as *arm's-length institutions*. "Arm's length" refers to the distance between head and hand, which appears to allow the hand a certain degree of autonomy, although it is ultimately controlled by the head. The arm's-length approach is intended to ensure that the museum is independent of partisan politics or corporate interest, and to encourage the institution to find additional means of support besides government, university, or corporate funds.

To continue the metaphor, the "arm's length" may be the distance from wrist to shoulder, or merely from elbow to shoulder, and institutional planning may consider whether the "distance" is sufficient or excessive. In our consulting practice we have sometimes recommended greater autonomy, but in other situations have suggested that the government concerned should take a more active role, in order to ensure adequate support for the institution.

Arm's-length museums differ from line department museums in that they normally have a *governing board* appointed by the senior political authority within that jurisdiction or by the president of the university or corporation. The government department, university, or corporation is usually represented on this board, along with representatives of concerned interest groups and/or the general public. This governing board is not merely advisory but actually determines policy and long-range plans and engages the museum's director. In museums at arm's length from government such a governing board is said to hold its responsibility for the museum as a *public trust*.

Museum staff may either be considered civil servants or employees of the university or corporation, or else they may be employed directly by the museum at arm's length. The collection and/or the land and buildings of a museum at arm's length may be owned by either the government department or the museum itself. Owing to a heightened perception of their autonomy, arm's length museums are sometimes more successful in attracting donations of both funds and objects for the collection than line department museums. Volunteers may also be more likely to support an arm's-length museum than a line department institution.

Government funding for museums at arm's length may be an annual allocation (as in line department museums), but it often takes the form of an annual dedicated grant rather than a departmental allocation. The amount of this annual grant is typically determined from year to year, thus making the arm's-length institution less certain of its annual budget levels than the line department museum. On the other hand, the arm's-length museum is usually entirely free to raise additional nongovernmental funds or even to attract grants from other levels or departments of government. Museums at arm's length typically do not have the line department museum's problem of their earned revenues going to a general government finance department, but are able to access both government and earned revenues freely for their own benefit—an advantage that is usually made evident in better-quality cafes and shops.

2.1.3 Nonprofit or Charitable Organizations

The term *nonprofit* refers to a legal status that in many countries exempts the relevant institution from some or all taxes. In Britain the term is *non-profitmaking*, and technically *not-for-profit* is the most accurate description. For our purposes we may use the terms interchangeably. The legal status that they indicate may also be described as a "charitable" or "educational" institution. The key legal requirement is that revenues in excess of expenses go toward charitable or educational purposes, not for profit. In the United States, such institutions qualify under section 501(c)3 of the Internal Revenue Code, and so are sometimes referred to simply as "501(c)3s."

The boards of museums incorporated as *nonprofit or charitable organizations* are governing, not merely advisory bodies. The board may be self-perpetuating or elected from the membership of the organization, or it may consist of both appointed and elected members. Whatever its specific form or size, the board collectively assumes legal and financial responsibility for the museum, subject to the laws governing this type of organization in each country.

Previously it was common for such museums to have constituent memberships, with the board as an executive body of the members, elected at an annual general meeting. Today, however, membership is usually just a program operated by the museum, with a separate set of bylaws governing the board's methods of recruitment and replacement of trustees. Membership programs are maintained as means of ensuring public support and achieving the museum's societal mission, as well as a minor revenue source.

To achieve charitable or nonprofit status, the museum organization will usually have applied for and obtained registration, letters patent, or a charitable tax number allowing it to provide tax-deductible receipts for donations and to receive other benefits allowed by government policy in each jurisdiction. Consequently, the museum organization must comply with a broad range of government regulations in order to maintain that status. For example, it may be necessary to establish a separate corporation to operate retail or catering, since the nonprofit museum itself may not be allowed to operate these directly. In the United States in recent years there has been a tightening of restrictions on what revenue-producing activities the museum may undertake, requiring that these must be directly related to the purpose of the institution: thus a museum may sell goods in its shop tax-free if they are related to its mandate, but must pay tax on the sale of goods that are deemed to be unrelated, resulting in the need to keep separate sales records for the two categories of stock.

- In Antalya, a major tourism destination in Turkey, the city is creating a new civic museum that it will fund to a high degree—but the museum will be established as an independent organization along civil society lines so that it can be more flexible and more responsive to public needs.

Children's museums, long a staple in America but a new and growing phenomenon elsewhere, are another museum type that is taking full advantage of this hybrid mode of governance. To take just two examples from opposite sides of the globe:

- In Vienna, the delightful children's museum named Zoom!, situated in the Museumsquartier, is strongly supported by the city but maintains a fully extended arm's-length control of its budget.
- In Manila, the outstanding Pambata children's museum—one of the leading institutions in the world in its commitment to helping street children and combating illiteracy—is entirely independent of government but generously supported by the city and by private donors.

For their part, some museums that were privately operated are becoming more oriented to civil society status by broadening their boards and expanding their connections to the community.

What these disparate examples have in common is a turning toward reliance on mixed sources of funding, resulting in institutions that are more accountable to a wider range of the public, and thus may become better institutional members of civil society.

2.1.6 Summary of Modes of Governance

Table 2.1 summarizes the four basic modes of governance of museums and galleries in relation to the six key factors identified. The fifth, mixed mode, or civil society, museum described in the previous section presents various combinations of these factors, depending on local circumstances.

Any change in the museum's institutional status must be carefully considered: a government line department museum may envy the freedom of an arm's-length institution, but is it prepared for uncertainty in its annual funding? On the other hand, a nonprofit or charitable organization struggling to finance the local public art gallery may be advantaged to move to arm's-length status by appointing civic representatives to its board. The management implications of the civil society mixed mode of governance are more fully considered in sections 2.5 and 3.1. Any decision to change status should be taken only as the result of a careful *institutional planning* process that examines all possible results of the change.

Table 2.1. Modes of Museum Governance

Factor	Line Departments	Arm's Length	Nonprofit	Private
Ownership	Government, University, or Corporation	Government, University, or Corporation	Association or Public Company	Individual or Private Company
Board or Trust	Advisory	Governing or Advisory	Governing	Advisory
Funds	Annual Allocation	Granted and Earned	Earned, with Grants and Endowment	Private and Earned
Donations	Less likely	More likely	Most likely	Not likely
Staff	Civil service or University or Corporation staff	May be civil service or museum staff	Association employees	Company employees
Volunteers	Difficult	Possible	Important	Rare

2.2   THE BOARD

Trusts and boards around the world hold their museums' collections and other assets in *public trust* not only for the public of today, but also for their descendants. They are *fiduciary* in character—a word describing trusteeship of property for others, meaning in the case of museums that trustees have an obligation to manage the property of others (in this case, the public) with the same diligence, honesty, and discretion that prudent people would exercise in managing their own property.

2.2.1 Board Roles and Responsibilities

As a consequence, although there may be many specific differences in the constitutions of museum boards around the world, governing boards have the following ten responsibilities in common. Advisory boards are generally expected to make recommendations on these same issues to a higher body, whereas governing boards make decisions on them:

1. to ensure the continuity of the museum's mission, mandate, and purposes;
2. to act as an advocate in the community (national, international, state, province, county, local, or community of interest) for public involvement in the museum;

- policy on public access to board meetings or minutes;
- financial accounting practices, spending and borrowing rules;
- responsibilities and means of selection of officers of the board;
- board committees;
- remuneration of board members and provision for expenses; and
- procedures in the event of dissolution of the board.

2.2.2 Board Committees

There are many sizes of museum boards. A large board of sixty to seventy people is sometimes considered desirable for fund-raising and community representation. Smaller boards of twenty to thirty people are sometimes considered to be more involved. Smaller museums in smaller communities may find even fewer members—seven to fifteen people—more efficient.

Most boards find it advisable to appoint their members (usually called *trustees*) to *board committees*, in order that the board can work on a wide range of issues simultaneously. In doing so, boards should set *terms of reference* to establish the mandate of the committee and its limitations. It is an important principle that while boards work through committees, it is the board as a whole that makes policy decisions. Committees may recommend but should not approve policies, and should report to the board regularly on the implementation of policies or plans. The following are among the committees most commonly appointed:

- *Executive Committee*: It may be advisable to appoint an executive committee to facilitate decisions between board meetings. This committee should normally include the board president or chair and the other senior officers and the museum director ex officio.
- *Nominating Committee*: This is a critically important committee that has two main responsibilities: first, the ongoing evaluation of board performance and making recommendations for changes in governance or board procedures; second, identifying strengths and weaknesses of the board and recruiting trustees who will strengthen the board.
- *Finance Committee*: It is often useful to strike a committee to focus exclusively on finances. This committee may have responsibility for capital fund-raising as well, but it is usually concerned only with ongoing operating funds. It normally works with staff to recommend the annual budget to the board, monitors financial reports, and ensures that the museum's accounts are audited.
- *Development Committee*: While the Finance Committee may be concerned with the operating budget, a Development Committee addresses the board's fund-raising role, including annual giving, corporate spon-

sorship, planned giving, and the many programs and activities the board undertakes to raise money. Specific subcommittees may be formed to spearhead special campaigns, such as acquisition funds, endowment development, or capital funds for renovation, expansion, or new construction projects.

- *Long-Range Planning Committee*: Long-range planning is a board function that is frequently delegated by the board to a committee that will work with museum management and planners to develop the strategic plan or the master plan as required by the board. The committee takes responsibility for the planning process, reports regularly to the board, and recommends the resultant plan to the board for approval. When a planning process or a capital project is underway, this group may become or may appoint a more specialized *steering committee* for that process or project.

- *Acquisition Committee*: Curators have the professional responsibility for collection development, but since additions to the collection affect the long-range future of the institution, many museum boards have established acquisition committees to which curators present proposed acquisitions for approval—sometimes only those above a certain monetary value. Such a committee can be instrumental in encouraging donations to the collection or finding sponsors for acquisitions that are beyond the museum's budget. The acquisitions committee is usually also responsible for approval of deaccessioning recommended by the curators through the director.

- *Membership Committee*: If the museum has a membership base, a dedicated committee of the board with its roots in the community can be very effective in recruiting new members and in sustaining a lively level of membership participation in the museum. This committee may be concerned with corporate as well as individual or family memberships and with encouraging members to increase their support of the museum by moving up to higher levels of membership.

Of course, boards may appoint additional committees as needed. However, some committees are problematic—exhibition committees, for example, can be appropriate if they focus on exhibition policy and on sponsorship for proposed exhibitions, but too often they go beyond the limits of a board's concern to make decisions on exhibition selection or priorities that should be delegated to staff. Such a committee can also present conflict-of-interest problems if its members include collectors whose acquisitions may be affected by the inside knowledge that their participation in an exhibition committee gives them.

The museum director is an ex officio member of all board committees and should give priority to participating in the executive committee and the acquisition committee. The director may share or delegate this responsibility to other staff members for committees that concern them: the chief financial officer may work with the financial committee, the head of development with the development and membership committees, the chief curator with the acquisitions committee, and so on.

2.2.3 Board Procedures

Boards malfunction when they attempt to direct the day-to-day activities of the museum, instead of delegating those decisions to staff. In some small museums or in the early phases of a museum's development it may be necessary for boards to undertake what are normally staff functions. When this is so, it should be explicitly understood and agreed that such activity is temporary, until staff can be recruited to fulfil those tasks.

Board members need training and development, just like staff and volunteers. Most museums find it useful to provide each incoming member with a *trustees' manual* that includes all the relevant mission, mandate, and policy statements and the board constitution or bylaws, as well as a history of the institution, current plans, staff organization charts, budgets and financial reports, a list of board roles and responsibilities, and an outline of the committee structure. The new trustee should attend at least one *board orientation session*, which should include a tour of the building and introduction to the division or department heads.

Board members need to be assured about the extent of their personal and collective liability for the museum's actions. This varies according to the legal provisions of each country, but in general the incorporation of a nonprofit society or similar association should have the legal effect of placing liability on the institution collectively. As part of their fiduciary responsibility, trustees also need to be assured that the museum's insurance is adequate for its risks and resources, and that they are personally protected from any allegations of liability for actions that the museum undertakes.

Museum boards should adopt a *code of ethics*, both for themselves and for the museum. A code of ethics protects the trustee as well as the museum's interests, and is written in the spirit of "Justice must not only be done, but must be seen to be done." The code should subscribe to relevant international conventions and national, state, provincial, or local laws affecting artifacts, specimens, or works of art, as well as to the Code of Professional Ethics of the International Council of Museums (ICOM) and parallel guidelines promulgated by the museum profession in each country, such as the British Museums Association's Code of Practice or comparable documents of the American Association of Museums. These codes of professional practice affect staff as well as trustees, and should be adopted as part of the board's code of ethics to govern the museum as a whole.

The board's code of ethics should also aim to eliminate conflicts of interest for trustees with collecting activities related to those of the museum. Obviously, it is an advantage for the museum to have trustees who are also collectors in its field, especially as it may result in future donations; however, since the museum itself is involved in the collecting field, it is important that the trustee should declare to the board his or her collecting activity, and of course any related business interests. A record should be kept of any advice given to the trustee by staff members affecting his or her collecting activity, and the trustee should normally be expected to give the museum first refusal on collecting opportunities that arise. The code should require a trustee to withdraw from any deliberations affecting his or her business interests or from which he or she might benefit, directly or indirectly. The code should also require confidentiality of the trustee, and collegiality with fellow trustees in pursuing the interests of the museum, as well as minimal requirements for attendance at meetings and museum functions.

It is important for the board to maintain appropriate relations with the museum director. The director recommends policies and plans to the board, implements approved policies and plans, and is responsible for the day-to-day management of the museum. The board should give the director unflinching support as long as its policies and plans are being implemented in a professional manner, and should not be involved in day-to-day administration. The board should expect from its director timely reports and recommendations, full disclosure of relevant information, and a commitment to the museum's mission that goes beyond personal enthusiasms or career goals.

Board relations with staff should be regulated by a board policy statement that may be included in the board's code of ethics. Normally, staff should report to the director, and the director should report to the board, except for staff delegated by the director to report to board committees. In a unionized museum there will be provisions for grievances in a collective bargaining agreement. The human resources department generally addresses staff problems and concerns. However, the code of ethics should also provide for extraordinary occasions of disagreement or conflict, whether these are professional concerns or grievances over employment conditions, so that the board may serve as an ultimate level of appeal within the institution. In such cases the policy should provide procedures so that the board can help to resolve the dispute in a constructive way that does not undermine the director but responds judiciously to staff concerns in light of the museum's mission and objectives.

2.3   MUSEUM STAFF

In this section, we describe the roles and responsibilities of the people who conduct the functions of the museum, define three alternative models of staff organization, and consider issues of working conditions and job satisfaction.

2.3.1 The Organization of Staff by Museum Function

The traditional organization of museum staff, still found in some older museums, was focused on curatorial departments determined by the academic disciplines represented within the collection. Each department might have not only its own curators but also its own conservators, preparators, and technicians. Such an approach resulted in the identification some years ago of as many as forty-five different systems of documentation in use at that time in the Victoria and Albert Museum—now entirely changed, of course.

The organization of museum staff today usually responds to a wider range of functions than the curatorial and relieves the curator of responsibility for many administrative and programming functions. In figure 1.2 we presented the six museological functions as two sides of a triangle, or as two divergent directions, held together by an administrative hypotenuse. Directional arrows added to the lines of the triangle may serve to indicate the inherent stresses in this model, which the museum administration must strive to make a creative rather than a destructive tension:

Figure 2.1. The Dynamics of Museum Management

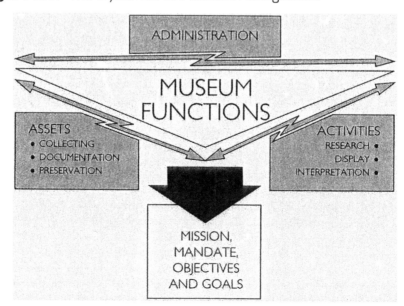

As noted in chapter 1, allowed to follow their own bent, each of the two divergent directions within the museum would contradict the other. The safety, preservation, and documentation of the collection could best be accomplished in a building closed to the public, with large areas kept in the dark for most of the time, while the study, display, and dissemination of information about the collection takes us in the opposite direction, toward maximizing public access in brightly lit open displays, including hands-on programs where possible. It is the task of administration to reconcile these two divergent aspects of the museum's functions, and to give their conjunction a positive and stimulating direction, which in figure 2.1 we have shown as the triangle's vector moving toward accomplishment of the museum's mission, mandate, goals, and objectives.

This triangle of museum functions suggests organization of staff into three divisions—one concerned with the museum's assets, another with its activities, and the third with administration. While the names of such divisions vary, these are commonly used:

- collections;
- programs; and
- administration.

Of course there are other ways of organizing museum staff. Some institutions group all the content-related staff together (collections and programs), then associate all operations and administration personnel (visitor services, retail, human resources, finance, information technology, and facilities), and cluster a third "external affairs" group (development, special events, communications, marketing). This may have advantages for larger institutions but tends to result in an administration-heavy museum, with two-thirds of the departments not concerned with the museum's content. The collection/programs/administration triangle of functions recommended here has the virtue of fitting all sizes of museums, from very small (where one to three people may be responsible for the three divisions) to very large institutions with many departments within each division.

This organization of museum functions into these three distinct "divisions" does, however, necessitate cross-divisional and interdepartmental collaboration throughout the museum, as the examples below demonstrate:

- Limiting the "assets" division to collection management functions tends to relegate site and building operations and maintenance to the administrative division. Since the security division is concerned with site and building operation, it is often located there as well. This means that curators and conservators must rely on these administrative departments to control the environment and safety of their collections, and they need to establish ways of working effectively with administration. Conversely, security officers and building managers responsible for building systems need to collaborate closely with curators and conservators to maintain the conditions that the collections need.

- Exhibitions are one of the principal activities or programs of most museums. Several decades ago, they were almost exclusively developed and certainly always directed by curators. Exhibitions obviously require significant participation by curators, registrars, and conservators from the collection management division. Placing them in a public programs division has sometimes resulted in the creation of such anomalous positions as "curator of exhibitions," or exhibition departments where exhibition planners and designers work together but curators in the collections department are consulted only when absolutely necessary. The administrative division is also concerned with exhibition development, ranging from security implications through cost controls to sponsorship and the provision of stock specific to the exhibition in the museum shop. Educational and publications programs similarly require curatorial input, and administrative controls. Multidepartmental collaboration for specific exhibitions, publications, and public programs is obviously required to get the museum's work done.

This issue of enabling staff to work across departments and divisions to achieve museum functions is pervasive and significant enough to be taken as an eighth criterion of museum management:

8. Does management facilitate interdepartmental cooperation and teamwork to conduct museum functions and create programs such as exhibitions?

2.3.2 Organizational Models

The following alternative organizational models for museum staff highlight different ways in which museum management can overcome compartmentalization and facilitate teamwork among museum staff:

- hierarchical pyramid;
- matrix organization; and
- task forces.

These models are by no means mutually exclusive and may be used in combination as required in the life of the museum. Thus the organization chart may be drawn as a hierarchical pyramid, with matrix organization and/or task forces being introduced as needed for specific functions or projects.

2.3.2.1 Hierarchical Pyramid

The *hierarchical pyramid* of authority is the form of organization found in most museums around the world. Figure 2.2 illustrates the three-division museum organization discussed in the preceding section.

In a small museum, one or two persons may perform all functions. If only three or four can be hired, these functions must be distributed among them. In a larger multidisciplinary museum, each division will have its own departments arranged to continue the hierarchy, as in the following generic examples in figures 2.3–2.5.

Figure 2.2. Typical Three-Division Organization

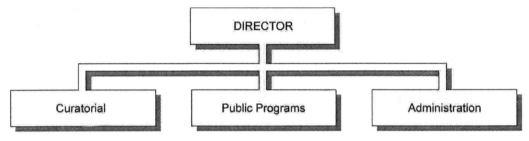

Figure 2.3. Collections Division

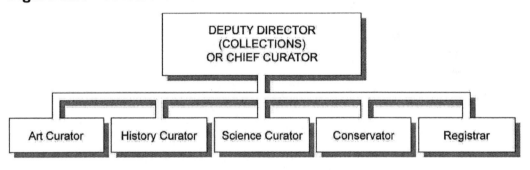

Figure 2.4. Programs Division

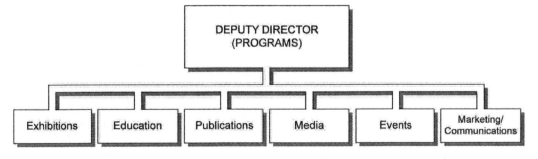

Figure 2.5. Administration Division

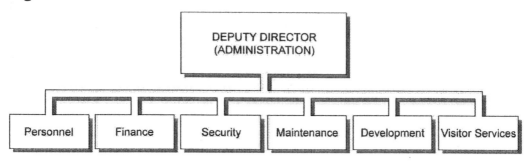

Museums with smaller staffs will assign more than one of these responsibilities (and others in each division) to single individuals, whereas larger museums will continue the hierarchical pyramid of each department as required. The following organization charts shown in figures 2.6–2.9 assume a relatively large staff, but may of course be adapted for smaller organizations by combining responsibilities.

A fourth department: If the museum is large enough to have four major departments reporting to the director, "External Relations" would be the fourth department, with its own deputy director responsible for:

- communications (which includes information technology and the museum's website as well as marketing); and
- development and membership (which are closely linked and may be grouped under one department).

This fourth department in larger institutions (shown in figure 2.6) reflects the more outward-looking civil society institutions that many museums have become, as well as their increasing dependence on multiple sources of funding, both public and private. Here again, however, collections and public program divisions are also leaders in public engagement, so interdepartmental collaboration is essential.

For those museums that develop the option of the fourth department, the deputy director for external affairs would have reporting to him or her the following positions:

- the development officer with the reports to that position, the development assistant and the membership manager and clerk, as in figure 2.9; and
- a communications officer with marketing manager, IT officer, and webmaster (as in figure 2.8) reporting to that position.

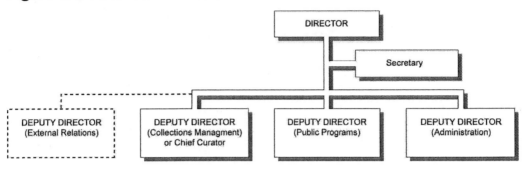

Figure 2.6. Senior Staff Executive

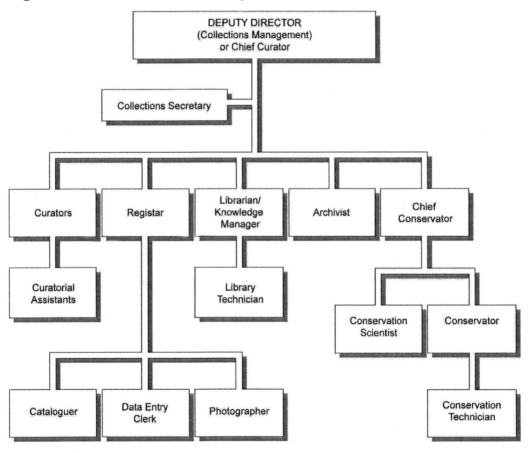

Figure 2.7. Collections Division Organization Chart

Figure 2.8. Public Programs Division Organization Chart

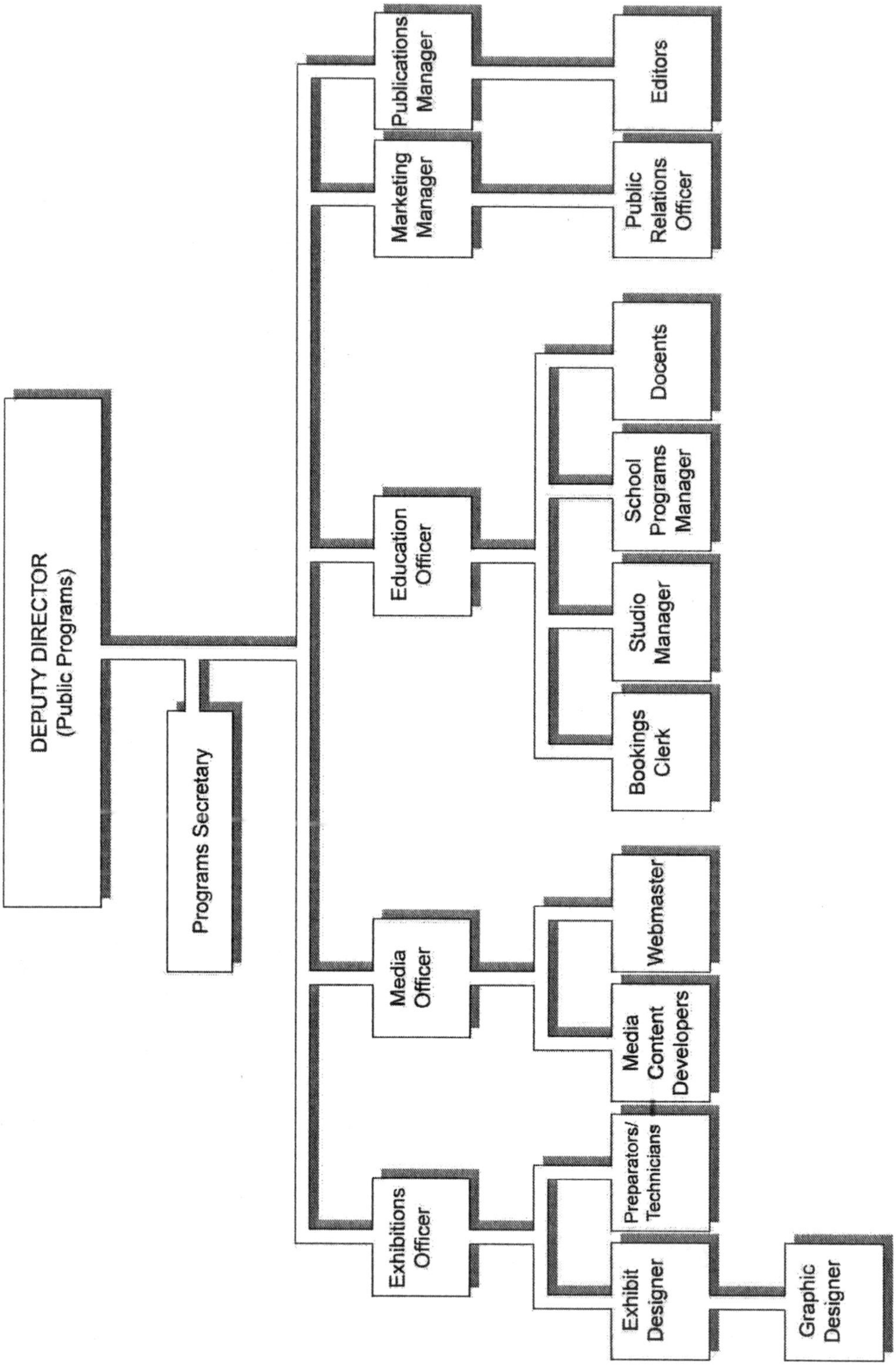

Figure 2.9. Administration Division Organization Chart

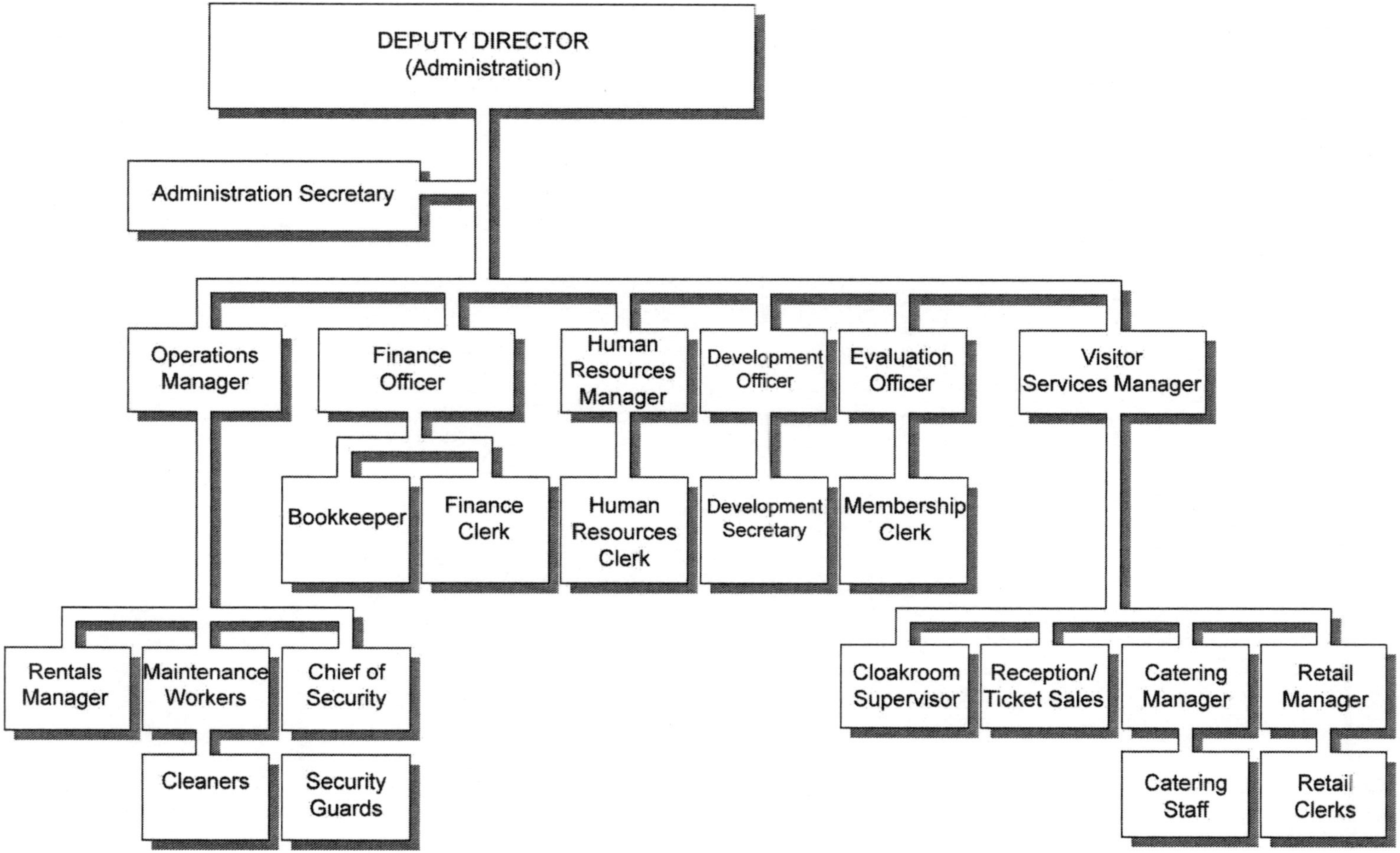

DEPUTY DIRECTOR
(Administration)

Administration Secretary

Operations Manager

Finance Officer

Human Resources Manager

Development Officer

Evaluation Officer

Visitor Services Manager

Bookkeeper

Finance Clerk

Human Resources Clerk

Development Secretary

Membership Clerk

Cloakroom Supervisor

Reception/ Ticket Sales

Catering Manager

Retail Manager

Catering Staff

Retail Clerks

Rentals Manager

Chief of Security

Maintenance Workers

Security Guards

Cleaners

2.3.2.2 Matrix Organization

A matrix is a format in which functions are arranged as axes of interaction. Since administration serves the other two divisions, one application of *matrix organization* to museum management could be expressed in the matrix in table 2.2, with the provision of administrative services indicated by the intersection of each administrative function with the other two divisions.

Another application of matrix organization to museum staff is the correlation of public programs and collection management staff. Table 2.3 shows this matrix for three public programming functions. The table shows that curators, conservators, and the registrar are all involved with exhibitions, whereas only the curators normally have a role in education and publications.

Combining the two matrices would give the image of a cube, with all three divisions shown as three interacting axes, as in figure 2.10. The successful interaction of all three sides of the cube provides for the most effective and efficient combination of the operational staff of a museum.

If there is a fourth, "External Affairs," department, obviously the interactions are all the more multisided, with communications, development, and membership officers relating to all other departments. With or without this addition, the cube indicates the multifarious ways in which museum staff must consult with other departments in order to have an effectively functioning institution.

2.3.2.3 Task Forces and Committees

As the preceding section indicates, many museum activities, including such important ones as exhibition development, require the cooperation of depart-

Table 2.2. Administration Matrix

Division:	Personnel	Finance	Security	Maintenance
Curatorial	X	X	X	X
Public Programs	X	X	X	X

Table 2.3. Collection Management Matrix

Public Programs	Curators	Conservators	Registrar
Exhibitions	X	X	X
Education	X		
Publications	X		

Figure 2.10. Matrix of Museum Organization

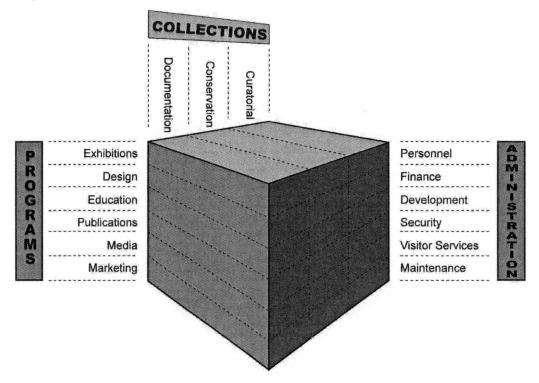

ments from all three divisions. This can best be achieved by combining representatives of each department in *task forces* dedicated to particular projects, as well as *standing committees* for general functions.

Exhibitions provide an important example: there is a need for a standing *Exhibition Committee* that may meet quarterly, with participation from all departments, coordinating all concerned to the upcoming schedule, which will affect everyone, including maintenance, retail, security, and finance as well as the more obviously involved departments. (This is a staff Exhibition Committee, not to be confused with a possible board Exhibition Committee, discussed in section 2.2.2.)

But in addition to this standing committee there is a need for a specific *Exhibition Task Force* for each major exhibition. This task force should combine the talents of all those responsible for the many aspects of the exhibition project. Each exhibition task force should include representatives of the following divisions and departments:

Collection Management
- curatorial
- conservation
- documentation

Public Programs
- exhibitions
- design
- education
- publications
- media
- marketing

Administration
- finance
- development
- security
- visitor services

Each department should be asked to nominate its representative. More important projects might require the attention of department chairpersons, whereas lesser projects should be seen as training opportunities for junior members of each department to participate. Contracted participants—such as an exhibition designer engaged for that particular show—should also be named to the task force.

The museum director should have final approval on the composition of the task force and should appoint the chairperson from among its members. Although the relevant curator might be the obvious nominee to chair many exhibition groups, some should be chaired by the Exhibitions Department representative, by the Education representative, or by the Marketing or Development representatives if audience development or membership recruitment are a major focus of the project. The committee may begin meeting monthly, should have regular reports from all participants—so that security, for example, is not left to the last minute—and should increase the frequency of its meetings as opening day nears. Crediting the members of the committee on exhibition literature or signage is an excellent way to inspire dedication to an outstanding result.

Similar combinations of standing committees and specific task forces may be developed for projects in documentation, education, information technology, visitor services, and audience development. The standing committee on Operations needs to meet weekly to review issues and match calendars, while the Communications group should meet monthly to review marketing plans and changes needed in the museum's website. Specific task forces will be struck from the committees as needed, often involving younger staff members who are not in the standing committee itself. These interdisciplinary groups supplement particular departmental meetings.

This standing committee and task force system has proved to be a most useful way for museums to address their complex tasks, ensure that their professional expertise is well deployed, and provide opportunities for growth in staff members' responsibility and confidence. It indicates the importance of a crucial factor in effective museum management—*teamwork*. Successful museum managers at all levels—from director to department heads—understand that in addition to all staff members' professional qualifications there is another key criterion for their success: the ability to work with each other effectively as a team. Good teamwork means accepting responsibility for making one's professional contribution with respect for other disciplines as well as one's own, communicating expectations clearly, promising only what can be delivered, and delivering it on time so that others can proceed with their part of the work. Teamwork can be learned, but must first be consciously identified and understood as an essential feature of the working life of a museum professional. Teamwork requires good leaders, but it also requires responsible followers, willing to differ when relevant, but dedicated to achieving the shared goal. Good museum managers find ways to recognize and reward effective teamwork, among both leaders and responsible followers.

2.3.3 Job Titles and Job Descriptions

Some museums are operated entirely by volunteers, while others have only one or a few paid staff. The same functions as outlined in these chapters will have to be performed by these smaller numbers of personnel. Thus if only three personnel are provided, it is very likely that one will focus on collection management, one on public programs, and one on administration. The subsequent addition of staff to one division or another will reflect the museum's priorities.

The outline of job titles and job descriptions provided in the appendix at the end of this book, however, assumes all of the posts listed in the organization charts in this chapter. It is unlikely that any museum would need all of these positions—it may be efficient to combine several posts into one—but the appendix is intended to give a reasonably complete checklist.

Job titles vary around the world. In China, for example, one may find "researchers" doing what "curators" do in a Western museum. One may also find "box makers" fabricating the storage boxes for artifacts, a position not known in the West. The job titles listed in this section are limited to the positions most commonly found internationally, with job titles most commonly used in English in Western museums.

Even within these limits, there is considerable variation of usage. The museum's chief executive, for instance, is usually called a director, but in some institutions may be called CEO (chief executive officer), executive director, president, chief curator, curator, or even curator/director. In the appendix we have tried to give some of the variants and have assumed the three or four divisions discussed in this chapter, plus the director's executive office, assuming further that each division is headed by a deputy director, with the provision that the deputy director (collections) will in many instances be called chief curator.

The number of positions also varies greatly. Even in larger museums some of the posts listed in the appendix will not be needed, or will be filled by persons who also occupy another post. In other places there will be more gradations, such as assistant curator positions between the ranks of curator and curatorial assistant. Notwithstanding all these qualifications, we hope that the list of job titles and job descriptions in the appendix will be useful.

2.3.4 Working Conditions

Once upon a time some of the senior people who worked in museums were amateurs in the best sense of the word, in a few cases not even requiring payment for their work. Over the past century, museum staff have struggled to be recognized as a profession with commensurate working conditions and remuneration. While in many parts of the world museum employees have made significant advances in both pay and conditions of work, progress has been uneven. Many people who preserve and interpret the world's cultural and artistic heritage are still unable to earn more than a marginal wage, and they struggle with poor working conditions.

On the other hand, museum employees in many countries today are often graduates of museum training programs, sometimes as postgraduate degrees in addition to their original disciplines in the sciences, archaeology, history, or art history. Conservators, registrars, and others are highly specialized experts in their fields. Directors and other administrators in some cases are accomplished museologists, and in others they have been attracted from the private sector as well as from senior academic positions. Courses are available to assist curators to become museum directors. Museum associations, private foundations, and government agencies offer in-service training seminars and conferences so that museum professionals can keep abreast of current developments in all disciplines and management philosophies. Online learning is a major tool of professional development that is only beginning to be fully exploited. Levels of compensation, at least in some of the larger institutions, are commensurate with the advancing levels of professionalism.

No matter how financially constrained the museum may be, it should recognize the value of its staff by adopting a *human resources policy* that addresses, within the museum's means, such issues as:

- statutory regulations
- salary

- benefits
- expense provisions
- probationary period
- hours of work and overtime
- statutory holidays, vacation, sick leave, maternity or paternity leave, and leave of absence
- training and professional development
- intellectual property provisions
- grievance and harassment procedures
- performance reviews
- termination conditions

Contracting (sometimes referred to as "contracting out") is often urged as an alternative to permanent employment by the museum. It has worked well in catering, and some museums have used it successfully for retail, cleaning, maintenance, and security. However, the museum's concern for long-term preservation of its collection and for dependable security mean that there are limits to this approach. Difficulties arise especially if the museum must subscribe to a government, university, or corporation policy to select the low bidder on every contract. The low bidder for a security contract may be the most dangerous for a museum! Low-bid security contracts often result in poorly paid, ill-trained, and indifferently motivated guards—with potentially disastrous consequences for the collection and a negative effect on visitors as well.

2.3.4.1 Diversity

A very large part of the world today consists of multicultural and multiracial societies. This presents a great opportunity for many museums, which could benefit from a diversity of backgrounds and viewpoints among their personnel. Yet many museums in these societies fall far short of reflecting the diversity all around them—on their boards; among their staff; and not surprisingly, therefore, among their visitors as well. The need for *inclusion* of both genders and all socioeconomic, cultural, and racial groups is a responsibility of museums and other civic institutions, and it also offers an exciting potential for their growth.

A concerted effort is needed to provide for a diversity among museum employees that reflects the diversity of the museum's community. Policies should be developed to encourage employment opportunities for visible cultural or linguistic minorities, and to ensure promotion opportunities for all throughout the organization. The goal should be to increase the number of visitors and to invigorate the creativity of the museums with the many perspectives and experiences that diversity brings. Experience has shown that this does not happen without the commitment of the board and senior management vigorously encouraging diversity at all levels.

Museums that preserve and display the culture of living societies must be particularly concerned to include members of the descendant communities among their staff. This may require special training programs aimed at enhancing the opportunities for members of those communities to acquire the requisite professional or technical skills. In South Africa over the past two decades there has been a particular challenge to develop such training programs for people who have only recently had the opportunity to take charge of the preservation and interpretation of their own culture. Elsewhere there is a pressing need for recruitment and training of local or national citizens in places where expatriates have been managing museums and other cultural institutions.

2.3.4.2 Training

Training programs instruct employees in how to do their job, whereas *employee development programs* open up new opportunities for staff. Both may be mounted in-house, or may be provided by sponsoring (partially or fully) employee participation in courses elsewhere. These may be museum training programs from the introductory to the postgraduate level, or courses in a wide variety of professional pursuits—technical or management skills that may be useful to museum staff members at all posts.

Instituting a *training and development strategy* for staff has always been important, but it has become essential in the twenty-first century, as museums meet the challenge of constant change, ranging from museum philosophy through technology to public expectations and marketing requirements. The successful museum of the twenty-first century will provide a constant learning environment for its staff as well as its visitors.

An important requirement of professional museum management is therefore to provide a training and development strategy that establishes general policies of support and can be related to the specific needs of each individual, from the director to the maintenance staff. The strategy, updated annually, should identify the training needs of the museum, including provision for planned changes in direction as well as the personal development plans of each individual, agreed in a consultative (and confidential) process of mutual identification of needs and resources. It is important for the director or the training officer (whoever is representing the museum) to ensure that the personal development plan meets the institution's requirements, rather than merely serving the career goals or enthusiasms of the individual employee; implementing such a strategy provides an outstanding opportunity to fulfill diversity policies at the same time.

One group that can benefit personally from a training and development strategy, and can then contribute far more to the employing museum, is the largest single sector on most museum rosters—security guards. These very numerous employees are also very often the ones who have the most frequent and prolonged contact with visitors: it is therefore most important that museums ensure that they understand what they are guarding, as well as how to guard it, and that they see a future for themselves within the institution.

2.3.4.3 Performance Reviews

Performance reviews of all staff should be directed toward evaluation of both effectiveness and efficiency in the employee's accomplishment of museum functions in relation to the museum's strategic goals and departmental objectives. The priority and weight given to various factors should be adjusted annually according to current priorities. The employee should do a self-evaluation as part of the performance review, and all review records should be held in confidence. The review should include both quantitative ratings and qualitative comments, and it should be linked to consideration of promotion and annual salary increments. The review should be done in consultation with the employee's immediate supervisor. The file on previous reviews, especially that of the previous year, should be reread by employee and supervisors participating in the review before each year's consultation.

2.3.4.4 The Role of Unions

In the realistic context of museums as (too often) relatively low-paid employment centers where professional recruitment and evaluation procedures and especially training and development opportunities can compensate somewhat for the low level of remuneration, *trade unions* may be seen as supportive forces in the workplace. In general, their pressure for higher pay can only benefit the profession, and they can be a powerful force for employment equity and improved training and development opportunities. Even where remuneration is appropriate to the professional qualifications of senior and middle management, there is often a need for such a force to upgrade the lower-level employees.

Unfortunately, trade unions are too often confined to the security staff, where confrontational policies on both sides can lead to the imposition of civil service or equivalent procedures that can result in inefficient operations. One government line department museum in Europe, for example, had to contend with extended lunch hours and breaks that necessitated doubling the number of guards required for its operation—a requirement that resulted in the regular closure of galleries to visitors.

Another difficulty often encountered, both for the museums and their unions, is the proliferation of multiple unions within one institution. The necessity to conclude separate *collective bargaining agreements* with several unions, often on different schedules, can challenge even the most dedicated human resources department—not to mention the complexities of multiple *grievance procedures*. If the union certification legislation in the museum's jurisdiction provides for separate unionization for guards, clerks, and technicians, for example, the museum may wish to encourage cooperation both among and with its unions to minimize the potentially harmful effects of more or less perpetual negotiations through coordination of agreement schedules and grievance procedures.

Unionized or not, museum personnel are sometimes concerned with the role of volunteers if these museum supporters appear to be supplanting staff positions in whole or in part. It is important to ensure that volunteer recruitment is aimed at tasks that are additional to those that the paid workforce can undertake. For instance, if the Education Department is mandated to train volunteer docents, interaction between the professional trainers and the volunteers should not be a problem; but if the volunteers are replacing former paid educators, there will almost certainly be strife.

2.4 THE ROLE OF VOLUNTEERS

Museums are at the heart of learning societies—all the more so as young people have to demonstrate experience to get their first job and as older people remain healthier longer. People of all ages are likely to have had multiple work experiences and may bring knowledge acquired in several different countries to the museum. Cultural institutions are best placed to leverage the talents of these accomplished individuals at all levels, but to do so they must put in place a well-conceived volunteer program. Although in smaller institutions a part-time volunteer coordinator may be sufficient to manage such a program, a full-time paid position is required for even medium-size museums to take sufficient advantage of this opportunity.

Volunteers are vital to the life of many museums, especially those operated by nonprofit or charitable organizations. Some museum workers believe that volunteers are not cost-effective because they require too much staff time for training and evaluation. This can be the case if the volunteer program is not well organized and controlled. If properly constituted, however, a volunteer work force can simultaneously link the museum to its community and provide invaluable support to the museum.

2.4.1 Operating a Volunteer Program

Museums in the start-up stage of development are frequently governed by volunteers (the board), managed by a volunteer director, and operated by volunteers. This is a particularly challenging situation in which there are distinct roles and a hierarchy; but all are equally unpaid. It becomes even more challenging when the museum begins to raise enough funds to hire paid professional staff. In all stages of museum development and in all sizes of museums, it is important to be aware of the distinct roles and responsibilities of volunteers:

- Board members are volunteers who are engaged in governance.
- A volunteer director is engaged in management.
- Task volunteers are engaged in unpaid staff positions.

This section is concerned with this latter category of volunteers, who play numerous roles in museums, including:

- *docents*, the most commonly encountered volunteer role, enabling the museum to provide guided tours of its collection to school parties and other groups;
- *hosts*, from general visitor reception to making special events possible by providing food service or refreshments;
- *retail sales clerks*, making feasible museum shops that would otherwise not contribute significantly to museum revenue in smaller institutions;
- *research assistants*, undertaking systematic research tasks for which time would otherwise not be available;
- *library assistants*, undertaking time-consuming sorting and shelving in the museum library;
- *data entry clerks*, assisting the registrar with the conversion of manual to automated catalog entries; and
- *restoration technicians*, often enthusiastically at work in transportation museums, but requiring careful professional supervision.

Museums that utilize volunteers in these or other roles should address them as workers who are paid not with wages but with other rewards—of *individual development* and of *social recognition*. The organization of volunteers must ensure that both of these rewards are attainable.

The first reward, *individual development*, indicates that volunteers should be part of the museum's training and development strategy. A *volunteer coordinator* is essential. The volunteer coordinator (who may be paid or voluntary) should maintain a roster on which the training needs and development aspirations of each volunteer are recorded, and the museum should undertake to assist the volunteer in accessing this development—not financially, but through providing training opportunities.

The second reward, *social recognition*, should be provided by the museum both on an ongoing day-to-day basis and in annual or seasonal social occasions that the senior staff and board members of the institution attend in order to present certificates or similar printed recognition of services rendered to the volunteers. The museum that understands the importance of volunteers will ensure that its senior staff and board members participate fully in such a recognition meeting, and that virtually all volunteers are recognized for their contribution.

Recruitment of volunteers should be undertaken with the same care as recruitment of staff. Volunteer posts should be advertised with job descriptions and qualifications listed, and those interested should fill out a volunteer application form. A *volunteer manual* that links the museum's mission and mandate to the museum's volunteer policy and to practical details pertaining to the daily work of volunteers (such as provision for out-of-pocket expenses) should be made available to those expressing an interest. For museums with membership programs it is important to insist that only members can volunteer, and that any volunteer committee must be part of the membership organization.

Interviews of potential volunteers should be aimed at determining the volunteer's interests, capability, and training needs as well as communicating the museum's requirements. References should be taken and checked, and health and criminal records investigated following the same personnel procedures as for any prospective employee. Less promising candidates should be politely declined in a letter thanking them for their interest. Some may be redirected to volunteering for tasks other than the post for which they applied.

Aspiring volunteers should then be offered a *volunteer agreement* (sometimes called a "volunteer contract," although it cannot be legally binding), completed to fit the needs of the museum to their circumstances, committing them to particular days and times for a specified period. With fulfillment of this contract in view, the volunteer should be enrolled in the requisite training program, provided by the museum's education department or other qualified staff; this course should include examinations, both theoretical and practical in nature, and it should be expected that some would-be volunteers will fail. Those who pass should be regularly evaluated, with further training and development planned. A trial engagement (three to six months), the length of notice required in case of the volunteer's resignation, and the museum's termination provisions in case of unsatisfactory performance should all be established in the volunteer agreement.

Long experience with volunteers has shown that such a program can be effective in recruiting, training, and maintaining a volunteer contingent with esprit de corps and commitment to the institution, while constantly developing volunteers' abilities and offering the rewards of social recognition as well. Far from resisting such procedures, volunteers welcome the diligence with which their efforts are treated, and respond with a higher quality of work and dependable attendance. With such a program the privilege of volunteering may proudly be added to the benefits of museum membership, and the museum will flourish with the full support of an active volunteer base.

2.4.2 Internships

Interns are a source of mostly youthful energy, enthusiasm, and newly minted knowledge that can be invaluable to a museum department. These are usually recent graduates, sometimes still completing education programs, who are willing to work for low levels of remuneration in order to gain the experience of working in the museum. In some cases universities or other schools are willing to pay the intern a stipend and grant them credit for working in museums. Thus they are not fully volunteers, but may join both paid and voluntary staff on a departmental team. As with volunteers, it is important to ensure that interns are engaged on a clear contractual basis that is not threatening to fully paid employees, and that their status is transparent to all who will be working with them. A certain number may go on to be hired for permanent positions, but it is important to ensure that all interns benefit from the experience of working in the museum, providing them with sufficient training and development opportunities appropriate to their time and role in the museum.

Volunteers and interns are no longer to be found only in Western countries. The Scientific Centre in Kuwait, for example, which combines an outstanding aquarium stocked from the Arabian Gulf with excellent science exhibits and an Imax theater, operates a school holiday program for teenagers to serve and learn as a revenue-producing program: the best of the students are then offered the opportunity to serve as volunteers on weekends or after school through the school year, receiving just enough compensation to pay for their lunches and transportation to and from the facility. The result is a constantly replenished group of eager, young, and knowledgeable interns and volunteers who animate the daily operation of the Scientific Centre, in a culture where many had doubted that a volunteer program could work.

2.5 CHANGING ROLES IN CIVIL SOCIETY MUSEUMS

As noted in section 2.1.5, over the past few decades there has been a slow, almost stealthy transition of museums from government line departments to civil society museums with multiple sources of funding and accountability to a much wider range of society, both private and public. Like most change in museums, it is not always by choice. This momentous change started in many jurisdictions with cutbacks in government subsidies or grants. In some countries, government subsidy to individual museums has declined by 20 to 50 percent over the past thirty years—even in places where the overall government subsidy to a much larger number of museums has increased. Where there are more museums, the leading institutions become steadily more professional and so want to do more, increasing their costs but also increasing public benefits. In many instances, the reduction in government subsidy is mitigated by allowing the museum to keep and use the revenues generated from admissions, shops, and other activities—revenues that previously were returned to the general public treasury by line department museums.

Paradoxically, the same governments have been willing to fund new museums and expand existing ones. But they are doing so not only for traditional reasons like the preservation of the heritage or scientific research, but to meet new goals, such as:

- participation in tourism, the world's biggest industry, and specifically in *cultural tourism*, its most dynamic sector;
- *social cohesion*—one of the world's biggest challenges, especially now that for the first time in human history more than half of humankind lives in cities where getting along and solving our problems together is necessary for survival;
- *urban redevelopment*—with former industrial sites and old power generating stations from London's Bankside to Istanbul's Golden Horn being transformed into museum locations;
- city (or country) *branding* to attract new industries and investment, especially in the "knowledge economy";
- stimulating the *creative economy* that brings added value to the economy; and
- competing with other cities or countries for one or more of the five preceding reasons.

This paradox—the decline in government subsidy to specific institutions even while the same governments are seeking more and better museums for economic reasons—can be explained in three ways:

- There are simply more museums—in general a very good thing, since it makes museums and what they offer more accessible to more people, and it shows that what they are providing is increasingly meaningful and valued.
- The growing professionalism of museum workers generates higher costs but also enables museums to offer far more to the public and to the care of their collections than they were able to do a few decades ago.
- But the decisive factor is the restructuring over the last thirty years of economies in all parts of the world.

This global restructuring has reduced taxes on wealth, sold off (some would say given away) government agencies, services, and natural resources to the private sector, and reduced government support for the public realm—including parks, libraries, and hospitals as well as museums. As a result, there has been an enormous growth of private wealth and its concentration among a relative few in every country. Governments increasingly see these individuals as potential museum supporters and their companies as potential exhibition sponsors. Thus the role and influence of boards has increased, as have the fund-raising responsibilities of the museum director and the development department.

The result is a significant change in the position of museums in the community. Because the former exclusively governmentally funded institution must now look outside for support—not only financial but also social, since social esteem is the basis for the financial interest—the museum becomes a more outward-focused organization with more links to the community. This is why we noted the growing need for a fourth deputy director in section 2.3.2.1—a deputy director for external affairs, comprising communications and development officers in his or her department. A good opinion of the museum in the community becomes much more important—not just for the curator's professional standing but also because it is ultimately important financially for the museum to be embraced by a community that understands its value and is proud of its collection and its accomplishments.

This affects not only the new deputy director for external affairs. The deputy director for public programs now needs more than ever to understand the tourism industry, and the head of education services needs to develop programs that welcome learners of all ages and ethnicities. Exhibitions become more of a dialogue, less of a monologue: in pioneering his remarkable public *Laboratoire* in Paris, David Edwards has proposed that he is presenting experiments rather than exhibitions (see his case study 3.3 in section 3.3.1.1).

An outstanding example is San Francisco's Museum of the African Diaspora, which Lord Cultural Resources helped to plan. Janera Solomon, who was part of our planning team there, writes in her case study 2.1 in this section of the experience of facilitating the community consultation that was part of the planning process, developing the concept of a civil society institution that is also part of the civic development of the Yerba Buena area around the San Francisco Museum of Modern Art, and so fits into the economic as well as the social development plans of the city. Janera's recollection of the planning process evokes the way in which a civil society museum can be rooted in that society's meanings, concerns, and values.

So a more vital type of museum is emerging—a more socially engaged, "outside-in" museum that demands new skills from its board, its management, and staff. This civil society museum requires that its personnel must be continually involved in training and personal development, as the museum becomes as much a learning as a teaching organization.

The extent to which this is happening depends on the extent to which funding sources become more varied as government subsidy declines. Whether this tipping point occurs at 75 percent or 50 percent government funding or lower is relative to the local culture, politics, history, and size of the museum. But enough instances have been observed that the overall direction is clear: museums are becoming civil society institutions, much more deeply invested in their communities as they piece together their support from self-generated funds, endowments, donations, and sponsorships as well as the still important government subsidy or grants.

Does the museum director and her or his team have a different role before and after this tipping point has been reached? The answer is a qualified yes, and that is the first topic of our next chapter.

LISTENING IN
The Value of Community Consultation
By Janera Solomon

When I joined the team working to develop San Francisco's Museum of the African Diaspora in 2001, there were many questions. Though "diaspora" had been a term used in academic circles since the 1960s, it was fairly new to the general public and to our team. Some were unsure of its pronunciation, and many asked, "What is diaspora?" and more importantly, "Who are the African diaspora?"—two questions for which there are many answers.

Community consultation is a process of discovery. We began by posing these questions to the public:

- How do we define the museum's themes and stories within such a broad subject?
- How could the museum be inclusive of so many perspectives?
- And how could we do so in ways that would avoid alienating visitors but rather engage them in universal questions?

There were many debates. We convened two national charettes, bringing together artists, scholars, critics, and other cultural stakeholders. Our challenge was to ask the right questions at the right time. That's what facilitation is really about, listening and knowing when to intervene with questions. As a team we needed to determine the questions we were going to ask. The better the questions, the better the answers.

Community consultation is a dynamic process, even more so in this case. We were discussing race, history, and culture, and we had to get through myths and misunderstandings. These discussions create an opportunity for the public to vet ideas; this is why the community consultation process is important. Opinions are scrutinized, questions are posed, and ideas are refined.

Our community meetings were more than theoretical musings on one idea versus another, or debate of historical fact. Instead, we heard stories, stories of humble beginnings, transition, and change. We heard words that later became the central conceptual framework for the museum—origin, movement, adaptation, and transformation—the experience of diaspora. Listening, I found, was the best way to facilitate my way through these ideological but deeply emotional questions.

As a community, client, consultant team, and public, we made some radical decisions. We would broaden the definition of "African." We would replace the popular understanding with a broader set of facts about the origins of humanity in Africa; a shift in thinking that enabled us to conceive of "Africaness" across time—from the premodern to the contemporary.

As a facilitator, I listen for consensus; these become our "big ideas." But points of conflict, the places where I don't hear agreement, become the questions that I continue to pose, through the process or within the program itself. These questions are passed on to the visitor through the exhibition and the visitor experience.

Community consultation is an ongoing conversation. Although the project ended three years ago, I'm still affected by dialogue, interactions, and exchanges. I've witnessed a change in community consciousness. Today, the notion of a Museum of the African Diaspora is much better understood and accepted. Together we found some answers.

Figure 2.11. Museum of the African Diaspora in San Francisco at night. The image in the facade is made of thousands of pictures contributed by people from around the world.

PHOTO COURTESY OF THE MUSEUM OF THE AFRICAN DIASPORA

CHAPTER 3

HOW
Methods of Museum Management

We are now ready to proceed to the methods of managing a museum. This long chapter answers the often-challenging question, "How?"

The triangle of museum functions in chapters 1 and 2 shows the management of assets and the direction of public programs as the two divergent sides of the triangle, held together—hopefully in creative tension—by administration. Leadership to impart movement to the entire triangle, giving it the direction toward accomplishment of the museum's mission, is the responsibility of the museum's chief executive, usually the director. This chapter therefore begins with the role of the executive within museum management.

3.1   THE EXECUTIVE ROLE

The executive role in museums requires both *management* and *leadership*: applying professional standards to doing the thing right (management), while inspiring the staff and board to do the right thing (leadership)—be it safeguarding heritage, ensuring that all members of the public have equal physical and intellectual access to the collections, or challenging staff to be more effective at communicating with visitors.

The director's role includes planning, policy formulation, approving procedures, and developing and maintaining relations with other institutions. It will be noted that many of these management functions are in fact shared functions with the board of trustees. That is why it is often said that an effective director spends 50 percent of his or her time working with the board. This section reviews each of these executive roles. How they are implemented will influence all aspects of museum operations and in effect create the museum's *corporate culture*.

3.1.1 Planning

The director is responsible for the disposition of a wide range of resources— collections, buildings, people, and funds. Planning is the primary means of determining how these resources should be deployed.

A *strategic plan* (in Britain often called a "corporate plan") is the most general level of planning, drafted with the purpose of organizing all aspects of a museum's activities into a coordinated direction articulated as goals to be achieved in the planning period. The mission, mandate, and current objectives and goals, as described in chapter 1, should be identified in the strategic plan and detailed for each museum division, along with a financial plan, including a budget and fund-raising targets, if necessary to achieve the objectives and goals during the planning period. If the plan is an update, progress on objectives and goals identified in previous plans should be reviewed. In addition to their value for internal management of the institution, strategic plans are very often used as supporting documents for funding or grant applications.

Since long-range planning is a role shared by board and management, strategic plans are generally prepared by a committee of management and trustees led by the director, and often assisted by consultants. It is important that all those who are expected to participate in the implementation of the strategic plan should be consulted in its preparation and should view the resultant plan as their own, because it takes their concerns and ideas into account. Clearly all ideas will not make it into the final document, but the planning process should clarify why certain goals and objectives had priority over others, and the director should be prepared to explain and discuss these matters frankly with trustees, staff, and volunteers if necessary. Strategic plans that are imposed from without or above without this consultation are often resisted (if not merely shelved); whereas, when long-range or strategic plans are formulated through consensus, there is the potential to elicit the wholehearted cooperation of all.

An outstanding example of a strategic or corporate planning process is presented here in Ian Blatchford's case study on "Strategic Corporate Planning at the Victoria and Albert Museum." As Ian's case study makes clear, the V&A consulted deeply with all those who would have the responsibility of implementing the plan, with excellent results.

STRATEGIC CORPORATE PLANNING AT THE VICTORIA AND ALBERT MUSEUM
Setting the Agenda, Thinking Backward, and Creating Good Luck
By Ian Blatchford

All organizations, whether in the public or private sector, struggle to find the right format for their strategic plan. This concern is partly about the process to follow in agreeing on objectives, but it also concerns the way in which those objectives are recorded and communicated. Too much detail and paralysis ensues because a plethora of objectives swamps really important targets, whereas a plan that is too vague and aspirational means that management is never truly accountable for specific objectives.

In 2003, the Victoria and Albert Museum (V&A) decided to adopt a new approach to planning, which would be a mixture of setting medium-term strategic goals (for a five-year period) combined with very specific objectives for the year ahead. Thus the current plan (2007–2012) sets short-term milestones (2008–2009), mid-term milestones (2009–2011), and then outcomes for 2012.

Setting these objectives proved to be very stimulating for the whole museum, with the director and deputy director hosting workshops with a wide group of colleagues, especially the crucial middle management who really deliver much of the museum's essential work. These workshops had unexpected benefits because they brought together people from all departments and disciplines (an obvious benefit) but also exploded our lazy assumption that people from the same discipline or department would share a common agenda. We recorded the top twenty priorities that emerged from these workshops, and all became part of the plan. Many staff were surprised that their feedback had such a direct impact on strategy. These priorities covered a wide range of concerns but were notable for their brutal reality about the need, for example, to invest in information technology and training, without which much of this strategic or corporate plan was fantasy.

People found it helpful to think backward, starting with the longer-term objectives and then filling in the detailed actions that would need to be completed in order to achieve the big-picture objective. Starting with the wider vision also helps to avoid two important risks:

- The first pitfall is that the whole plan is driven by the current agent of a major funder (in the case of the V&A it is the British government's Culture Department), whereas a good plan should be thinking about new or emerging agendas and thus shaping government policy sometimes, rather than always reacting to it.

- The second risk is that the plan might be simply a list of "everything we are doing" (a very common fault in strategic or corporate plans) without providing a sense of priorities and themes. The 2012 outcomes allowed the museum to think about a "balanced score card" so that its objectives are a healthy mixture of stewardship (acquisitions, conservation), scholarship and research, public access, and business excellence and efficiency.

It is easy to understand why plans fall into the second trap because it is natural for colleagues to feel that if their core work (e.g., building maintenance, core conservation, and the like) is absent from the plan then is it not valued. We took great care to explain that the strategic objectives are only possible because we are able to assume a level of core excellence in essential museum activities.

Thinking backward also assisted in making decisions about resource allocations, because staff found it a more imaginative approach than the "zero-based" budgeting so adored by accountants. The new plan is also popular because it only sets deadlines and numerical targets where they really matter. Previous annual plans set deadlines for each quarter, but when we took a hard look at these landmarks it became clear that many of the deadlines were pointless and created perverse concentration on very short-term "box ticking," which was of no strategic importance.

A simple example of how the new plans work is that we have set ourselves goals for audiences (through site visits and the Web) that we want to achieve by 2012, and the plan contains a series of cumulative steps over 2007–2011 aimed at achieving them. Staff felt that this gave them a much clearer of idea of how exhibitions, collection digitization projects, and new gallery capital projects play their role.

The new plan was launched in tandem with our "CulturePlan" initiative, which aimed to explore more efficient and accountable ways of working as an organization. This project encouraged colleagues to offer ideas on how decision making could be more transparent and how cross-disciplinary working could become more natural. It must be admitted that we all approached this cautiously and with a degree of skepticism, but in reality it has been wholly positive. It certainly helped that we engaged an external branding/culture consultant to initiate the project and provide a degree of objectivity.

Any strategic or corporate plan rests on the assumption that people will articulate clearly, honestly, and quickly any concerns about resources, pressures, and priorities, rather than commit to a project in the secret hope that it will go away. CulturePlan has ensured that colleagues are more confident about sounding an early warning about project difficulties or emerging priorities.

Creating the new plan was very hard work, but it has been worth the effort. Most of the time it simply keeps the museum on course, and is useful in repelling distracting ideas or proposed partnerships. Nevertheless, the environment changes, and new opportunities can be tested for their fit within the overall objectives. Museums often have a reputation for being slow to assess new proposals, and the strategic or corporate plan can help the organization to become more flexible. That just might, in turn, enhance the chances of good luck striking.

Figure 3.1. The John Madejski Garden, which opened in July 2005 (designed by Kim Wilkie)

IAN BLATCHFORD

The term *strategic plan* describes both a type of plan and the planning process to arrive at the plan. This planning process involves determining the best future for an organization by studying its situation in a changing environment through the use of both external and internal consultation and research:

- *External* consultations—including interviews with cultural, political, and business leaders or other members of the community; "workshop" meetings with people who support or use the museum such as donors, funders, teachers, and frequent visitors; and focus groups with those who do not use the museum—help planners understand the museum's public role, how it serves the community, where it fails and how it can be improved.
- *Internal* consultation includes interviews and workshops with staff, volunteers, members, and trustees, and helps in assessing the institution's strengths and weaknesses in relation to the museum's mission, and the opportunities and threats facing it.

Retreats, as part of a strategic planning process, are extended meetings at which trustees and senior staff withdraw for a day or more to:

- consider long-range directions and key issues and challenges both within the institution and in its global environment;
- review the mission statement and revise it if necessary; and
- identify a relatively small number of strategic directions (usually no more than three to five) that can then be translated into long-range qualitative institutional goals (as defined in section 1.2).

Based on those goals, specific quantitative objectives (described in subsection 1.3.4) for each division or department, along with a budget and timetable, are developed by management and staff. The strategic plan as a whole is finalized by the board. It will then be implemented by the entire institution, and progress should be evaluated annually to ensure that the organization stays on target or that the plan is amended.

The strategic plan is usually for three to five years, and may be the "ignition" for other planning activities, such as a master plan if some major capital development is foreseen. Some institutions combine the two, with the strategic plan setting the overall qualitative direction and the master plan then applying its conclusions to an analysis of the museum's collections, space, or facility needs. (Much more detail on the strategic planning process is provided by authors Gail Dexter Lord and Kate Markert in their 2007 book, *The Manual of Strategic Planning for Museums*, also published by AltaMira Press.)

A *master plan* is more long term (usually for around twenty years) and more detailed than a strategic plan, and it focuses on the museum's resource requirements of space, facilities, personnel, and funding and the means for fulfilling them. It should include the following elements:

- *institutional plan*, addressing both the museum's governance structure and its relations with its entire institutional context (government, educational institutions, other museums, private sector, tourism, and so on), as well as the museum's mission, mandate, and statement of purpose;
- *market analysis*, which may comprise the results of visitor surveys as well as demographic and sociographic analyses of the community—resident, school, and tourist—aimed at identifying the museum's target markets;
- *collection analysis*, projecting growth as well as present dimensions and directions of the museum's collecting activities, including current and desired levels of density of display and storage of the collections, and issues of collection management and care;
- *public program plan*, projecting the activities that the museum wishes to undertake or has been undertaking, ranging from exhibitions through interpretation of its collection to education, publications, extension services, outreach and such visitor services public amenities as toilets, shops, or catering, in relation to the museum's target markets;
- *communications strategy*, dedicated to attracting those target markets to the museum, not merely through advertising and other marketing methods, but through visitor services and activities that will meet the museum's objectives and motivate visitors to return;
- *staffing plan*, projecting requirements for human resources in order to operate the desired level of public programs with the collections identified in the foregoing sections of the plan;
- *facilities plan*, deducing the space and facilities required for the collections in storage and on display, for the public programs and amenities, and for the needed support facilities and work spaces for staff;
- *capital cost projection*, the amount needed to upgrade or build the requisite space, to provide furnishings and equipment, or to build the planned exhibits;
- *attendance, revenue, and expense projections*, forecasting all sources of income and categories of expenditure, with a view to identifying the need for subsidy or other fund-raising;
- *funding strategy*, to meet both capital and operating fund requirements from public, private, and self-generated sources; and
- *implementation schedule*, designed to move the museum from its present situation to the one outlined in the master plan.

The interconnectedness of the components outlined in this description demonstrates the benefits of completing the entire master plan. However, when no major capital development program is foreseen, it may be useful to undertake only some of the component parts—for example a collection development strategy or an institutional plan, for sectors that are considered to be weak relative to the museum's mission and goals, and need to be improved.

For proposed new museums, relocations, or expansions, a *feasibility study* would cover the same ground as the master plan, except that it should conclude with a statement of the project's feasibility. This must be based on a set of assumptions about the quality and size of the proposed institution, its location, marketing, management, freedom from debt, and the like. Feasibility of museums is not the same as feasibility of a private-sector project, where profit is the criterion; for public museums it is usually a question of establishing the level of annual subsidy, grants, donations, endowment, sponsorship, or other fundraising that would be required beyond the potential for self-generated revenues, and a judgment as to the likelihood of such annual financial support.

Plans developed as a method of managing specific activities—such as exhibition plans (3.3.1), education plans (3.3.3), and marketing plans (3.3.6)— are the shared responsibility of management and staff (not of management and board), and are therefore considered later in this chapter.

3.1.2 Policies

While plans are a method of management directed primarily toward future accomplishment, *policies* are instrumental to regulating both the fulfillment of present museum functions and the achievement of a desired future condition at the requisite level of quality. Both plans and policies should be aligned with the museum's mission and mandate statements.

Policies are formulated in order to ensure standards of quality and public accountability in the accomplishment of museum functions. They are therefore a shared responsibility of management and board, in which management through the director is responsible for policy formulation and for presentation of policy options to the board, while the trustees are responsible for ensuring that the policies are consistent with the museum's mission and goals, and that the institution has the resources needed to implement them.

The precise number and names of museum policies vary. Among the policies required by most museums are:

- *collection policy* (sometimes called "collection management policy"), including acquisition, deaccessioning and loan policies;
- *conservation policy*, which may be included in a collection management policy;
- *documentation policy*, another that may be part of the collection policy;
- *education policy*;

- *exhibition policy*;
- *human resources policy*;
- *public access policy*, including policy on access for the disabled;
- *communication policy*, including the interpretation of the collection, but also extending to way-finding in the building, graphics, Internet and Web communications, marketing and media;
- *research policy*, which should also include policy on intellectual property;
- *security policy*; and
- *visitor services or customer care policy*.

Policies should identify the museum's goals in relation to each of these functions and should establish the level of quality to which the museum is committed in the implementation of its policies and plans. Since policies relate to ongoing functions, they should be drafted by the senior staff responsible—so that the chief of security, for instance, should be asked to draft the security policy—with the director serving as editor and joining in any revision required to align the policy with the museum's plans.

Policies should then be recommended by the director to the board and should not express professional standards that are unrealistic in terms of the museum's budget, space, technology, or staff limitations, but should project attainable levels of excellence in each function, given the museum's mission and resources. They should be comprehensive, relating to all implications of the fulfillment of that function.

Once approved by the trustees, policy implementation becomes a staff responsibility, delegated to the respective managers for the policy area. However, trustees retain responsibility for monitoring the policies, so the director should report regularly to the board on their implementation with recommendations for policy changes if required in order to ensure that no museum functions are neglected and that policies are more than wishful thinking. Since many museums find that they need about ten to twelve policies, it is convenient to review and report on one policy per month: thus a board that meets monthly may consider a different policy document and a report on its implementation, along with any recommendations for changes, at each meeting—collection policy in January, exhibition policy in February, security policy in March, and so on—ensuring that through the year all policies have been considered, reviewed, and changed if necessary. In this way the board retains an energetic role in the governance of museum functions, and policies remain relevant and implementable.

3.1.3 Procedures

A museum's procedures are its established ways of doing things. Many museum functions must be discharged in a systematic way—such as documentation of a new accession, or security measures. The *procedures manual* is the main means of codifying and communicating the systematic means of conducting museum functions and related tasks.

Like policies, procedures are related to museum functions, but they are more specific and more quantified because they are linked to the attainment of specific quantitative objectives for those functions, whereas policies are related to longer-range qualitative goals. Procedures manuals record the steps in the activity as recommended by the museum in order to realize the level of quality desiderated in its policies. The subject matter of procedures manuals may range from welcoming and ticketing procedures through documentation forms and condition reporting to security routines and—a particularly important one—an e*mergency procedures manual.*

One area where procedures manuals should be used with special caution is in *visitor services.* It is important to remember that each visitor is an individual, and that the service required by that individual visitor may or may not have been anticipated in the visitor service or customer care manual. Staff serving the visitors—including security guards—should be regularly reminded that service to the individual visitor, as long as it is within the guidelines of the museum's policies, may override the strictures of a procedures manual.

Curatorial research, exhibition planning, and design are examples of other areas where procedures manuals may not be appropriate. Even here, however, there may be certain segments of the work that can best be accomplished by following a set routine that will most often obtain the level of quality desired. Library practices, for example, may benefit from being the subject of a procedures manual. *Checklists* in procedures manuals are always valuable: Have the artifacts for the exhibition been identified? Have the loan agreements been sent and received back? Has their documentation been reviewed? Has their condition been checked?

Procedures manuals should be prepared by the responsible museum officer, who may find that many manuals are required to provide guidance for all the activities occurring in that department. Procedures manuals are often simply a point-form listing of steps that any employee, including new recruits, should follow in carrying out a specific activity; but they should always link those steps to the quality level articulated in the relevant policy. They should be consistent with that policy and should be reviewed and approved by the director, who should ensure that they will result in implementation of the policy. Whenever the policy is changed, therefore, the procedures manual should be updated.

3.1.4 Reports

With policies and procedures in place, day-to-day management of the museum is conducted with regular *reports* on all aspects of their implementation. As the saying goes, "management never gets what it expects, it only gets what it inspects." In the well-managed museum, reporting relationships and schedules for reports are clearly defined and understood at all levels. Each department head and deputy director should regularly be reviewing reports and summarizing them at larger intervals for the next level in the hierarchy. For instance, the admissions clerk should be reporting cash and attendance figures daily to the visitor services officer, who will be summarizing these reports weekly to the public programs officer, who in turn will prepare a monthly summary for the director, who will report on attendance quarterly to the board, which will issue an annual report based on these cumulative figures.

Reports should provide not just *quantitative data*—visitation, revenue, relative humidity variations, budget versus actual costs, acquisitions, donations, membership, and so forth—but should also provide a concise *qualitative analysis*—marketing impact, visitor satisfaction, progress in collection development, significance of research results, and so on. The incisive ability to identify key factors in any area of museum activity relative to the museum's objectives for that function distinguishes outstanding staff members from the merely competent.

The relationship between plans, policies, procedures, and reports as methods of management is summarized in table 3.1.

3.1.5 Relations with Other Institutions

The most inspired plans, excellent policies, and impeccable procedures may not avail if the museum is not functioning effectively in its institutional context. Museums are not isolated institutions, but in almost all cases exist within

Table 3.1. Methods of Management

Management Method	Relevant to	Time Reference	Drafted by:	Approval by:
Plans	Mission, goals, and objectives	Future	Director and management	Trustees
Policies	Functions and goals	Present and future	Director and management	Trustees
Procedures	Functions and objectives	Immediate and present	Staff	Director
Reports	Fulfillment of functions	Recent past and present	Staff	Managers and Director

a network of related agencies, public and private. The other institutions that impinge on museums usually include:

- levels of government and government agencies (3.1.5.1)
- other museums and museum associations (3.1.5.2)
- educational institutions (3.1.5.3)
- specialist societies and foundations (3.1.5.4)
- the tourist industry (3.1.5.5)
- the private sector (3.1.5.6)
- communities of interest (3.1.5.7)

Three levels of intensity may be distinguished among these relationships:

- The most basic is simply a matter of good professional practice—participating in the relevant museums association or a marketing consortium of area attractions, for instance.
- A more critical level to the survival of the museum is the creation and maintenance of relationships related to funding—relations with governments, foundations, sponsors, and donors.
- The most advanced level is the establishment of *partnerships*—collaborations between institutions entered into for mutual benefit. These may be between museums sharing an exhibition, between a museum and a school combining for an education program, or a *public-private partnership* designed to support the very establishment and operation of the museum itself.

In each instance it is important to determine who the partners are that will be most beneficial; how the relationships serve the museum's mission; what the impacts on staff, space, and budget will be; whether the partnership needs to be exclusive; and so on. Creating and sustaining the right mix of relationships with a judicious balance of the museum's finite resources is a significant challenge at all levels of museum management. The following sections consider each type of relationship in turn.

3.1.5.1 Levels of Government and Government Agencies

Museums are inherently "political" institutions: history museums communicate the meanings of our past; art museums present works of art that often comment on the meaning or values of our personal and social lives; and science museums interpret what we think we know about the world around us. Museums are intensively involved in communicating values and ideologies about the meaning of their collections. These ideologies are usually implicit, but they can become explicit very quickly in a temporary exhibition on a politically sensitive subject—or one that suddenly becomes sensitive because of the content of the exhibition.

Further, museums are "political" in the sense that they are very often funded by, or form part of, a government service. Whether they are government line departments, at "arm's length" from government, independent non-profit associations, or even civil society institutions with a mixed funding base, museums are very often dependent on government funding programs and policies, including myriad tax policies and government grant programs.

Museum management must therefore be concerned with the museum's position in relation to city, county, state or provincial, and ultimately national, government—not only to ministries or departments responsible for culture and heritage, but also those concerned with tourism, education, and taxes. And if the museum's mandate touches on science, the military, transportation, or agriculture, these government departments may become important as well. In many jurisdictions the ministry or department administering employment grants is among the most important to the museum. Managing the museum's relationship with government is a major responsibility of the museum's director and trustees.

In some jurisdictions one national, state, or provincial museum has been assigned responsibility for the administration of the general museums service, or the distribution of grants to other museums. This often leads to perceived conflict of interest problems, at least in the eyes of the other museums, so that it is usually preferable to establish a separate entity for grants administration, and often for other centralized services as well.

Such government line departments or quasi-governmental agencies responsible for museums have in many instances developed a high level of professionalism in assisting museums. Many have wide-ranging responsibilities for archaeological sites or architectural heritage preservation as well as museums. Some have established accreditation or registration programs that have been instrumental in encouraging or requiring museum trustees to ensure that their institutions meet professional standards. Others, like the state museum services in Germany, provide consultants to assist museums technically. Most employ grants officers whose task is to ensure that public funds are effectively and efficiently spent in their constituent museums.

Other government agencies, such as the Canadian Heritage Information Network and the Canadian Conservation Institute in Ottawa, have established internationally recognized standards in their respective disciplines. Independent organizations—such as Britain's Museums Documentation Association, and in the United States the Getty Conservation Institute—are also actively involved in research and standard setting that influences museums far outside their country's borders. Museums in historic buildings may be concerned to meet standards established by their own or other countries' national trusts or parks administrations, as well as international accords between governments respecting the conservation of historic sites. The United Nations Educational, Scientific and Cultural Organization (UNESCO) is another source of international standards through such mechanisms as controlling World Heritage Site status.

As noted in section 2.5, in recent years many governments faced with fiscal restraints have moved to make museums more self-reliant in obtaining funds. Some museums that were formerly "free" to the public have found admission charges necessary, while others, like Britain's national museums, have been given additional subsidy in order to allow them to offer free admission and encourage greater social inclusion. Many museums have been obliged by changes in government funding patterns to give much more attention to their shops, food services, and rental capability, and increasingly to seek donors or sponsorships in the private sector. Managing such transitions is often challenging and can be done much more effectively if the museum maintains a positive relationship with all relevant governments. In some cases governments at various levels (such as a city's parks department) can provide important help of a nonmonetary nature, such as providing buildings, grounds, and maintenance staff.

Another long-range concern is the government's attitude toward museum expansion or renovation. Growing collections are constantly generating the need for more space, and professional standards require upgrading of facilities. Politicians and government officials may view such tendencies with alarm, especially in times of fiscal restraint; yet in periods of high unemployment, especially in regions of chronic employment problems, the responsible development of museums or historic sites as cultural tourism attractions may be a politically expedient as well as a meaningful initiative that can be launched with government support. In many places, as noted in section 2.5, museums have become part of a determined government program to change the image as well as the economic basis of a community. Bilbao, Glasgow, and Manchester are among examples usually cited, while the regional government of Nord-Pas de Calais looks forward to the establishment of an outpost of the Louvre at Lens in northern France. In the famous case of Bilbao, the success of the Museo Guggenheim Bilbao made it possible for the governments of the area to go further and support the expansion and renovation of the local fine arts museum.

Worldwide, it is clear that museums and their governments are closely related, and wise museum managers will pay close attention to this relationship. Maintaining an independent viewpoint in their exhibitions, publications, and other programs is a challenge that varies from country to country, but is present everywhere. Respecting professional standards while sustaining good relations with all levels of government around the world requires an essential ingredient of great leaders—courage.

3.1.5.2 Other Museums and Museum Associations

Museums are not directly competitive in the sense that private-sector attractions usually are. Because a very high proportion of museum visitors also visit similar or related museums in the same area or elsewhere, museums do not compete with each other, but can stimulate greater interest and activity among all their visitors, even when they have related or overlapping mandates in the same market.

Thus museums have everything to gain by cooperation with other museums: this may involve *partnerships* with similar museums, or *pairing* for marketing purposes with entirely dissimilar ones, in order to reach a wider audience. A military or transportation museum, for instance, might be advantaged to form a marketing partnership with a decorative arts museum nearby, in order that both might widen their market by offering a mutual discount on each other's entry fee. In many cities or regions, museums and other attractions have associated together in a marketing consortium. In Richmond, Virginia, and Cleveland, Ohio, museums went further to form *cultural collaboratives*, aimed at finding ways to economize through joint ordering of supplies, or sharing of specialized staff.

Sharing exhibitions, either one-to-one or via area organizations such as a regional museums' association or a group of science centers or children's museums in different cities, is a long-standing means of cooperation among museums. More recently, the Solomon R. Guggenheim Museum Foundation in New York has led the way in sharing its entire collection with associated museums established for that purpose around the world. Following that lead, a consortium of nine French museums has entered into a long-term relationship with Abu Dhabi in the United Arab Emirates, whereby collections from the Louvre and other national museums of France will rotate on long-term loan over a twenty-year period, while the "Louvre Abu Dhabi" builds its own collection. In England the Tate has established branches at Liverpool and St. Ives in addition to its two London locations, to make its collections more accessible.

Many museums and museum professionals relate to their colleague institutions through museum associations. At regional, state, provincial, and national levels these have been instrumental in the development of the profession, in English-speaking countries especially. Their conferences, seminars, and publications are among the most important means of training and professional development for their members, both as institutions and as individuals. Some, like the American Association of Museums, have established accreditation or registration programs that have succeeded in raising professional standards for both institutions and individuals.

The International Council of Museums (ICOM) is the worldwide equivalent. In some countries, the national chapter of ICOM plays a similar role to that of museum associations elsewhere. For others, the specialized international committees of ICOM, such as the International Council on Conservation (ICC) or the International Association of Transportation and Communications Museums (IATM), are the vital link with fellow professionals or institutions with related concerns. The triennial conferences of ICOM, the annual meetings of its international committees, its journal, *Museums International*, and the many newsletters of its committees, are for many the very lifeline of the profession. ICOM's ethical standards and guidelines are also instrumental in supporting professional practices in many countries.

The influence of ICOM has been restricted in some countries by the practice of appointing only a few representative individuals to attend conferences, instead of recruiting members throughout the profession. Democratizing ICOM membership, and encouraging widespread participation in its committees through its publications, is of long-term importance in the development of the museum profession in these countries, along with the encouragement of national or regional museum associations. Professional development is very much tied to the existence of these organizations, whose conferences and publications provide a venue for presentation and discussion of issues of mutual concern, as well as stimulating career development for younger members of the profession.

3.1.5.3 Educational Institutions

Educational services are usually an important part of a museum's institutional role—sometimes in the view of government and almost always in fulfilling its own sense of mission. The museum's relationship to universities, colleges, and schools at all levels is therefore another important dimension of its institutional context that requires adroit management. The possibilities may range from cross-appointments of professors for museum research or curatorial duties to signing a contract with the local school board to provide a certain number of tours to school parties for a fixed level of reimbursement throughout the school year. Some museums have found it advantageous to propose a "time-share" agreement with schools, whereby the museum is open every morning, for instance, only to school groups for their educational use. Others have gone further to form "museum schools," as documented in a case study in Barry Lord's book, the *Manual of Museum Learning* (2007). Museums can also participate in teacher training programs, with teachers in training receiving credit for well-prepared school tours of exhibitions.

In establishing relationships with educational institutions, the museum director or education officer should remember that the museum can be an excellent venue for *informal* learning, while the schools and universities usually provide the preferred setting for *formal* education. Retaining this distinction of roles usually helps to ensure that each institution does what it can do best, without attempting to supplant the other.

3.1.5.4 Specialist Societies and Foundations

Museum research programs, such as field archaeology activities, are sometimes rooted in their relationships with universities. Others may be developed with special interest groups, such as an entomological society or a local historical association. Public programs may be developed with a broad range of groups, from local Scout troops to cultural or linguistic minority associations. Committed museum managers at all levels of staff should be continually exploring the museum's potential to extend its services by working closely with community organizations of all kinds.

In some cases such cooperation may have important fund-raising implications. This is especially true of working with *foundations* that have special interests. Some of these, like the Getty Foundation or the Gulbenkian Foundation, have programs that are focused exclusively on museums, whereas others have broader educational or research objectives that the museum can meet. Museum managers need to be constantly aware of the prospects for working with national or international foundations of relevance to them. A project that is beyond the reach of a local museum may become realizable with the aid of an international foundation.

3.1.5.5 The Tourist Industry

As museums have been obliged to be more self-reliant, many have taken a greater interest in tourism. With tourism emerging at the turn of the century as the world's biggest industry, and with cultural tourism increasingly recognized as a very dynamic sector of that industry, museums must take full advantage of their prominent roles as tourist attractions. Even relatively small museums can play a part in extending visitors' length of stay to a region of otherwise limited appeal, and the director should lose no opportunity to communicate to political and business leaders the potential or actual value of the museum's role in tourism.

Cooperation between museums and the tourism industry is therefore of vital importance to both. In general, staff in cultural institutions, including museums, have had limited understanding of—or even sympathy for—their tourist markets, and often barely tolerate tourism operators. These operators in turn are often unaware of the realities facing the museums and other cultural attractions on which they may be dependent for their livelihood. Wherever possible, museums should take the lead in bridging this gap, learning to work with tourism operators to mutual advantage.

Tourism has many motivators—visiting family or friends, sports, business, or shopping—but *cultural tourism* is among the strongest of them, and can easily be combined with any or all of the others. Thus it is important for museums to seek ways to include themselves in the tourist industry—a discounted museum ticket or a special offer at the museum shop provided at hotel check-in can be beneficial for everyone, including the tourist!

Sustainable tourism is an important concept that is being developed in many of the more responsible tourist attraction centers. It begins from the recognition that tourism can be destructive of the very resource that attracts it—as perhaps most tellingly demonstrated at some of the world's great historical or archaeological sites. The imposition of special taxes on hotels, restaurants, or other businesses benefiting from tourism, and the provision of those taxes directly to those responsible for the preservation of the heritage, is one way that tourism and the cultural or heritage sectors can work together to ensure that tourism becomes a truly renewable resource industry.

3.1.5.6 The Private Sector: Public/Private Partnerships

The tourism industry is only one area within the private sector that is of interest to museum managers today. Museum membership programs routinely include *corporate memberships* that encourage companies to join in order to gain such benefits as free admission for employees, discounts at the museum shop, or reduced rentals on meeting spaces. The prestige of the company's association with the museum is typically acknowledged on a plaque near the entrance.

The private sector is most important as a source of donations or sponsorships. Museums seeking such support need to develop a *sponsorship policy* in order to ensure that their standards of scholarship and objectivity are not compromised by the sponsors' interests. This has proven important, for example, among science centers with commercial sponsors for exhibitions affecting consumer preferences, such as exhibits on food or health choices. With such a policy clearly articulated and understood by all from the beginning, however, sponsorships can be instrumental in making possible exhibitions, publications, or other programs that could not otherwise be attempted.

Sponsorships need not be on a grand scale. One public art gallery in western Canada, for instance, had success in developing an exhibition sponsorship program to appeal to small local professional firms. Companies were offered a range of exhibitions each year for an affordable fee, and they became accustomed to choosing and taking an active interest in shows that appealed to their management, coming to the exhibition opening for public acknowledgment of their assistance and a chance to meet the artists.

Working with the private sector can be a challenge to trustees and museum professionals, who must ensure that the public interest continues to be served. It can also offer new opportunities to the museum to become directly involved in the economic development of its community. If the local economic development priority is to provide jobs in the telecommunications industry, for example, the regional history museum might contribute an exhibition on the history of communications in the area, while the local science center presents educational and interactive exhibits on the principles of telecommunications, both sponsored by the industry. The Science Museum in London devised an excellent example of this kind of programming on a national scale, with a decade-long series of exhibitions on new and old materials used in manufacturing, sponsored by the British steel industry. Disciplined by appropriate policies, museums can find ways to serve the public interest in collaboration with the private sector.

Private-public partnerships are the most advanced form of relationship between the private sector and a public institution like a museum. Their allure is sometimes illusory: the branch of the Royal Armouries at Leeds, for example, was established in the forlorn hope that private sector partners could find a way to make it a profitable operation. More successful are the partnerships between real estate development and museums, whereby the developer provides the base building and a significant capital contribution in exchange for planning permission from the local authority or permission to build condominiums, hotels, or offices in excess of regular planning guidelines. These partnerships are often brokered and monitored by the local and regional governments. The next challenge is for the museum to receive ongoing annual support from the commercial development in recognition of the very real contribution the museum makes to quality of life and to property values. Key in these partnerships is to ensure that the private sector pays for operating costs either annually or through an endowment fund, in addition to the initial capital outlay, in exchange for the rights to proceed with some adjacent lucrative development.

3.1.5.7 Communities of Interest

Thus far we have discussed relationships with other organizations or corporations. However, museum management also needs to be conscious of their actual or potential relationships with a broader, more amorphous group that may be called a "*community of interest*." Specialized museums are usually keenly aware of such communities—the yachting community for the National Sailing Hall of Fame, or train spotters for railway museums. But in fact all museums have a relationship with a community of interest that can be developed to mutual benefit. For a local history museum this may be on its doorstep, although even in that case there may be some historic events of national or global significance that broaden the community of interest considerably. Art museums share an international community of interest in their subject but may also focus on specific sectors of it, such as wildlife art or Asian art. Ethnographic, archaeological, and anthropological museums have particularly important relationships with their communities of interest, which include the *origin communities* of their collections: the South Australian Museum in Adelaide, for instance, has an intense relationship of service to the aboriginal community, as the Museum of the American Indian in Washington has with the native peoples of the Americas.

The advent of the civil society museum, noted in section 2.5, makes the cultivation of relationships with the museum's community of interest of particular importance. Given its reliance on a broad range of funding sources, public and private, it is most important that these museums remain prized by their natural communities of interest, both within their geographical location, and globally. A conscious effort to cultivate these relationships can be fruitful: a museum with an important collection of West Coast North American Indian artifacts, for example, might begin by establishing partnerships with the contemporary nations that are the "origin communities" of that collection, but through that relationship might extend to a much wider group of programs with indigenous people worldwide, bringing Maori people and artifacts, for instance, from New Zealand to participate in international exhibitions or research programs.

3.1.6 Meetings, Meetings, Meetings

"Is this meeting necessary?" The director of a large American museum confessed several years ago that there were at least thirteen meetings *per week* that she was supposed to attend, from annual general meetings through monthly board meetings and staff meetings to meetings of task forces and a seemingly endless round of internal and external committees. Needless to say, she had developed the habit of delegation. But were all those meetings really necessary?

Looking around a meeting room of a dozen staff members or trustees assembled for two hours, it is possible to calculate not only the *direct cost* of the meeting to the museum in person-hours, but also the *opportunity cost* as its participants are prevented from performing other functions while attending the meeting. The impact of e-mail, voice mail, and computerized bulletin boards have already weakened the tyranny of the meeting over corporate life somewhat, as we all have become accustomed to asynchronous methods of communication. Conference calls and video conferences are another way of making in-person meetings less frequent. By the end of the twenty-first century we may well look back on the previous era as one dominated by the face-to-face meeting, whereas it may now be possible to limit the number of such occasions to those situations where person-to-person communication and collegiality of the group are essential.

However, section 2.3.2.3 has already established the importance of standing committees and project-specific task forces for museum management. And since they can enable people to work together to achieve institutional goals, meetings often *are* necessary, and it is management's job to ensure that meetings are productive by utilizing such simple tools as an *agenda* and *minutes*. If the meeting is virtual, via conference call or video, these tools are all the more important.

All participants in the meeting should be invited to contribute to the agenda in advance of the meeting. One director is known to have cancelled all further meetings when he realized that only he was setting the agendas, and that all participants were deferring to him for decisions. The purpose of a meeting is to share viewpoints and to gain collegial commitment to common purposes; this collegiality should begin with the agenda and continue throughout a truly participatory process of discussion.

In order to prevent such discussion from becoming dilatory—and again recognizing the considerable opportunity cost represented by the meeting—the agenda should be *timed*, and the chair must keep the meeting on schedule. Time allocations should be checked with all participants at the outset and adjusted during the course of the meeting only by majority consent.

Minutes should be kept, preferably by someone who serves only that role in the meeting, with requirements for *action* indicated and allocated to individuals or groups in the margin. If these action lists all point to the same person, it is obvious that the meeting was not necessary, but a reconsideration of work loads may be! Minutes should be distributed within forty-eight hours of the meeting, with another forty-eight allowed for corrections so that the actions arising from the meeting may be readily implemented, and agreements reached may become the basis for future action. Minutes should be understood as a planning and management tool, not as a passive record. Reading the minutes at or prior to the next meeting should then point to the fundamental issues to be resolved.

3.1.7 Communication

The meeting is one form of communication utilized by museums. In section 3.1.4 we have already emphasized the importance of another form, regular reports. In general, the museum manager must be continually addressing both *formal* and *informal* means of communication.

3.1.7.1 Formal Communication

There are three degrees of formal communication among those concerned with the management of a museum:

- notification;
- consultation; and
- delegation.

Whenever a decision is taken, the museum manager must determine who needs to be *notified* of the decision. For example, the decision to extend the time period of an exhibition, or simply to open the museum for an evening event, will almost certainly require notification of the security staff and probably of the food service, ticketing, and shop staff as well. Failure to notify all those affected by such decisions *promptly* is one of the cardinal sins in museum administration and one of the most common complaints of those who have to live with the consequences. Notification should not be casual but should be formally controlled and stated within the museum management system by official notification memoranda that must be dated, timed, and signed by the relevant museum officer.

Consultation is a higher level of formal communication because it involves the opportunity costs of a meeting or some form of written input from those consulted. Considering a possible decision, the museum manager must determine whether notification of that decision would be sufficient, or whether it requires consultation with those affected before it can be taken. If consultation is thought to be worthwhile, the manager must truly *consult*—that is, to listen and take the ideas of those consulted on board. Another management deficiency is to create the appearance of consultation when all that was really intended was notification. It adds the injury of wasting time to the insult of not listening to people's views and leads to cynicism among staff, which is then most harmful when management really *does* want to consult them.

The value to the institution of the decision under consideration should be proportionate to the person-hours devoted to consultation. A major decision, such as eliminating admission charges where there have been some before, may require months of carefully considered consultative meetings, whereas a decision to add a new line of stock to the shop may be accomplished by consultation with the relevant curators and the retail manager in half an hour. In either case, the consultation should not be casual but announced in advance and consciously undertaken by all concerned.

Delegation is perhaps the most important formal means of communication, since it is most directly connected with accomplishing the museum's functions. Like the other formal means of communication, it should not be done casually but should be made explicit by the delegating officer to the person to whom the task is delegated. Assumed or vaguely comprehended delegation is the root of many of the communications problems that afflict museum workers. Both delegators and delegatees should insist that the act of delegation be recorded, with the extent and limitations of the delegated responsibility made clear.

3.1.7.2 Informal Communication

Careful notification, consultation, and delegation may be of little use unless the corporate culture of the museum also encourages a healthy climate of *informal communication*. This involves an awareness of the art of *creative listening*, which starts with an understanding that listening is an active, rather than a passive, endeavor. Personnel at all levels, including trustees and volunteers, should be encouraged to understand that listening to each other is a creative task and that it is useful to "check back" with each other by saying, in effect, "What I hear you saying is . . ." Only when the original speaker confirms that what has been heard is what was said can we be sure that effective communication has occurred.

Even more important for an effective management culture is attention to *motivation*. Proper notification, consultation, and delegation, even in a climate of responsible listening, are not enough: the museum manager should also determine whether all those concerned with a policy or procedure have been sufficiently *motivated* to carry it out. Respect for each of the individuals concerned, as well as a linking of particular actions or procedures to the long-range goals of the institution, is essential to motivating those of good will to undertake the desired activities wholeheartedly.

Above all, there must be sufficient motivation for individual *creativity*. In particular, it is vital to respect the need for creativity among curators and others concerned with developing exhibitions, education programs, publications, media, and special events, as well as those concerned with marketing them. Plans, policies, and procedures must *facilitate* creativity, not stifle it. The effective museum manager should ensure that the corporate culture of communications in the museum is one that *welcomes* the original idea and that seeks to determine how it can be achieved, rather than why it can't be realized. This criterion of encouraging creativity is the ninth and ultimately the most important measure of museum management.

9. Effective museum management respects and sustains creative solutions to the museum's problems and creative responses to the museum's opportunities among trustees, staff, and volunteers.

3.1.7.3 E-Mail

In museums, as everywhere else, e-mail has revolutionized both formal and informal communications. Even workers located in offices next to each other find it useful to record their communication via e-mail, especially since they can then notify others of it by copying to them. The workday and the workweek have of course been extended, as e-mails can reach us at any time. We enjoy both the advantage and the disadvantage of being reached immediately wherever we are—on vacation or attending a conference on the other side of the world. Mistakes that would have been caught and erased in the old days of signing letters and mailing them are now sent before they can be reconsidered, resulting in a chain of e-mail corrections or qualifications to all concerned.

An *e-mail protocol* should be part of the museum's corporate culture. The automatic habit of pressing "reply to all" especially needs to be checked by considering whether in fact everyone on the original list really needs to know the sender's reaction to the message. On the other hand, sending a message or replying to only one person when several others are mentioned or affected by the e-mail means that the recipient must now forward the message when in fact the original message could have notified all concerned at once.

Copyright, intellectual property, and legal issues specific to museums should be addressed in an e-mail protocol, along with requirements for saving or deleting messages. There should also be a way of indicating which messages in the judgment of the sender should be printed and saved on paper. These considerations are particularly important in regard to acquisitions, contract negotiations, and external relations.

3.2 COLLECTION MANAGEMENT

Collections are the defining attribute of museums. Their management is at the heart of any museum's operations. Adding to them judiciously is the most fruitful way in which a museum can grow. Documenting them fully and caring for them well is, in the long run, the fundamental criterion of a well-managed museum, since the ability of the museum to provide meaningful experiences for the public today and in the future depends on its care for its collections and the information about them.

This section begins with a consideration of the role of the curator or keeper (3.2.1) and reviews the components of collection policy (3.2.2) and the steps toward forming a collection development strategy (3.2.3) before addressing the issues of collection care—documentation (3.2.4) and conservation (3.2.5).

3.2.1 Role of the Curator

Despite the centrality of collections, the position of curator (sometimes called "keeper" in Britain) has been somewhat embattled in recent years. This was originally due to the reorganization of museums from curator-led departments to the more functional administration outlined in chapter 2. This tendency has been intensified by the increasing emphasis on public programs and visitor services and by the realization that exhibitions and other museum activities require input from many other professional disciplines as well as curatorial.

Yet, with a greater emphasis on visitor-centered exhibitions and other public programs and services, the curator's role need not be, and should not be, marginalized. On the contrary, the role of the curator in the twenty-first century should be integral to the success of the museum in achieving its public mission.

One of the difficulties with the role of the curator has been limited comprehension of its primary qualification and activity—*connoisseurship*. The intimate knowledge of a collection, whether it be mollusks or Monets or mummies, is rooted in an ability to see, to make distinctions, and above all to make judgments, about objects. This is connoisseurship, and it is as essential to a science, military, or transportation museum as it is to an art or philatelic collection. A scholar, however academically qualified, is not a curator; the curator is not simply a researcher and is not focused on written evidence, as many academics are, but roots his or her knowledge in the works of art, artifacts, specimens, or archival documents of that discipline.

The qualified curator brings such connoisseurship to the task of adding to the collection. Curatorial acquisition is a creative response to opportunity, disciplined by the necessities of the marketplace, the museum's acquisition budget, and the shape of the collection that the curator has in most cases inherited from precursors. Curatorial success at acquisitions requires inspiration, dedication, patience, opportunism, and a knowledge of sources that is both extensive and detailed.

To sustain their abilities, curators need time for research. They need to research potential acquisitions, proposed exhibition subjects, and the knowledge base for publications or media productions that the museum wishes to undertake. Research may be done in the curator's office, in the museum library, in private galleries or artists' studios, in fieldwork, or on visits to other museums and private collections abroad. The most common complaint among curators of all kinds is the lack of time for consistent pursuit of research objectives.

Case study 3.2 in this section, by Willis E. (Buzz) Hartshorn, director of the International Center for Photography in New York, on "The Curatorial Voice in Museum Management" is an evocative and representative account of the importance of sustaining and supporting the curatorial role as a critical factor in effective museum management. The case study makes clear the long-term rewards for giving priority to scholarship, research, and publications in the rigorous context of public programming—a demanding but successful high-quality exhibition program.

THE CURATORIAL VOICE IN MUSEUM MANAGEMENT
By Willis E. Hartshorn

The photographer Cornell Capa founded the International Center of Photography in 1974. A Hungarian immigrant displaced by World War II who became a successful photographer for *Life* magazine, Capa saw the need for an institution devoted to photography and had the determination to create one out of whole cloth. He intentionally wanted a center, not a museum. He felt museums were musty places full of dead objects. He wanted a place that would be alive in the present. As the brother of famed war photographer, Robert Capa, his commitment was to photojournalism and documentary photography. His belief that photography could affect social change profoundly shaped the exhibition and collection policies of the ICP.

The early years of the institution were economically challenged, which had a direct impact on the programs. On the theory that change would drive attendance revenue, exhibitions were rotated every six weeks, usually two per period. For the curators, the job was about volume, and the challenge was to create quality with limited means and time. As the institution matured, along with the standards of scholarship in the history of photography, this way of working became less and less acceptable.

Figure 3.2A. Museum Interior, International Center of Photography, New York

© NORMAN MCGRATH
WILLIS HARTSHORN

Figure 3.2B. Installation of Robert Capa: This Is War: Robert Capa at Work, International Center of Photography, New York

PHOTO BY JOHN BERENS

When Capa retired in 1994, I became the director. I had for ten years been a curator at ICP and was keenly aware that support for the exhibition and collection programs was still our greatest challenge. At the same time, there was increased competition from other institutions in New York City who were beginning to collect and exhibit photography—the Whitney and Guggenheim had newly entered the field—while the Museum of Modern Art and the Metropolitan Museum had expanded their long-standing commitments to photography. Even though we were a small institution, we had to benchmark our exhibitions with the photography programs at these much larger and better-funded institutions. The only way to remain relevant was to enhance our programs with an investment in scholarship. If we did not, ICP would never achieve the levels of support we needed to survive, let alone grow.

To meet this challenge we needed to invest in staff and be sure they had the resources needed for research, travel, and the time to do scholarly exhibitions. Over a three-year period we doubled the number of full curators to four, added three assistant curators, and modestly increased the support staff. We were fortunate to hire curators with established reputations, who had known and respected each other for many years. They

Figure 3.2C. Installation of Dark is the Room Where We Sleep: Francesc Torres, International Center of Photography, New York

PHOTO BY JOHN BERENS

also had distinct voices, with strong interests in different aspects of contemporary and historic photographic practice. As part of our strategic planning process, we began, through a series of conversations, to shape a program that respected the founder's commitment to photojournalism but also encompassed the multiple histories of photography, considering the medium not only from the point of view of art history, but also of cultural history, commerce, world events, and politics. This was a critical affirmation of vision and direction that would eventually reach all departments in the institution, particularly our higher-level education programs and the faculty who work closely with the curators.

As the director, the most ambitious decision I made was that the program would drive funding, not the reverse. If the scholarship was good, the project would find the support it deserved. This theory has proven to be remarkably true. The fact that an outside exhibition had funding was not a determinant in our taking it, as it had been in the past. This is not to say that we always raise the necessary funds or don't often rely on exhibitions from other institutions or outside curators. As in the beginning, funding remains our greatest challenge, but it has less impact on programmatic decisions.

In order to provide curatorial staff time for researching the exhibitions and development staff time to secure funding, we reduced the number of shows and extended the length of the exhibition periods, giving us three changes per year rather than the four that had become normal. The fear was a decline in attendance, shop sales, and press. This has not been the case. We initiated biweekly meetings—one to discuss fund-raising and another to discuss the status of projects. These increased communication between development, curatorial, education, and marketing personnel.

As the scholarship of the exhibitions increased, the reviews became more numerous and consistently enthusiastic, and the board took greater pride in the programs and the staff. This encouraged funding from individuals, donations of work, and expanded participation in the exhibitions and collection committees. It brought more serious collectors to the institution and an increase in potential board prospects.

During this period we were also engaged in a major capital campaign and relocation of the institution. It was difficult to maintain the focus on programs during a time when the institution was engaged in such a transformation. But this seemed vitally important. Too often in other institutions the pressures of relocation and expansion had resulted in new galleries with underwhelming exhibitions. It was to our great advantage that we were able to manage both aspects of institutional growth, each helping to justify the other.

With the support of trustees and the enthusiasm of the curators, we began a publishing program that produces up to six books a year, allowing every major exhibition to have a catalog. We are beginning to identify collection-based publications to expand our offerings. Importantly, the catalogs preserve the work of the curators and photographers, contribute to our knowledge of photographic history, and allow for an audience that might not be able to see the exhibitions. A motivating concern of the trustees, the publications have also served to increase our visibility as an institution internationally.

An institution is only as good as its programs. Exhibitions and publications are particularly powerful because they reach the largest public. They are a sure way to build or damage your reputation. One bad exhibition is equal to dozens of good ones in shaping public opinion. For the International Center of Photography, investing in our curatorial staff has been a key part of a larger strategic goal of becoming more vital, influential, and internationally recognized. The perception that our programs are making a significant contribution to the field has helped to build the morale of the staff and board, at the same time that it has elevated the reputation of the institution.

Research is the unseen motor of all museum programs. Without adequate and accurate research, public programs can be misleading at best, dead wrong at worst. Poorly researched acquisitions can litter the collection with irrelevant or unimportant examples—or worse, with copies or fakes. The most sophisticated high-tech multimedia programs depend on the quality and extent of the museum's research—some of them literally transposing the collection database into a publicly accessible format.

Since their responsibilities continually draw their attention to the museum's need for research, curators have devised various ways of finding time to undertake it:

- One strategy is to focus attention on a relatively narrow or even esoteric research program, often unrelated to the museum's programs, in some cases even unrelated to the collection. With this approach, the curator plays a minimal role in the public functions of the museum, in some cases publishing results of his or her research in academic journals unrelated to the museum's publications program.
- The opposite strategy deeply involves the curator in the museum's public programs, but as a result, he or she may be dragged from one research topic to another, usually in support of the exhibition program. For these curators it is difficult to find time for research on acquisitions, and their research work may become cursory, constantly moving from one exhibition topic to another.

Neither of these extremes is desirable, or necessary. The solution of an enlightened museum management is to support long-term curatorial research by establishing a *research policy* and by encouraging the development of *research plans*:

- A museum *research policy* should have the following components:
  1. A museum's research policy should establish that museum's commitment to research in relation to the museum's mission and mandate.
  2. It should commit the museum to provide the personnel, time, library, travel budget, and other resources needed for effective research, commensurate with the museum's budget and other resources.
  3. The research policy may make some of these resources—such as travel for fieldwork—contingent on the researcher getting grants to pay for them. The policy should articulate the extent and the limits of the museum's responsibility, and encourage the individual researcher's role.
  4. It should address not only curatorial research but research by other staff members—conservators, education officers, and others—who will be expected to undertake research.

5. It should outline the museum's policy toward outside researchers' use of museum facilities, whether they are visiting scholars studying the collection or secondary school students writing an essay.
6. The policy should articulate the museum's position on copyright and intellectual property, usually making a distinction between the results of research done on museum time and personal research that some museum staff may undertake independently.
7. Most important, the research policy should insist that all museum-sponsored research, even if theoretical, should ultimately relate to museum collections or programs, and must form part of the execution of a research plan by each individual researcher on staff.

- *Research plans* prepared by museum personnel in response to their museum's research policy should have the following characteristics:
  1. Individual research plans should be prepared by all museum staff members (not only curators) who wish to undertake museum-sponsored research.
  2. The plan should indicate the relationship of the projected research to museum collection documentation or public programs.
  3. The research plan should include a time framework for its accomplishment.
  4. Research plans should be prepared annually, with a time framework likely to be in months or years.
  5. Research plans should be drafted by the researcher, reviewed by the deputy director for that division, and approved by the museum's chief executive officer (usually the director).

The value of having both research policy and plans in place is that the museum management can then consider changes in research direction with due regard for the long-range implication of altering its research time commitments. If, for example, the director decides that a new exhibition must be organized for next year, and therefore advises a curator to undertake the requisite research, that curator should respond with reference to his or her research plan, observing what effect the change in research direction will have on the objectives and timing of the formerly agreed research plan; a decision can then be made as to whether this alteration is in the long-term interests of the museum. On the other hand, if a curator suggests a research plan that is not meaningfully related to the museum's collection documentation or public programming needs—but perhaps reflects his or her personal interests—the deputy director for collections management or the director can work with him or her to redirect the research so that it is of greater benefit to the institution.

Given the centrality of curatorial research to all other museum operations, it is extremely important to establish a sound research policy and a system of research plans as the basis for the curatorial role in both collections management and public programming activities. Neglect of this area (which is lamentably common) results in the worst kind of inefficiency for the museum—waste of one of the museum's most precious human resources, the expertise of its personnel. With policy and plans in place, however, it becomes possible for curators to take a responsible and creative place in all aspects of the museum's operations, and to make the fruits of their connoisseurship fully available to the institution.

Acquisitions: In view of the importance of collection development, many museum boards appoint an *acquisitions committee* from among their members. Such a committee, which should meet with the relevant curator, is useful as a means of channelling trustees' efforts toward encouraging donations or bequests to the collection in accordance with the museum's collection development strategy. Since acquisitions lead to increased operating costs and ultimately to space and facilities requirements, the acquisition committee should also function as a committee of recommendation for major acquisitions, defined as accessions above a certain monetary value. The acquisitions committee should be empowered to approve acquisitions up to a certain value, but above that value its recommendations must go to the full board for approval. Collections committees with broader powers are not recommended, since they inevitably become involved in day-to-day museum operations that should be delegated to the curatorial staff.

3.2.2 Collection Policy

The museum's chief instrument of collection management should be its *collection policy*—sometimes called a *collection management policy*. The clauses of a collection policy should address the following issues.

1. The museum's commitment to maintaining the collection as a *public trust*, for which it will provide conscientious care indefinitely, should be declared. The status of the collection as a public trust means that the public has entrusted it to the care of the museum's board and staff, who have the responsibility to preserve and present it for public study and enjoyment.
2. The range and limits of the collection related to the museum's mission and mandate should be defined.
3. Usually the policy establishes beginning and end dates (if it is a historical collection), the geographical range (if relevant), and the materials (for example, ceramics or glass) to be collected.
4. A qualitative statement of the objective of the collection should be stated: an art collection may be said to be restricted to *outstanding* examples,

whereas a natural science collection may aspire to be *comprehensive* or *systematic*, while a history museum's collection may aim at a *representative* sample of a particular period. Some historical collections are centered on exceptional items related to great events or individuals, whereas others focus on objects typical of their time and place. The collection of a museum in a heritage building may be restricted to objects that were actually used in the building, or may extend to objects of the type used there.

5. The policy may also determine whether artifacts must have been *made* in a particular district or era or merely *used* in that place or period, or both.

6. Natural history collections that aspire to be systematic must be further specified as to whether they will include merely one example of each species, whether they include definitive *type specimens*, or whether they aim at an example of each stage of development of each species.

7. The *criteria* for inclusion in the collection should be specified. These go beyond the foregoing general statements of the collection's range and quality to identify such particular requirements as:
   - size;
   - demonstrated authenticity;
   - an established provenance;
   - the legal issue of clear title; and
   - either display condition or a condition that the museum has the resources to restore and maintain.

8. Monetary value levels requiring different levels of approval—curatorial, acquisitions committee, or acquisitions committee recommendation to the board for approval—should be specified.

9. Criteria may also distinguish between objects for different parts of the collection. For example, original documents, tapes, and other media related to the subject matter of the museum may belong in the museum's *archives*, but material in print or other media that is collected only because it provides information about the rest of the collection will be found in the museum *library*.

10. Approved *acquisition methods* should be specified, which may include gifts, bequests, purchases, fieldwork, deposits from other museums, and acceptance of acquisitions from government programs or agencies responsible for cultural property protection.

11. The collection policy should establish the museum's position on *ownership* of the collection, including acquisition procedures for donations (gift agreements) and purchases (receipt requirements). Usually the collection policy disallows gifts "with strings attached," and requires that donations must be transferred wholly and entirely, without qualification as to the museum's use of the acquisition.

12. The museum's policy with regard to tax deductions for donations of objects to the collection should be articulated in this document. This should be written to comply with the legal requirements of the country, province, or state in which the museum is located, identifying who can determine evaluations (not the curators but an independent evaluator), and under what circumstances the museum will provide tax deductible receipts, if it is qualified to do so.

13. *Ethical* commitments of the museum and its trustees with regard to acquisitions should be included, such as the museum's commitment to international conventions, national laws, or treaties, including policy regarding objects from indigenous cultures and policy regarding the repatriation or restitution of objects to their origins.

14. Ethical guidelines adopted by the trustees regarding potential conflicts of interest with their own or staff personal collecting activities (as discussed in chapter 2) should also be included in the collection policy.

15. There should be a statement of the purposes for which objects may be collected, leading to a classification by purpose, usually including:
    - A *display collection* acquired for exhibition and interpretation purposes;
    - A *study collection* acquired for purposes of comparative or analytical research (such as archaeological shards from a museum dig, or zoological specimens in spirit jars); and
    - A *reserve collection*, which may consist of objects pending assignment to either of the first two classifications, duplicate or secondary examples assigned to hands-on educational programs, or objects pending deaccessioning.

16. The collection policy should indicate that the display collection and study collection are to be preserved indefinitely, whereas some of the items in the reserve collection may not be.

17. Some museums acquire a *contemporary collection* of the potential artifacts of tomorrow (while they are still inexpensive and plentiful), and hold these items in reserve for a period of years (say, twenty), after which they may be either transferred to the display or study collections, or deaccessioned.

18. The reserve collection may also be used for unwanted objects that the museum is sometimes obliged to accept, at least temporarily, as part of a donation that includes other objects needed for the display or study collections; if possible, the donor should be persuaded to give only the desired pieces, but when faced with an "all or nothing" offer, it is convenient to assign the unwanted objects to the reserve collection (as long as this is explained to the donor and recorded in the gift agreement), so that the museum need not make the commitment of long-term preservation of unsuitable material. Objects in educational hands-on collections, which may be seen as part of the reserve collection, will

deteriorate from repeated handling and are thus not going to be preserved indefinitely. This is why it is useful for the collection policy to state the museum's commitment to preservation of the display and study collections, while allowing for the reserve collection to be subject sooner or later to deaccessioning.

19. The museum's policy on *deaccessioning* should be included in the collection policy as a means of collection management. Although some would resist any such inclusion, it is far better to have a sound policy in place than to pretend that the museum will never need to dispose of unwanted items.

20. Certain objects—or the entire display and study collections—may be declared exempt from deaccessioning in perpetuity, with deaccessioning restricted to items in the reserve collection alone.

21. The deaccessioning section of the collection policy should make it clear that in general the museum collects objects only for their indefinite preservation, and therefore that deaccessioning is to be regarded as an exceptional activity. Both the International Council of Museums and many countries' museum associations have published suitably cautious statements on deaccessioning, which may be quoted: "There must always be a strong presumption against the disposal of specimens to which a museum has assumed formal title," as the ICOM Code of Ethics puts it.

22. Criteria for consideration for deaccessioning should be listed, including:
    * objects that do not fit the museum's mandate;
    * objects that have been found to be spurious;
    * objects acquired illegally or unethically;
    * objects due for repatriation or restitution to their origins;
    * duplicates that are inferior to more recently acquired examples; and
    * objects in a condition that is not cost-effective to restore.

23. The steps to be taken in the event of deaccessioning should be spelled out, providing rules such as the following:
    * Only curators can initiate deaccessioning.
    * The process must be fully documented with the reasons for deaccessioning according to this policy fully recorded.
    * The museum's information about the deaccessioned object must be retained.
    * Approval procedures for deaccessioning should always involve the director, and may also require the attention of the trustees.

24. Acceptable options for disposition of deaccessioned items should be indicated, with alternatives listed as the following:
    * A sequence of "first refusals" should be laid out aimed at keeping the object in the public domain, if possible within the country, state, province, county, or municipality.

- Destruction of objects should be done only by curators in the presence of the director, and recorded.
- In the event of sale, any revenues from the disposition of deaccessioned objects must be used only for new acquisitions or collection care—never for the museum's operating costs.

25. The museum's policy on *loans* should be included in the collection policy, distinguishing between long-term loans or *deposits* of items from other museums or collections, and short-term loans (both incoming and outgoing) for temporary exhibitions:
    - The clause on *long-term incoming loans* is usually written to persuade prospective long-term lenders to become donors instead, and may go as far as to forbid long-term loans from individuals entirely, while admitting the possibility of deposits from other collections or museums (which will be restricted by their own collection policies and therefore only able to deposit objects on long-term loan).
    - For *short-term outgoing loans* it is usual to identify the approvals required (such as registrar and curator for most, but the director or even the board for some objects, with still others never to be loaned), to specify that the museum will lend objects only to institutions able to provide an equivalent level of environmental and security protection and insurance, and to require that the borrowing institution fill out a satisfactory *facility assessment* form and provide condition reports at each packing and unpacking point. The policy may also require that couriers must accompany certain loans to supervise their installation and demounting.

26. The museum's policy on *appraisals* usually protects curators from being asked for monetary evaluations, especially if tax deductions for potential donations are involved. Sometimes curators may appraise up to a certain market value, with higher values being referred elsewhere.

27. Procedures for *documentation* of the collection are usually included in collection management policies, describing the entire process from arrival of the object in the museum (possibly with a temporary receipt while it is under consideration) through the numbering system and information fields to be captured for each item, requirements for gift agreements or receipts, procedures for multiple objects within one accession, and the responsibility of the registrar to record collection movement, loans, and relocations from storage to display or back again. This may be extensive enough to justify a separate *documentation policy* (see section 3.2.4).

28. A collection management policy usually also addresses *conservation*, requiring a condition report for each new acquisition and the subsequent maintenance of such reports throughout the object's life in the museum, and providing that any treatment of the object will be recorded. This section

may also require that a conservator's recommendation be considered prior to acquisition, to ensure that the object meets the museum's requirements that its collections be either in display condition or in a state that can be cost-effectively restored. The policy may state the museum's objectives in conservation—whether simply to retard the object's deterioration optimally, or to return it to a specific prior condition, for instance. As with documentation, larger museums are likely to find it preferable to elaborate a separate but related *conservation policy* (see section 3.2.5).

29. The museum's commitment to the *security* of its collections should be articulated in a collection management policy. This security section of the policy may incorporate a *risk management strategy* that identifies threats to the collection and the measures that the museum takes to meet them. For example, this section might include a commitment to two-hour firewalls and doors on the collection storage rooms, the conditions under which the museum will place its collections under sprinklers (at home or on loan), or the staff levels permitted to enter the collection storage rooms or to handle the collections.

30. *Insurance* provisions are an important section of a collection management policy. In some countries, government museum collections are self-insured. Some offer indemnity programs according to which the government will cover the cost of any harm or loss, making insurance for international exhibitions unnecessary up to a pre-agreed value—but only if the institution qualifies for the program. More generally, the policy should identify the range of insurance coverage and conditions affecting the collection, including third-party liability, deductible levels of reimbursement for loss or damage, inventory requirements, and the museum's procedure for recording insured values, reviewing and changing them regularly, and communicating current values to its insurers.

The collection policy should be a public document that the curator may invoke when necessary in the museum's dealings with prospective donors or vendors. It is most useful as a means to resist would-be long-term lenders, "all or nothing" donors, or well-meaning trustees whose proffered donations or bequests do not fit the museum's mandate. It should also be used within the museum as an organizational principle—so that all objects are assigned to display, study, or reserve collections, for example.

3.2.3 Collection Development Strategy

Collections absorb two-thirds of a museum's operating budget and generate major long-range space and facilities needs that eventually require expansion and capital costs (see Lord, Lord, and Nicks, *The Cost of Collecting*, 1989). The development of a museum's collections is therefore a significant concern for the management of the institution. A *collection development strategy* addresses this concern.

A collection development strategy, to be drafted by the curator in consultation with the registrar and the conservator for approval by the director and the trustees, should begin with a *qualitative analysis* of the collection. An aesthetic evaluation may be of interest in the case of an art collection, but a qualitative collection analysis for museum planning and management purposes is not primarily concerned with such evaluation. Rather, it begins by identifying such features as:

- the scope and range of the collection;
- its international, national, or regional significance;
- its outstanding pieces;
- its representative or systematic character; and
- its uniqueness.

The qualitative collection analysis should then proceed to consider the potential for enhancement of the collection through acquisition—which may be limited by sheer availability, the museum's acquisition budget, and other factors. This is because *the purpose of the qualitative analysis in a collection development strategy is to project the trajectory of the collection's intended growth*—where we are going, and how we will know when we get there (if ever). The Sigmund Freud Museum may know that there are no more artifacts available associated with its subject matter, whereas a contemporary art museum may project an unlimited trajectory qualitatively that must be addressed quantitatively for planning and management purposes. The qualitative analysis should establish the museum's *collecting horizon*, and its *qualitative priorities* on the road to that horizon.

The collection development strategy should then proceed to a *quantitative* analysis that includes:

- the present size in numbers of objects of the collection as a whole and in all relevant categories, such as collection department, artifact type, historical period, materials (important for planning conservation needs), percentage registered and cataloged, and use classification—display, study, and reserve collections;
- the history of the growth of the collection in number of objects (not merely accession numbers) from as early in the museum's history as possible, again in relation to the same categories, and with both annual averages and the most recent *collection growth rate* computed, not in percentages (as is often erroneously advised) but in actual numbers of objects accessioned;

- the current *display/storage ratio* (by collection department if applicable), and curatorial recommendation of a more acceptable proportion if the present ratio is not satisfactory;
- current *storage densities*—objects per square meter or square foot, or square meters or square feet per object, depending on the relative size of the objects in the collection (locomotives or postage stamps)—by object type or materials, together with the registrar's and conservator's recommendation of a more acceptable density if the present level is too crowded; and
- current *display densities*—again, objects per square meter or square foot, or square meters or square feet per object, whichever is more appropriate—in the permanent collection exhibition galleries, linked to an identification of the dominant display mode in that gallery (aesthetic, thematic, environmental, systematic, interactive, or hands-on, as described in subsection 3.3.1.1).

A *design year* needs to be determined—the year by which the collection development strategy should be fulfilled—usually about twenty or twenty-five years in the future, since projections beyond those limits are likely to be highly speculative. Any factors anticipated to affect collection growth between now and the design year should be noted—an anticipated bequest, hiring an additional curator, or opening a new curatorial department, for instance—and their effect on the present collection growth rate should be quantified. Many curators find such projections difficult, but in fact past growth rates are likely to be indicative of future averages, with whatever qualifications may be due to developments that can be anticipated and gauged in proportion to past experience. Thus adjusted, the growth rate (again computed in actual numbers of objects, not as a percentage) may be projected to the design year, for the collection as a whole and for each collection department and material type.

The next variables to be determined are the preferred display/storage ratio and densities. In order to project these, the director and curators in consultation with the conservators, exhibitions officers, and designers (and sometimes a museum planning consultant) must decide on the most suitable and stimulating *display modes* (see also section 3.3.1.1):

- The *aesthetic* presentation of an art collection has a relatively low density—paintings and sculpture in a gallery with adequate viewing distance for visitors.
- A *thematic* presentation, linking objects contextually and interpreting groups of them together, is likely to be denser.
- *Environmental* exhibits (such as a furnished period room) will have still more objects per square meter or square foot.

- A *systematic* display mode, such as a visible storage gallery, provides the highest display densities, usually only about one-third less than the closed storage density for similar material.

Since the size of museum objects and the nature of museum displays varies so widely, each museum must determine its own density variables, and it may then undertake to increase public access to its collections by including at least some display modes of higher density (such as visible storage for suitable collections). Total display space may be distributed by percentage—so much gallery space for aesthetic displays, so much for thematic, and so on.

The collection development strategy may now project the museum's space and facility needs as far ahead as the design year, respecting the agreed growth rate, display/storage ratio, and display modes. It should also be possible to project the number of objects that will be in the collection as a whole, how many will be in storage, and how many on display in each mode. The object is not to get such projections exactly right, but rather to see the implications of proceeding with collection development at the present or projected pace and to gauge the importance of monitoring that intake in order to achieve the museum's qualitative priorities within these quantitative guidelines. If the results of the collection development strategy are acceptable within the museum's present resources or anticipated capacity for growth, they may stand as the basis for a master plan; if not, it may be necessary to adjust expectations—either in the rate of acquisitions, or in the intended plans for display. If, for example, the collections are projected to grow by 40 percent over the next twenty years and if 5 percent of the collections are currently on display, it is unlikely that even an expanding museum can retain the 5 percent display ratio at the end of that period; between now and then, of course, a building expansion can provide a higher proportion of objects on display.

Since many museums are currently concerned to increase public access to the collections, it may not be advisable to restrict plans for display—quite the opposite; it may be possible to enhance public intellectual access through the use of contemporary technology instead of relying solely on the provision of additional exhibition gallery space. Even so, the result of a collection development strategy may be to project collection development limits for curators.

These restraints should not be viewed as inviolable laws, but only as useful *guidelines* on the basis of which the museum can plan its space and facilities development, and project future capital and operating fund requirements. The collection development strategy should refer back to the qualitative analysis with which it began and translate these guidelines into *priorities* for collection development. Curators should be encouraged to attend to agreed *qualitative priorities* within the *quantitative guidelines* established by the strategy.

Yet the museum must remain open to opportunity. Specific departments may be allowed or even encouraged to exceed the guidelines when significant collection development opportunities are at hand. The purpose of a collection development strategy is not to inhibit such creative growth, but to ensure that decisions about the museum's acquisitions program are made in an informed and deliberate manner so that the institution can continue to provide for its collections in a professional way.

3.2.4 Information Management

Information has been defined as "reduction of uncertainty." For a museum, uncertainty about the meaning, status, or significance of objects in its collection amounts to the loss of their value, since the museum must be certain enough of their meaning to display, publish, or in other ways communicate that meaning to the public. Retention and management of information is thus a central concern of all museums.

In British museums the documentation of information about the museum's collection has historically been a curatorial function. In the United States, the position of *registrar* has evolved to specialize in managing the documentation base, even though the information usually originates with curators. In recent years, a number of major British museums have found it advisable to appoint a registrar; the change reflects the growing scope and complexity of both documentation and information management in museums. In this section, therefore, we assume a registrar, understanding that in museums without this position curators or curatorial assistants may be undertaking these tasks.

Given its commitment to the public dissemination of information about its collection, the management of that information is in many ways just as important to the museum as the management of the collection itself. Furthermore, the *documentation* of an object in the collection is of limited utility unless it can be related to the *location* of that object. The documentation of museum collections therefore means more than their mere registration or cataloging; it also means management of the location and movement of all objects in the collections. Hence the registrar should be responsible for the museum stores and for loans and their insurance, and must be involved in all exhibition planning, in addition to the management of information about the collection through the compilation of records and the provision of access to them.

Some would go still further and suggest that museums are essentially about the distribution of information. While the primacy of the object in the museum is indisputable, certainly the conversion of formerly manual records to computers, the digitization of automated data (including imaging), the provision of both staff and public access to the data, the possibilities of relating the database to other information systems within the museum, and the proliferation of databases as a means of sharing information within a museum and among institutions all point to the growing need for a more integrated approach to *information management*, of which documentation of the collection is only one important aspect. In some museums a director of communications has been put in charge of all verbal communication by the museum—oral, printed, or electronic.

Examples of the information that museums manage and the officers directly responsible for it are given in table 3.2.

This list indicates the need for information planning and the advantages to be gained from its integration across departments and divisions. Ticketing records, for instance, may be used as a mailing list for membership programs, a

Table 3.2. Information Management

Information Resource	Officer Responsible
Registration of acquisitions	Registrar
Collection catalog	Registrar
Collection management records	Registrar
Photographic negative and digitization files	Photographer
Museum library catalog	Librarian
Archives	Archivist
Condition reports and treatment records	Chief Conservator
Building systems records	Building Manager
Ticketing records	Visitor Services Manager
Membership records	Membership Manager
Fund-raising and development records	Development Officer
Current accounts and financial records	Finance Officer
Exhibition development schedules	Exhibition Officer
School party visits	Education Officer
Digital publishing files	Publications Manager
Interactive and multimedia programs	AV Technician
Computerized show controls	AV Technician
Evaluation records	Evaluation Officer
Personnel records	Personnel (HR) Manager
Volunteer recruitment and evaluation records	Volunteer Coordinator
Office automation	Chief Clerk
Interoffice communication	Chief Clerk

fundraising campaign, and a volunteer recruitment drive, while the media officer may need to convert the catalog entries for a group of objects into a visitor-friendly database for a visible storage exhibition. When one considers, in addition to the officers responsible for them, the multiple *users* of these information systems—from curators' research of the collection catalog to providing public access for interactive and multimedia programs—the need for information management to coordinate the many persons involved becomes apparent. It is also obvious that *task force* project teams (see section 2.3.2.3) are required to coordinate information management, with the registrar playing a leading role on these teams while focusing on documentation. Here again, a director of communications may be a key position providing leadership and coordination.

When the first edition of this manual was published in 1997, attention was focused on the possibilities for interinstitutional cooperation digitally, pointing to opportunities for sharing information *between* as well as within museums. The 1995 *Report of the Commission on the Future of the Smithsonian Institution* called on that museum complex to become "the leader in establishing such a world-wide computer linkage." Since that date, museums around the world have made data and images of all or at least significant parts of their collection virtually accessible to everyone on their websites.

Today, the emphasis is much more on the provision of digital information to visitors in the museum and to users worldwide. Visitors are snapping digital pictures of museum exhibits and their labels with their mobile phones, or using their iPods to pick up and keep information that a few years ago would have been available to them only in a printed catalog. Virtual exhibitions are now routinely produced, either as part of a major physical exhibition in the museum or independently. Millions of users of the museum's digital programs now supplement the thousands or millions who actually visit the museum.

Technological literacy is therefore a must for museums as they adapt and integrate interpretative material with new media. Museums are able to leverage these forums as platforms for visitor engagement and promotion of institutional programs. Some examples include:

- digital features directly linked to curators' computers for real-time content updates;
- interactive opportunities through advanced radio-frequency audience response technology;
- a descriptive tour of Tate Britain's permanent collection available on an audio program for the visually impaired;
- capability for visitors to "bookmark" images of selected objects during tours so that they can download, print, or e-mail them to themselves after the tour; and
- podcasts with interpretative content and interviews available for download.

All of these developments are constantly impacting museums' information systems, in institutions where the registrar may have converted a card catalog and a registration book to a computer database only a few years ago—or in some cases may only be preparing to do so! Museums at whatever stage of automation need a sound information policy and an information system plan.

The museum's *information policy* should include the following:

- It should at the outset address issues of intellectual property for all types of information—spoken, written, published, digital, and broadcast, within the institution and among its staff.
- The policy should indicate the museum management's orientation to the use of its databases, or other dissemination of museum information, particularly images. The *digitization* of information, including imagery, has changed the way that we understand the concept of "reproduction" or "replication." The practical questions of encouraging open access to at least some parts of a museum's database, and how to control such access (if control is either possible or desirable) should be addressed in the policy. Certainly there is an opportunity for broadening public access, but there are also risks of misuse of imagery; questions of copyright; and potential revenues, now or in the future, that should be addressed in the policy. Contemporary art museums, where living artists may claim an interest in the information or the images, have a particularly acute challenge.
- The information policy should assert the museum's commitment to documenting its collection accurately and comprehensively, retaining all pertinent information in an accessible format indefinitely, and providing public access as appropriate. Certain information—prices and insurance values, for instance—should be kept confidential, but visitor access to most other information—including nonvisitor access electronically—can be and is being provided, not only to scholars but also to the general interested public. The nature of knowledge about the collections—no longer the preserve of curators and registrars, but accessible to all—and the nature of publication or dissemination of that knowledge have radically altered.
- The information policy may very well have to be adjusted as technology, legislation, and the international flow of information evolve.

Having resolved, at least for the present, a satisfactory information policy, the museum should be able to develop an *information system plan*, possibly with the help of specialists in this field. Planning for an information system is most efficiently done after conclusion of a strategic plan or master planning exercise that has identified all museum functions and priorities:

- An information system plan begins with a list of all information-related functions (like the foregoing list in table 3.2, but prioritized).
- It then determines which components can be efficiently integrated in the near future, ensuring as far as possible the necessary compatibility of systems so that further links can be forged later.
- An *information model* may be devised, showing in graphic form the current tasks and consequent information flow, and desired improvements in these patterns. Merging of software programs is likely to be involved here.
- It should then be possible, with some specialist consultant assistance, to list functional requirements of the information system and use these as a guideline to preparing specifications for both hardware and software.
- Costs—in terms of training and development as well as money—must also be computed, and the plan may have to be adjusted to realistic parameters—although the potential of sponsorship by hardware or software companies should not be discounted.

With both an information policy and an information system plan in place, the registrar may need to upgrade the *documentation procedures manuals* to ensure that they are compatible with the entire system. Procedures manuals are usually important for both registration and cataloging. In addition to the steps involved in making a satisfactory record of a new accession, these manuals must provide very explicit instructions for the catalogers and data entry clerks who will be using them. The steps in the registration procedures manual should include at least:

- *entry* of identification, source, and history in a secure and permanent file;
- *numbering* of both object and record;
- *acknowledgment* to the source of the acquisition;
- formal *transfer of title* by gift agreement or receipt;
- addition of the object to the museum's *insurance* coverage;
- an initial *condition report* by the conservator; and
- the initial *location* record for the object.

Although a wide variety of registration systems have been employed throughout the museum world—forty-five different ones were found to be in use at the Victoria and Albert Museum when it commenced automation of its records many years ago—most museums today register acquisitions by means of what is called the three-part numbering system. It comprises:

- a three-digit number referring to the year of acquisition—009, for example;
- a period and a number referring to the number of the acquisition in the present year—so that 009.13 refers to the thirteenth accession made in 2009;

- another period and a number referring to the object within that accession—so that 009.13.4 refers to the fourth object donated by the source of the thirteenth accession of 2009; and
- if necessary, a lower-case letter designating part of an object, so that 009.13.4a might refer to a teapot, while 009.13.4b might refer to its lid.

Such a number system that is unrelated to any object categories has been found to be most durable for collections of all kinds. Some collections may need to correlate it with other conventions. There is an international registration system for stamps, for example, and archaeological collections may need to correlate finds with the universal geographical site reference system. Many natural history collections find it preferable both to document and to organize their holdings by genus and species, while coins are classified by country, ruler, material, denomination, and date. Others may have inherited a historic system that remains viable—although any system must admit of infinite change, as the conceptual bases of classifications of objects of all kinds are continually evolving. Thus, it has not proved useful to base a documentation system on the periods of art history, for example, since the very basis for the period classifications is questioned and revised from time to time by the discipline itself.

Numbers may be applied to very small objects, or ones where all surfaces are of equivalent aesthetic importance, by means of tags. Unbleached cotton labels may be discreetly sewn into costumes. For most other objects numbers may be applied on the base or in a comparable inconspicuous place in varnished drawing ink on an acetone base coat; conservators recommend that the base coat should include a 20 percent Paraloid B72 solution, and that the area where numbers are applied must have adequate ventilation for the safety of those working there. The Registration Procedures Manual should detail the numbering process, and recommend suitable places for locating numbers uniformly on the type of objects in that museum's collection. *Bar codes* are a still more permanent method of tagging objects, now increasingly in use in museums.

The documentation procedures manuals should also refer to the museum's *location tracking* method. This should be initiated at registration with the *entry documentation*, and maintained for each acquisition throughout its retention in the museum, regardless of when or whether it is subsequently cataloged. The manual must determine who is allowed to move objects in the collection, and what procedures they must follow, to ensure that others will be able to find the objects subsequently. All storage and display locations should be codified for easy reference. In the event of loans, the manuals should provide an approved *exit documentation* procedure, which must be checked by security officers as well as collection management personnel.

Maintaining a sound location tracking practice is essential for the success of a collection *inventory*, which is vital to security as well as to collection management. Government line department museums may be expected to meet auditors' requirements for inventory of their collections. But all museums should undertake inventories in regular rotation, with every object even in large collections being checked at least once every few years. Insurance policies may require regular inventories.

Cataloging is a more extensive recording process than registration, and many museums that keep up-to-date with their registration have a backlog in cataloging. While registration records a limited number of data fields—name and function of the object, its source and provenance, place and date of its origin, its materials, and a brief description, for instance—the museum catalog aims to record a full sense of its significance in relation to other objects in the collection, in other collections, and in the world at large. While the registrar and data entry clerks may be able to register an object with input from the curator, the catalog entry should be fundamentally a curatorial concern. It should include references to relevant literature and reproductions—much of which may be standardized for groups of similar objects. Developing a comprehensive catalog of a collection is a museum's major responsibility that should not be forever postponed due to the deadlines of temporary exhibitions or the opportunities to add still more acquisitions.

The *automation* of collection records often throws a spotlight on hitherto little-known lacunae in the museum's catalog. Early endeavors to transfer records to computers attempted complete catalogs, trying to record comprehensive information about a necessarily restricted number of objects; experience has shown that entry of only a few key fields from the registration records for a large number of objects is far more efficient and effective, as long as the system allows further information to be added in the future. In this way the registration records and the eventual complete catalog can be integrated in one automated system.

The *nomenclature* used to record museum objects has become an important subject in itself, particularly as computer word search programs facilitate access for everyone, from curators to visiting scholars and schoolchildren. Standardizing terminology internationally, not only for technical terms but for color references, for example, will help to smooth global access to the world's growing collections database. Some disciplines, such as the natural sciences, have inherited conventions such as the genus and species classifications, whereas others are still in the process of development. In Britain the *Social History and Industrial Classification* published by the University of Sheffield in 1983 may be helpful for collections of that kind, while in the United States *The Revised Nomenclature for Museum Cataloguing* published by the American Association for State and Local History in 1988 (based on the earlier edition by Chenhall) is almost universally employed for historical collections of artifacts—

but some Australian museums have found it necessary to develop their own standard guide for their historical collections.

Many software programs designed for museum registrars' use are available. Some museums that chose their systems many years ago subsequently had difficulty in acquiring imaging capability or providing public access, and had to reconvert. Waiting for the ideal software or upgrade is not a solution, however; instead, the registrar or curators, often with specialist consultant advice, should undertake systematic development of an Information System Plan to ensure that all possible specifications have been considered, and should then either make a commitment to the best system on offer, or may prefer to develop a program unique to the museum's needs, but compatible with as broad a range of applications as possible. The capacity of some computer programs to accommodate nonalphabetic languages may also be important—for Asian art and archaeology collections, for example.

Data entry to convert manual records to computer software programs has been labor-intensive. One major British museum reported that trained workers there could input only seven 1,000-character records per hour from cards or book entries. Such data entry almost always involved reconfiguring the original record into the format required for the computer. Merging or migrating from one computer program to another today is much less challenging, at least in terms of person-hours. Although this work is largely accomplished in many major institutions, it is important to remember that it is still underway in many smaller museums and those in developing countries.

Digitized *imaging* is another important step in the upgrading of museum records. In many cases this has required rephotographing an entire collection. The benefits for both the museum's documentation system and interpretation of the collection to the museum public are usually sufficient, however, to justify such an undertaking. Advances in digital photography have made the manipulation of images so much more effective for all museum purposes. *Digital asset management* programs are needed to optimize use of both word and image data, including possible leasing for other uses.

Public access to documentation is a growing field of applications. Visible storage has been made far more attractive, since a simplified keyboard or touch-screen monitor can provide interested visitors with access to the museum's complete (or nearly complete) catalog information about the objects on view. The amount of information available to the visitor about a collection shown in this way is far greater than what could be communicated via a label and museum graphics in a contextual or aesthetic exhibition. Multimedia applications can animate such catalog data, and bring it to life for visitors at all levels of familiarity with the subject matter. Virtual exhibitions can take that digital imaging and information to thousands of users worldwide, many of whom may never visit the museum.

The future is bright for museum documentation and information systems. This is an area where museums have already changed extensively and rapidly in recent years, and where the pace of change may be expected to continue. Information systems provide the exciting interface of the museum's knowledge base and its users. Some visitors may take home spoken interpretation, music, or pictures from an exhibition on their mobile phones, while others are snapping personal memories in the galleries on theirs. Virtual exhibitions are now regularly planned and presented as part of most major exhibition projects. Users far from the museum routinely access data and imagery from home. The very nature of the museum as a public institution is being transformed. Yet the desire to see "the real thing" grows apace. Museum managers will have to be fully informed and aware of the manifold possibilities as the digital information age continues.

3.2.5 Managing to Preserve the Collection

Preservation of a museum collection entails the indefinite provision of security (considered as an aspect of facility management in subsection 3.4.2.3), and conservation, the subject of this section. A complete museum conservation program should comprise:

- preventive conservation (3.2.5.1);
- investigation and treatment (3.2.5.2);
- restoration (3.2.5.3); and
- conservation research (3.2.5.4).

In addition, the preparation and installation of museum objects for exhibitions—the work of the museum's *preparators*—should be closely integrated with that of the conservators.

3.2.5.1 Preventive Conservation

The aim of the conservator is to preserve the museum object and to retard any change in its original qualities as long as possible. This is to be accomplished in the context of a public museum, which wishes to make the object visible to the public. Thus the conservator's ideal of a black box with unvarying temperature and humidity and no light must be compromised to meet the needs of the visitors, and of staff who wish to study the object from time to time. A *conservation policy* should establish the long-range qualitative standards for this endeavor, particularly with regard to preventive conservation measures.

Over the past few decades conservators have increasingly shifted their emphasis from treatment of objects to concentrate on the prevention of deterioration by maintaining conditions as supportive as possible of the long-term intact survival of the museum object. *Preventive conservation* is the applied science of providing an environment that minimizes the object's deterioration in the public museum context. Its focus is on the following key environmental factors:

- temperature and relative humidity;
- air filtration;
- light;
- pests;
- handling; and
- emergency procedures.

Temperature and relative humidity: These two climatic factors are closely interrelated; relative humidity (RH) is the ratio, expressed as a percentage, of the absolute humidity of sampled air to that of air saturated with water at the same temperature. Organic materials respond to fluctuations in temperature and relative humidity, especially the latter. Continued fluctuation results in a weakening of the organic material. Textiles, paper, leather, and wood are among the objects commonly found in museum collections that are particularly susceptible to such deterioration, which can present special difficulties in objects of mixed organic and inorganic materials. If RH is too high for too long, mildew and mold are additional hazards, along with corrosion of metals.

As noted in subsection 3.4.2.1, the standard for environmental conditions for many museum collections of organic or mixed materials in temperate zones is usually a diurnal constant of 50 percent RH plus or minus 5 percent year-round at 20 or 21°C (68–70°F) plus or minus 0.5°C in winter, which may be modulated upward by 0.5°C per month to 22 or 24°C (72–75°F) in summer. For new buildings constructed to withstand such conditions, especially in a temperate maritime climate, this standard need not present a major problem; for historic buildings, or other structures not built to sustain such a standard, especially in continental climates, 55 percent RH is likely to be the best that can be maintained, or it may be necessary to adjust humidity from 55 percent in summer to 40 percent in winter by three monthly 5 percent steps in RH settings each spring and fall. If engineers still find such limits constrictive, or the museum finds their maintenance too expensive, allowance can be made for wider variations for, say, 5–10 percent of operating hours during a year, with the standard maintained for the rest of the year. Metal and paper collections require a lower RH, around 40 percent, while collections that have originated in the tropics may have a higher hydroscopic content, and may require 65 percent RH.

Once the standards are agreed upon, it is the conservators' responsibility to monitor these environmental conditions closely—traditionally with psychrometers or hygrothermographs, but more commonly today through computerized building management systems (BMS) by digital means of recording RH and temperature. Monitors should be positioned to record conditions at all levels of galleries and stores, and in major display cases. Simultaneous records should be kept of outside climate conditions and of internal spaces that do not benefit from the museum's heating, ventilating, and air-conditioning (HVAC) controls designed to maintain this collection environment. Zones that do not normally contain collections may be maintained at human comfort levels for those who work in or use them.

The climate controls are usually maintained by a ducted air handling system that provides heated or cooled and humidified or dehumidified air as required. Unmodified replacement air is normally kept to a minimum, and building engineers must provide not only insulation, but also a vapor barrier of 0.04–0.08 perms to prevent water vapor from dampening the insulation, and an air barrier to stop air from leaking into the fabric of the building from the interior. Fenestration, if present at all, should be triple-paned, with panes at least 1.3 centimeters apart, and skylights, if present, may be buffered with an area that provides a halfway zone between the exterior climate and that in the galleries or stores. Section 3.4 indicates some of the challenges related to the building that arise from the climate-control requirements of preventive conservation.

Air filtration: Dust and air pollution are other environmental factors affecting the condition of the object, which are especially obnoxious in the industrial or high-traffic areas where many museums are located. Fortunately these can be controlled with an appropriate system of filters—ideally a 25–30 percent efficiency prefilter (according to the American Society of Heating, Refrigeration and Air Conditioning Engineers' [ASHRAE] dust spot efficiency test section, ASHRAE test 52-76), followed by a medium 40–85 percent efficiency filter, and a 90–95 percent after-filter. This bank of filters should be positioned so that both outside and recirculated internal air passes through it. (Electronic air filters should not be used, because the ozone they generate can be harmful to the collection.) For gaseous pollutants, the standard test is to place polished metal "coupons" around the museum for long periods of time, and then to analyze any corrosion products that form on them. Activated charcoal filters are preferred to eliminate or reduce air pollution.

Light: Deterioration of color due to natural or artificial light is another concern of conservators. An ability to set light levels at 50 lux (5 footcandles [fc]) is essential for exhibitions of works on paper, drawings and watercolors, feathers and other light-sensitive organic materials. A level of 150–200 lux (15–20 fc) is usually recommended for oil or acrylic paintings and other moderately sensitive objects, while ceramics, glass, stone, and most metals are among the items that are not particularly light sensitive, and can therefore sustain 300 lux (30 fc), resulting in a *contrast ratio* of 6:1 from the most brightly to the most dimly illuminated object on display. The challenge for architects and lighting designers is not just that these levels must be maintained in dedicated galleries (50 lux or 5 fc in a photography gallery, for instance), but that in a gallery that will be showing works in all media, they must be attained side by side in many instances.

A prime concern is the duration of exposure, with conservators recommending withdrawal of light-sensitive items as necessary to keep lux-hours down; *rotation* of objects on display should accordingly be planned into all exhibitions containing works on paper or textiles, and the number of hours exposed to light should be carefully controlled. Standards ranging from a maximum of 120,000 lux-hours to 50,000 lux-hours have been proposed for highly sensitive 50-lux (5 fc) items, such as works on paper or textiles; for its Turner paintings in the Clore Gallery, Tate Britain aims to restrict annual exposure to 500,000 lux-hours per annum, at a constant of 100 lux (10 fc).

Ultraviolet light is another concern, with standards recently dropped to <10 microwatts per lumen from the previous level of 75, due to technical improvements in the UV filters built into fluorescent light tubes or made available as film or laminations for window glass. The choice of both fluorescent tubes and incandescent lamps—and now the availability of fiber optics—provide the conservator, the curator, and the exhibit designer with a wide range of illumination possibilities, and although many aesthetic factors (such as a color rendering index minimum of 85) may be considered, the preventive conservation requirements of lux and UV control must be paramount.

Pests: Rodents and insect pests are among the enemies of the conservator. Good housekeeping is the best defense against them. Poisons and chemical treatments are also of value, but must be mitigated by consideration for any effects they may have on the object. Fumigation of new accessions used to be widespread in museums, but has been found to be highly problematic due to risks to staff and the consequent need for licensing of operators in many jurisdictions. An *anoxic isolation chamber*, using nitrous oxide for instance, is an effective and less noxious way of eliminating insect pests.

Handling: The preventive conservator should be concerned with the training of all museum personnel who will be allowed to handle artifacts. They should develop procedures manuals that prescribe safe practices for handling, movement, and installation. The use of unbleached cotton or white gloves, for example, should be prescribed for all artifacts except for a small class of items (such as intricately carved lacquer, for example) where it is not well advised; handling and installation techniques designed to sustain support for the object at all times should be made relevant to the needs of each collection and the materials in it. Dusting or cleaning procedures must be detailed, along with instructions on who is to undertake such work at what level. Requirements for museum vehicles, vans, and dollies should also be specified in the manual, ensuring padding where necessary to protect works of art, artifacts, specimens or archival materials in transit. If the museum has a costume collection, storage, display, and handling procedures are likely to be very particular and detailed in the manual.

Emergency procedures: Conservators should confer closely with the chief of security to ensure that the effects of emergency procedures on the collection are fully considered. For example, conservators should ensure that the appropriate type of sprinkler system is installed and that procedures in the event of sprinkler discharge are well understood by those whose actions will affect the collection. A fire, flood, earthquake, hurricane, or tornado will equally be the conservators' concern. The chief conservator should certainly be a member of the emergency action team.

3.2.5.2 Investigation and Treatment of Objects

Although preventive conservation has become an increasing concern, the investigation and treatment of museum objects with a view to preserving them is still an important part of the work of any museum conservation department. The conservation studio is the usual locus of this work, unless the objects in the collection are too large to be moved there.

Investigation and treatment may range from a *condition report*, mandatory if the object is to be loaned or taken from store onto display, through routine cleaning to extensive investigation and nonharmful tests of objects in order to determine treatments needed to conserve them, followed by treatments that are sometimes prolonged. These techniques can be extremely various, ranging from relining a painting on a "hot table" to preserving waterlogged wood by soaking it in tubs of polyethylene glycol over many months or years. Conservation laboratory equipment to undertake such investigation and treatment is highly specialized, and is constantly subject to technological upgrade, so equipment budget allocations are a recurrent concern.

In larger museums specialized labs may be required for paper conservation, paintings, metals, archaeological materials, waterlogged wood, or other types of objects or materials in the collection. Collection storage rooms should similarly be organized by medium so that all works on paper may be stored together and all textiles and all metals enjoy the same dedicated RH and temperature settings.

Planning and management of this investigation and treatment is a challenging task of assigning priorities and attempting to maintain them, usually in the context of pressing demands for temporary exhibitions or loans that the museum wishes to make. A *conservation treatment plan* should be drafted by the chief conservator, and requests for variations from it should be considered in consultation with the deputy director for collection management and the director or curators. The museum can then balance the pressure of exhibition and loan needs with its long-range concern for the treatment needs of its collection.

Some conservation treatments may be harmful to those undertaking them. The laboratories must therefore be furnished with exhaust devices to eliminate harmful chemicals from the atmosphere, and the museum's first-aid center, including eyewash and shower facilities, should be adjacent to the laboratories in the event of splashes or other accidents.

3.2.5.3 Restoration

While conservation treatment is focused on the preservation of the object, or at least on retarding its deterioration, the *restoration* of museum objects is aimed at returning them to a previous condition—either an original state or some other condition that is preferred, usually for purposes of display. This activity needs to be controlled by both a *restoration policy* and a carefully considered *restoration procedures manual*.

The museum's restoration policy should clarify its philosophical intent in restoring objects. It should make clear that lacunae in the original object must generally remain visible (by painting them with a neutral color, for instance), rather than attempting to conceal or fabricate them as if the object were intact. This policy is extremely important for retaining both the integrity of the collection and the trust of the visitor, who will recognize that the museum has taken pains in restoring the object to allow him or her to distinguish what is original from what has been supplied in the conservator's laboratory.

There are exceptions and qualifications, however. The policy may appear to be straightforward enough if the object is a prehistoric pot being reassembled, with unpainted areas indicating where the museum has supplied material to hold the shards together. But if a relatively small area of a painting is being restored, the purpose is usually to match the original artist's intention and hue as closely as possible; areas of the canvas will be left untouched only if they are large enough that it has been decided to let the visitor see where the original artist's work is no longer visible. The policy may become even more contentious where machinery is being restored, or if a recovered shipwreck is to be prepared for display; the museum's intent to communicate clearly to the visitor what is original and what is not must be applied responsibly but imaginatively in each instance.

One important principle common to most conservation treatment and restoration policies is *to do nothing that is irreversible*. This entails written and photographic documentation of treatments in detail, and prior investigation of how to remove or undo treatments if this should become necessary in future.

Restoration policy and procedures manuals are particularly important in institutions where volunteers participate in restoration work—as commonly encountered in transportation and military museums, or in agricultural museums and heritage villages. The well-meaning intentions of such volunteers are sometimes directed toward "restoring" vehicles or machinery to a "band-box" finish that they never had when in use. The restoration procedures manual should require them to proceed with work only under professional supervision, following a step-by-step plan written by the responsible curator or conservator. Documentation of each step in the restoration process, by photographic and written reports, is also of the utmost importance where volunteers are involved.

3.2.5.4 Conservation Research

The job descriptions provided in the appendix include both conservators and conservation scientists. The latter employees, if a museum is large enough to employ them, should focus exclusively on conservation research. However, conservators may also find it valuable to include research as part of their job descriptions.

In the discussion of research plans (in subsection 3.2.1), it is noted that they are needed for conservators and others in the museum doing research as well as curators. Conservators or conservation scientists should therefore be asked to draft such plans, with an indication of likely time requirements for each project. As with curators, these research plans should be useful when the inevitable pressure to respond to an exhibition schedule or new acquisitions leads the director or the chief conservator to consider redirecting their efforts. The plan will allow all concerned to note the effects of such a redirection and to decide collectively if the interests of the museum are best served by the change.

Conservation research is a particularly important aspect of museum operations, whether it is directed at the testing of new materials proposed for display, at contemporary conservation and restoration techniques, or at investigation of the materials and methods of manufacture of the artifacts or works of art in the collection. Museum management should aim to ensure that conservators have the time, space, facilities, and equipment to undertake such research and that the results of their inquiries are published and disseminated to other museums and collectors.

Such research needs to be planned carefully, in consultation with those in academic institutions or in other museums who may be working on related pursuits. Museum conservators need to participate fully in international conferences and subscribe to all relevant journals in order to ensure that they keep abreast of contemporary developments and do not set out to "reinvent the wheel." Participation in the computerized *International Conservation Network* (ICN) and the *International Conservation Committee* (ICC) of the International Council on Museums (ICOM) are two important ways for museum conservation scientists to keep abreast and to communicate their results to others.

3.2.5.5 Exhibit Preparation

Preparators (sometimes simply called technicians) belong to one of the more underrated professional groups in the museum. Yet their work in preparing museum objects for display or loan and installing, dismounting, and returning them to stores brings together both the conservation and public aspects of the museum in specific relation to the collection. They should be encouraged to work closely with the conservators, especially in ensuring that all support materials used in display or storage are pretested, or are known to be safe. If they have mount-making abilities—creating the supports for artifacts, specimens, or works of art—they can save the museum much time and money if they are given time to do this highly specialized but essential work.

3.3 PUBLIC PROGRAM MANAGEMENT

Public programs encompass all those activities that increase public access to and involvement with the collections: they enrich the visitor's experience, enhance enjoyment and understanding, attract new audiences, and encourage return visits. In the twenty-first century two qualities characterize the successful management of public programs: visitor responsiveness and creativity.

Visitor responsiveness refers simply to the fact that museum programs are for people. Unlike educational institutions that offer courses as part of degree studies or accreditation, museums offer programs that respond to people's interest in self-directed learning—"life-long learning" as it is often called. From the scholarly symposium to the Saturday afternoon treasure hunt, from the website to the planetarium laser shows, museum programs respond to the interests of the public.

Does this mean that museum programs are designed by survey? No, they are designed by professionals who are steeped in the museum's mission and who also understand the interests and needs of the public. Continual evaluation, including surveys, is the only way to ensure that programs are visitor responsive (rather than staff responsive) in their content, quality, format, and method of delivery. But the programs must originate from the museum's mission.

Creativity is the "wow" factor. It is the inspiration of a docent, the juxtaposition of two paintings never before seen in the same gallery, the new meaning an object theater display gives to artifacts of everyday life, the wonder of electricity when the visitor creates an arc of light, the magic of being in the presence of museum objects that are beautifully displayed, the enthusiasm of an information desk clerk. Museum managers who nurture creativity in their staff and respect the creativity of visitors will best be able to facilitate creative public programming. David Edwards's case study 3.3 in this section, "Innovation as Culture," places creative innovation at the heart of his center, Le Laboratoire in Paris.

This section explains how to manage public programs and related visitor services and activities in such a way as to encourage and sustain visitor responsiveness and creativity under the following headings:

- Exhibitions (3.3.1);
- Interpretation (3.3.2);
- Learning (3.3.3);
- Extension and Outreach (3.3.4);
- Publications (3.3.5);
- Marketing (3.3.6); and
- Visitor Services (3.3.7).

As noted in section 2.3.1, visitor services would be part of an Operations Department, while publications and marketing would be part of External Affairs in larger museums that have those departments. Here, however, we present them in the context of public programs not only because they are often grouped together in this way in three-department staff organizations, but more importantly because they are best managed within the context of visitor-oriented public programming.

3.3.1 Exhibitions

Exhibitions are the museum's main forum for interacting with the public. Indeed, the public most often judges the success or failure of a museum by its exhibition program. An exhibition policy and the exhibition development process are two important tools for managing a creative and visitor-responsive exhibition program—and museum managers need to use both of them.

3.3.1.1 Exhibition Policy

The *exhibition policy*, which is formulated by the museum's leadership, is the principal management tool for establishing:

- the objectives of the exhibition program;
- the philosophy of presentation; and
- the number, frequency, size, and scope of temporary exhibitions.

It is equally important for the staff and the museum's supporters to under-stand the *objectives* of the exhibition program—for example, the particular bal-ance between scholarship and visitor attraction, the relative emphasis on exhibitions of local, regional, national, and international significance, the role of research in the exhibition program, and the degree to which the museum endeavors to increase public access to its collections through rotation and spe-cial exhibitions. In his case study 3.3 in this section, entitled "Innovation as Culture," David Edwards proposes a highly creative balance between art and science as the objectives for Le Laboratoire in Paris.

INNOVATION AS CULTURE
By David Edwards

Labs are places of experience. We enter to explore. Each minute in a functioning lab is like a page of a smart novel that loses meaning without reference to what came before and what is about to follow.

Art, like science, is such an experience, and yet we encounter art and science in our museums more frequently as outcome, as product—dug up, carved down, highly edited—the result of a mysterious process of creative thought and engagement.

Process, of course, is hard to define, to classify, or to curate. It can seem to be beside the point. Sometimes, however, it is not. Occasionally, processes of exploration, discovery, and innovation matter more than any result these processes ever produce. This seems to be increasingly the case in culture as in industry and in society generally speaking. The pace of change in the "post-Google world" imparts transience to works of art, industry, research, and social enterprise to such a degree that results or products, as in the canonical research lab, appear mere points along an intriguingly winding curve. This curve, the engaging drama, has replaced the dots that make up the curve, the words and the clever sentences, as the predominant reference of value, and anything discrete and definitive seems increasingly suspect.

What is this creative process? As I argue in my book *Artscience: Creativity in the Post-Google Generation* (2008), idea development in culture, industry, education, and society can be conceived as a kind of experimentation, where the catalyst for change, for movement—for innovation—is a fusion of those creative processes we conventionally think of as art and as science. This fused process, what I call *artscience*, is the basis of a new kind of culture center we have opened in central Paris.

Le Laboratoire, located in Paris's *premier arrondissement*, invites the public to experience the creative process that drives innovation and value, in culture as in industry, society and education, as a fusion of art and of science, producing tangible—if transient—art and design outcomes. These outcomes or "works-in-progress" result from experiments conceived of and directed by leading international artists in collaboration with leading international scientists. Le Lab is a kind of off-Broadway, or pre-museum, aiming to catalyze change in culture, industry, society, and education with partners who invest in the exploration process more decidedly than in the guarantee of any outcome this process might produce.

Figure 3.3A. View from the walkway of French plastic artist Fabrice Hyber's installation Food for Thought at Le Laboratoire, Paris, October 2007–January 2008

PHOTO BY BRUNO COGEZ

Artscience Experiments

Works of art and design resulting from a confrontation with science, or at least with technology, fill art and science museums today. The works of art and design that result from experiments at a culture lab possess a narrower definition. At Le Laboratoire particularly we look for novel ideas of art and design that cannot be properly formulated without a sustained encounter with a pioneering edge of science. We then help broker encounters between artists and scientists that permit concrete idea formulation. Once ideas are formulated, we invest in development of the experimental projects that result. In this way, artscience, the process of creative thought that synthesizes aesthetic and analytical methods, becomes a catalyst for *innovation* and a basis for *partnership*.

Innovation can occur in cultural, industrial, and humanitarian contexts. For example:

- In a first culture experiment at Le Laboratoire, the French plastic artist Fabrice Hyber worked with the Massachusetts Institute of Technology (MIT) scientist Robert Langer to explore the possibility of sharing the experience of being a stem cell that produces a neuron. Hyber came

Figure 3.3B. The American photographer James Nachtwey's Attention! exhibit at Le Laboratoire, Paris, February 2008–March 2008

PHOTO BY BRUNO COGEZ

Figure 3.3C. View through a window glass of the exhibition of Bel Air, an innovative plant-based air filter designed by Mathieu Lehanneur and later commercialized as the air filter "Andrea." Exhibited at Le Laboratoire, Paris, October 2007–January 2008.

PHOTO BY BRUNO COGEZ

up with the idea that falling through a giant hourglass might produce an experience reflective of cellular division, the central process in neuronal production. He created several large inflatable hourglass objects, one through which the public could fall, with a mattress underneath. There were barrels of fermenting grapes and apples, which produced another sensory experience of cellular transformation, and a giant bubble-gum axon, which you could touch (see figure 3.3A).

- The French designer Mathieu Lehanneur collaborated with me to design an object that would make plants "smarter." An air filter emerged, more efficient than anything tried with plants before, which later traveled to the Museum of Modern Art in New York for the *Design and the Elastic Mind* exhibition. In the spring of 2008 *Popular Science* magazine selected Lehanneur's filter as an "Invention of the Year" (see figure 3.3C).

- The photographer James Nachtwey collaborated with the scientist Anne Goldfeld, cofounder of a major AIDS and tuberculosis clinic in Cambodia, and other medical scientists around the developing world. This led to a powerful photography exhibition, within which seventy

- scientists from around the world gathered with funding from the Bill and Melinda Gates Foundation to explore a new collaborative pharmaceutical model for addressing the health care crisis in impoverished countries (see figure 3.3B).
- The Michelin-starred chef Thierry Marx collaborated with the colloid physicist Jerome Bibette to invent a new form of flavor encapsulation, while art and science students at Harvard University worked with me to invent a way of eating by aerosol.

In all these examples, art, like science, was process and the outcome—whether contemporary art installation or industrial design object—remained unpredictable until the end. The outcome was not entirely beside the point, but it was less meaningful without reference to the experimental process that brought it about. It's this experimental process I explore in the "Séguier Novels," published with the Ecole Nationale Supérieure de Beaux Arts de Paris, including *Niche* (2007) and *Whiff* (2008).

Why Partners Invest

Experimental projects like these potentially affect culture, society, industry, and research. They also produce surprise and learning. Both possibilities drive partnership at a culture lab, as they do in most science labs. Le Lab's current partners include:

- an international bank, which brings twenty-five to thirty investment bankers from around the world each quarter to reflect on innovative experiments at the interface between art and science and on what this means to the bank;
- an international nongovernmental organization (NGO) interested to find innovative ways to approach global health;
- universities aiming to provide innovative experiential education; and
- a major new Asian museum, interested to produce innovative cultural programming.

Partners invest in the experiments of a culture lab as they do in the present value of tomorrow's potential. This value derives from a process of creative engagement that widens the scope of culture as we conventionally think of it, being intuitive and analytical, inductive and deductive, comfortable with uncertainty, thriving in ambiguity, and yet able to frame a problem and produce tangible solutions with measurable meaning.

The *modes of presentation* used in its exhibitions define the ways in which any museum communicates with the public through the medium of the exhibition. Today, there are many choices of modes of presentation. Some museums take advantage of all of them. Some (like science centers or many children's museums) focus mostly on a single approach. Still others take one approach for the permanent collection and use temporary exhibitions as an opportunity to experiment with various modes as seems appropriate. We briefly describe six of these modes of presentation here:

1. Contemplative or "Aesthetic" Mode: In this mode of presentation, museum specimens, artifacts, or works of art are presented aesthetically as individual objects for contemplation, with the intention of enhancing the visitor's affective experience of the object. This approach is most common in art museums and galleries, but it is used to good effect in many other types of museums to evoke a sense of wonder or awe, as, for example, in the dramatic display of a piece of moon rock in a science museum.

2. Thematic or Contextual Mode: In this mode objects are grouped together to show their relationships with each other, while graphics or other interpretive devices place them in their social, historical, cultural, or scientific context. Sometimes referred to as *didactic displays*, exhibits in this mode are commonly found in archaeology, history, and natural history museums.

3. Environmental Settings: Room settings or large-scale walk-in dioramas of natural environments recreate or evoke the time and place in which the artifacts or specimens displayed in them were originally found. This mode is almost universally found in historic houses and decorative arts museums, as well as in many natural history museums.

4. Systematic Mode: The comprehensive display of museum objects to demonstrate type variations or a range of comparable specimens was the dominant form of museum exhibition in the Victorian period. Today it is found in *visible storage* installations, which offer a systematic display of all or most of the objects of a particular medium or type in the museum's collection, accompanied by computer terminals where the entire catalog entry on each object is keyed to the display by a simple numerical guide to the shelf and individual object. In section 3.4.1.2 Georgina Bath provides case study 3.8 of visible storage at the Smithsonian American Art Museum in Washington, D.C.

5. Interactive Exhibits: This mode of display involves the visitor in dialogue with the exhibit. Touch-screen computers utilizing multimedia technology have been particularly effective not only in helping visitors to explore scientific principles in science centers or design principles in design

museums, but also in allowing them to explore the image catalogs of the entire art collections of many art museums today.

6. Hands-On Exhibits: This mode of display encourages visitors to learn through physical, kinaesthetic experience. Mechanical and physical devices can be very effective, especially in the children's (or family) gallery of any museum—demonstrating color mixing in an art museum, the lever in a science museum, or how sails are hoisted in a maritime history museum, for instance. Once the exclusive mode of science centers and children's museums, today many types of museums offer *touch tables* or *discovery boxes* where visitors of all ages can feel the weight of an ancient bronze or touch the glaze on a Korean ceramic, where duplicates, secondary examples, or replicas are used.

Underlying the contemporary approach to museum exhibition is a fundamental shift away from the idea of the museum as representing absolute authority in its field to an understanding that the museum presents and interprets facts, concepts, or theories that are sometimes contentious or even contradictory, and may reflect the convictions of various experts as well as those of the curators. The objective is to present the evidence so that the visitor may understand alternative explanations or theories and develop a somewhat better-informed opinion about them. In its annual rehang of its permanent collection in London, for instance, Tate Britain not only changes the themes of the galleries, but through its audio guides and publications aims to involve the visitor in the real intellectual excitement of art museums, where different perspectives lead to new or renewed understanding of the art on view. Science museums similarly aim to present the evidence for evolution in an open-ended way so that visitors with religious apprehensions about the subject can consider it for themselves and reach a better-informed conclusion.

Another fundamental shift is away from the museum as a closed institution where curators know all to an open one that invites both the specialist and the broad public to contribute their knowledge and information. This has the greatest impact on exhibition planning, but there may also be a visible effect in the galleries, and on museum websites, where visitors may be invited to record their comments on the exhibits in graphic or electronic form. The museum's exhibition policy should set out guidelines on issues of authority and openness for museum staff in addressing these complex matters during the exhibition development and design process.

Temporary Exhibition Policy: The sources, number, duration, frequency, size, and scope of temporary exhibitions are all cause for continual debate among museums. How many exhibitions of local significance, how many of regional import, of national importance, and of global origin and character will vary with the type and specific situation of each museum. Balancing a regional artists' association's annual exhibition with shows of greater range—or replacing one with another—can be a controversial decision for a local art museum.

Many museums offer too many changing exhibitions, leaving the staff too little time for other activities and not allowing the public time to communicate news of the exhibition by word of mouth, the most powerful form of publicity if it is given time to have effect. The duration of travelling shows is often too short due to constraints imposed by lenders, but the museum's own temporary exhibitions should be planned for longer stays so that they can be effectively marketed.

Size and scope are still more controversial, with continual dire warnings of the "end of the blockbuster," despite its continuing presence. Its advocates point to the great opportunities that the *blockbuster* offers for scholarship as well as audience development, whereas its detractors complain of the drain on staff and the distraction from other aspects of the museum's mission. Meanwhile such large major exhibitions remain one of the great attractions museums can offer to their public. Many new museums and expansions have been fuelled by the desire of their stakeholders to participate in the world of these major international shows. Here are five guidelines that may be useful in evaluating whether a major exhibition is worth doing:

- Re-presentation of artifacts and/or works of art as a result of new research. This may offer a juxtaposition of works not often seen together; a new thesis about the artist, the group, or the theme; or re-presentation by means of what the French call mise-en-scène.
- A transformation experience: in other words, surprise and discovery of new attitudes, values, or appreciation of meanings. This is the essential visitor experience that exhibitions can deliver.
- A self-directed experience. Visitors may choose an audio or human guide, but the possibility of a self-directed experience is always there.
- Engagement of visitors of all types: scholars, learners, artists and people in the art business, relaxation seekers, escapists, cultural tourists, first-time visitors, or diligent students.
- Transparency as to the sources of the exhibition's viewpoint. As a medium of representation, the exhibition is actually ill-suited to the omniscient presenter (even though we have been accustomed to this approach in the past). Exhibitions are more suited to a multiplicity of voices.

An exhibition policy should provide general guidance on all these issues so that the museum's exhibition schedule may be consistent with its mission and with the objectives of the exhibition program. The policy should consider the different types of exhibitions available to the museum and set a range for the frequency and scope of each type, including such issues as:

- rotation of sensitive objects for reasons of conservation;
- small feature exhibitions to provide public visual access to new acquisitions, current research on the collections, and collection resources in storage, including such features as one-object exhibitions in which individual works of art or artifacts are displayed, supported by a great breadth and depth of information about their making and meaning;
- major thematic exhibitions from the museum's collection, possibly supplemented by borrowed works, which may be designed to travel or may be exhibited only at this museum;
- loan exhibitions of various sizes, originated by another museum, a museum consortium, a private sector organization, or government agency, if these are consistent with the museum's mission; and
- large, high-profile exhibitions that are so spectacular they attract a huge audience—blockbusters—not only art exhibitions but also archaeological and natural history exhibitions. The policy on these exhibitions should include attention to how the museum hopes to sustain its membership and attract return visits from those who are attracted by the big show.

The two-year chart in table 3.3 is a useful tool for ensuring that the exhibition policy maintains an appropriate balance among these many possibilities. The column at the left indicates whether the content of the exhibition (whatever its origin) is local, regional, national, or international in character. The types of exhibition for a notional regional museum are ranged across the top as an example.

The example in table 3.3 is for a museum with a strong regional history mission, mandate, and collection. The policy guideline seeks to mount nineteen exhibitions over a two-year period. Four of these would rotate the museum's important collection of textiles and works on paper produced in the region. Six small exhibitions would focus on new acquisitions, current research, and items of local or regional significance from the collection. Over the two-year period the museum will mount four larger exhibitions on

Table 3.3. Guideline for Two-Year Exhibition Schedule for a Regional Museum

Scope	Rotation	Small	Thematic	Loan
Local		3	2	
Regional	4	3	2	2
National				2
Global				1

broader themes, two on local and two on regional subjects. The museum will also borrow five larger exhibitions over this two-year period, three of which will have national or global reference, providing the community with a "window on the world." Toward the end of this two-year period, staff should evaluate the effectiveness of the program, and the director should recommend changes to the policy if it is felt that a greater or lesser number of exhibitions of the various types is required, or if there is a demand for more exhibitions of global or national scope.

It is worth underlining here that the board's role in regard to exhibition policy is not to debate the exhibition program, but to debate and formulate policy on program objectives, modes of presentation, and these guidelines for the exhibition schedule, then to provide oversight to ensure that the director and staff are creatively fulfilling the institution's exhibition policy.

3.3.1.2 Organization of the Exhibition Development Process

An exhibition is a medium of communication that is the museum's main method of communicating with its public. To communicate effectively through such a social medium requires all the resources of the museum—and often involves resources from outside as well. Its exhibition development process is the method that the museum employs to coordinate all these resources so that exhibitions open on time, within budget and to the desired level of quality.

3.3.1.2.1 Exhibition Committees

In section 2.3 we described two types of exhibition committee. A third "advisory committee" may also be considered for some exhibitions. The three options are as follows:

- Some museums favor board exhibition committees that meet with the director and curators to consider exhibition policy; these are sometimes counterproductive, however, as they often encourage trustees to get involved with decisions about exhibition content, instead of focusing on matters of policy.
- Standing exhibition committees of staff representing all departments (since everyone is affected by the exhibition schedule) that meet monthly—or at least quarterly—to review the upcoming schedule and the results of recent exhibitions. This committee, which reports to the director, should also recommend members of exhibition task forces for major shows being planned. The director or a senior curator may chair this committee, but in any case it is the director who has the final decision-making role in deciding

whether or not to proceed with a particular exhibition. (See *The Manual of Museum Exhibitions* [2002], edited by Gail and Barry Lord, for more details on how exhibition ideas are developed in museums.)

- For some exhibitions, an *advisory committee* may also be needed. These may be committees of academics, collectors, and scholars in the field of the exhibition whose knowledge will enhance the quality of the show. Or they may be an advisory group based in the community of interest relevant to the exhibition, locally or globally, who can ensure that the exhibition responds to community sensitivities. An exhibition on a specific ethnic culture, for instance, may involve members of the present-day community of origin of that culture. The results can be significant in ensuring enthusiastic participation by that community as visitors or donors, as well as giving a particular relevance to the exhibition that it would not otherwise have. However, these committees often also involve the museum in divergent views of what is significant about a culture or in contentious accounts of history. The key to successful advisory committees is often the director's personal commitment and involvement and always a sincere intention not merely to listen but to implement suggestions or to explain why not, and to achieve consensus concerning other solutions.

3.3.1.2.2 Exhibition Task Forces

Section 2.3.2.3 indicated the importance of task forces for museum management. Here we apply that approach to the development of exhibitions. Some loan exhibitions that are "package" shows coming from one source and small displays of new acquisitions or current research may not require a full task force project team. For all major exhibitions originated by the museum, however, there should be a specific task force project team that combines the talents of all those responsible for the many aspects of the exhibition project. Each team should include representatives of the following functions in the museum:

Collection Management
- curatorial
- conservation
- documentation

Public Programs
- exhibitions
- design
- education
- publications
- website

Administration
- finance
- development
- security
- visitor services
- marketing

The idea of exhibition task force project teams is that they are project-oriented and nonhierarchical (as outlined in section 2.3.2.3). In selecting personnel to serve on a particular task force, therefore, department heads should take account of the knowledge and ability of each staff member, rather than their position or title alone. Where outside contractors are involved—in exhibition design, for example—they should also participate in the exhibition task force meetings.

Department heads should recommend their representatives to each exhibition task force, but the director should have final approval of the composition of the project team and should appoint its chairperson and project manager. Although the relevant curator may be the obvious choice to chair an exhibition in his or her area of competence, in some cases the exhibition department representative, an educator, or a conservator may be a suitable choice. While the chairperson may control the content of the exhibition, a separate *project manager* will be needed for larger exhibitions, and may be an experienced consultant contracted from outside the museum. The director delegates penultimate decision making on the budget and schedule to the task force. The chairperson and the project manager report to the standing exhibition committee and the director, who is an ex officio member of the task force and may join its meetings at any time to review progress to date.

Depending on the exhibition timeline, the team might begin by meeting monthly but will need to meet more frequently as opening day approaches. Regular reports from all participants should be heard at each meeting—so that security concerns, for example, are not left to the last minute. The project team is the forum for staff ideas and creativity, so all staff should feel welcome to present ideas and suggestions on the exhibition to the project team. Crediting the members of the team on exhibition literature and a graphic in the gallery is a good way to inspire dedication to an outstanding result.

The challenges experienced by exhibition task force project teams are legendary: the members of the team are required not only to bring their own professional expertise to the table, but also to be skilled in working cross-functionally and to understand the needs of all other disciplines, usually under time and budget pressures. The team leader needs to be both a skilled facilitator and a determined project manager. These are *not* necessarily the same abilities required to achieve a PhD in art history or palaeontology, nor to be a talented exhibition designer. Training in teamwork is often required, and an experienced project manager contracted from outside the staff may be the best way to achieve the result everyone wants to see.

3.3.1.3 Stages in the Exhibition Process

Where do exhibition ideas come from? The director's leadership, curatorial research, and suggestions of the educators are among frequent in-house sources. If the museum is interested in developing the quality and involvement of its security guards, a suggestion box in their changing room is a good idea, since the attendants have the opportunity to observe public interest, or lack of it. A visitor suggestion box in the lobby, and/or on the museum's website, inviting exhibition suggestions, is also recommended. And of course many exhibition ideas come from outside the museum, from the *zeitgeist* of current interests and concerns.

Just how the exhibition evolves from a vague idea to opening day will differ from museum to museum, depending on the size of the institution, the balance between in-house capability and contract services, and the corporate culture of the museum. Here we may delineate some basic steps that are followed by many museums. (See *The Manual of Museum Exhibitions* [2002], edited by Gail and Barry Lord for more details.)

3.3.1.3.1 Exhibition Concept Plan

At this stage, the idea for an exhibition has received some tentative level of interest among the museum leadership, so it may be developed by its proponents into a concept plan that articulates:

- exhibition objectives in relation to the museum's exhibition policy;
- scholarly significance of the exhibition and research or documentation required;
- visitor interest in relation to the museum's target markets;
- what the exhibition will look like (verbally) and the amount of gallery space required;
- a general indication of the type of artifacts, works of art, or specimens available in the museum's collections, with reference to their present condition and need for conservation;
- sources of potential loans and the likely availability of those;
- potential use of media and potential for a parallel virtual exhibition on the museum's website;
- initial cost projection;
- potential sources of funding or sponsorship; and
- initial projection of schedule.

This *concept plan* should be submitted by the exhibition's proponents to the standing exhibition committee, who may recommend it to the director for a go/no-go decision. If the initial cost projection is very high, but the exhibition is considered to be desirable, the concept plan may be given to the development director to seek a sponsor for all or part of the cost. The development director is likely to ask for preliminary *renderings* or even a *model* that suggests what the exhibition will look like, even at this early stage, in order to interest potential sponsors.

Formative evaluation can begin at this stage and may be sustained throughout the following stages. The term means, quite simply, evaluation while the exhibition is taking shape or forming. It is intended to ensure that the exhibition works from the visitors' perspective. One useful approach is to convene representative focus groups that consider the exhibition concept and its subsequent phases of schematic and more detailed design as they emerge. They might include a selection of likely users of the exhibition—teachers, students, museum members, or visitors selected at random. They might simply be asked to respond to a survey, or as plans progress they might be "walked through" the plans, the text, and the storyboards to identify areas of miscomprehension or confusion. If the project is a major new permanent collection exhibition, the museum may be well advised to employ an outside evaluator.

3.3.1.3.2 Interpretative Plan (Design Brief)

Once the standing exhibition committee and the director have approved the exhibition concept and it has been added to the exhibition schedule and budget, an exhibition task force is established, and the project team starts work. The first step is to write an *interpretive plan*, sometimes called a *design brief.* This is an important document that will guide the exhibition development process right through to opening day.

The interpretative plan or exhibition brief articulates:

- objectives of the exhibition;
- intended visitor experience;
- levels of interpretation (for children, adults, and specialists, for instance);
- component-by-component description of the exhibition, including:
    - communication objectives of each component—major artifacts, specimens or works of art, display cases, interactive exhibits, demonstrations, and theatrical presentations;
    - means of expression to communicate these objectives (multiple means for each objective), utilizing all appropriate display modes (see section 3.3.1.1);
    - diagrams of visitor flow patterns on gallery layouts; and
    - initial concept sketches or renderings to give the feel of the exhibition.

If there is to be a parallel virtual exhibition on the museum's website, the interpretative plan should also provide an outline of that feature.

Curators or educators are often expected to draft the interpretative plan, although some larger museums will have *interpretative planners* on staff. Often the museum may choose to contract an experienced outside consultant specialized in interpretative planning, with the exhibition concept plan serving as the *terms of reference* for a *request for qualifications* or a *request for proposals* to select this person, who may be part of a museum planning firm or an exhibition design studio.

Whoever produces it, the interpretative plan will be reviewed by each member of the exhibition task force until the entire team and the director reach a consensus of agreement about it. This is the point at which all members of the project team should be consulted: it is as important to have the comments of the chief of security as the chief conservator, and as important to get the input of the visitor services director and the marketing and retail managers as it is to obtain a sign-off from the curatorial department.

Once the interpretative plan has been recommended by the project team and approved by the director, each member of the task force can begin to develop plans for his or her own area of specialization: the selection of artifacts, works of art, or specimens by the curators; a schedule for condition reports on them by the conservators; a schedule for the requisite loan forms by the registrar; a marketing plan by the communications department; any special security arrangements by the chief of security; and so on. If the museum has in-house exhibition designers, the interpretative plan becomes the basis of their design; if not, it becomes the *Design Brief* for a competition to select the exhibition designers (unless the interpretative planner was part of a design team already selected). This competition may be for design only, or it could be for a *design-build* or *turnkey* contract for both design and fabrication.

3.3.1.3.3 Schematic Design

Schematic design refers to the period during which designers are drawing up the layout and design of the exhibition to fulfill the interpretative plan. This is usually a combination of floor plans, sections, elevations and three-dimensional views (often called "presentation drawings") of each exhibition component. There are usually several reviews until the designers (whether in-house or outside contractors) develop a solution that the exhibition task force chairperson can sign off on. Once this level of approval is reached, these drawings are not only useful for the exhibition design process but may also be invaluable to the marketing and development departments, especially if a sponsor is being sought for the exhibition. A preliminary "fly-through" graphic illustration of the experience of the exhibition may now be possible, which is even more helpful to all concerned—marketing, development, education, and others.

If the exhibition is to include a theatrical presentation, the schematic design stage is where a *script* and *treatments* should be developed, advancing beyond the interpretative plan's means of expression to draft a story line and propose treatments of specific themes. This document, usually developed by a specialist in the cinematic or theatrical techniques being proposed, is attached to the schematic design and should be considered and eventually approved along with it. If there is to be a parallel virtual exhibition on the museum's website, text and images for it should also be prepared in draft at this time.

Here the value of the initial interpretative plan becomes apparent. The more accurate the interpretative plan, the less time it will take for the design team to develop an appropriate solution, and for the exhibition task force to recognize and approve it. This is an important factor in staying within the exhibition schedule and the budget, as the schematic design should also be the basis for a more advanced costing by a museum planner or cost consultant with museum exhibition experience.

This is equally the "sketch stage" for all the specialists on the team. The educator, for example, can now draft a learning program based on the exhibition, making sure that there is sufficient provision for the space required by the groups of schoolchildren or adults expected to tour the show, and providing for any adjacent hands-on labs or classrooms, as well as learning stations in the exhibition itself, such as performance areas for demonstrators. The security chief is able to look for surveillance issues *before* design is finalized. The retail manager can begin to plan the special exhibition shop, and start to order the stock for it. Visitor services can consider whether there is sufficient space for queues and any special ticketing arrangements that are needed. Depending on the size of the project, schematic design can take from three months to a year, with the final product being approved by the task force and the director before detailed design or design development can start.

3.3.1.3.4 Design Development

As soon as schematic design is approved, *design development* should begin. Design development elaborates the schematic drawings into complete designs for buildable exhibits, vitrines (display cases) for specific objects, and locations for paintings or graphic panels. Some design practices distinguish design development from a subsequent stage of *detailed design* for larger projects, whereas others see the two as closely intertwined, especially for smaller projects. At this stage the script and treatments of the theatrical presentation should be elaborated into *storyboards* illustrating scene-by-scene what the viewer will see on the screen or on stage.

This is also the stage in which the text of all graphics and labels and any audiovisual scripts should be drafted for repeated editing to fit the space, as well as being subjected to the formative evaluation focus groups to test for clarity. Questions are often more effective communicators than assertions, and there is a paramount need to avoid the academic or technical jargon that creeps into the museum's language but may mystify the visitor, in addition to limiting the text of a graphic panel to sixty words or less so that a majority of visitors will pause long enough to read it. Curators usually initiate text, but the interpretative planner and/or the educators should massage it for length and clarity, with the final version submitted to the curator to check back for accuracy. If the museum has a chief of communications or a publications director, it is also valuable to have them edit the text from the viewpoint of the museum's house style. Graphic designers (either in-house or contracted) will meanwhile be developing a graphic style for the entire exhibition that provides a comprehensive format and size guide for all levels of printed communication, from the exhibition title and gallery names through graphic panels to labels, monitor screen text, and publications, all planned in relation to the levels of communication identified in the interpretative plan. They should also be preparing the final version of the text and images for the parallel virtual exhibition on the museum's website, if one is planned.

With all of these activities in development at the same time as the educators and the marketing staff are developing their plans, it is not surprising that, depending on the size of the project, the design development stage takes three months to a year after schematic design has been approved.

3.3.1.3.5 Construction and Installation

Signed-off approval of detailed design is really the last point at which the exhibition task force or the museum director can make changes. Thereafter, *construction drawings* are prepared on the basis of the detailed design. For the audiovisual and theatrical components, a final recording schedule or shooting script is developed on the basis of the approved storyboards.

The construction drawings are then assembled with all other instructions to contractors, creating a bid, or tender, package that is issued with a request for proposals from exhibition fabricators. These may be issued as one large contract, with the understanding that the fabricator will employ various subcontractors, or the museum may prefer to manage separate contracts for such elements as display case construction, computer hardware and software programs, model and mannequin making, audiovisual production, and so on. Mount making—building the supports for artifacts or specimens that might range from a gold ring to a reconstructed drinking vessel, or from a trilobite fossil to a whale's skeleton—is a specialized field in itself, which may be assigned either to in-house technicians or to an outside contract with a good track record for that very specialized work. Audiovisual production for the museum's theater or within the exhibition gallery is usually a separate contract with its own timeline, hopefully coordinated with the rest of exhibition fabrication and installation so that it will be "alright on the night" of the exhibition opening.

The contractor selection process should be managed according to the museum's procurement policies by the museum's purchasing department or responsible financial officer, in close consultation with the exhibitions department and the task force. The museum should not be tied in advance to accepting the lowest bid—frequently a low bid may indicate simply a lack of understanding of the complexity of the project, a lack of experience commensurate with the quality the museum expects, or an attempt to win the job at a low price, counting on change orders to increase the actual expenditure to what is really needed. This applies equally to the audiovisual producer and to any other separate components, if they are not grouped as subconsultants under the main fabricator.

Once the construction and installation process has commenced, the exhibition task force can intervene for quality control only at previously agreed points, when a prototype is being presented for approval, or an inspection of a particular phase is prearranged. Keeping within the budget and the schedule is important at this stage, with hard decisions having to be made if, for instance, certain materials are not available in sufficient quantity, so that substitutions are proposed, or if expensive change orders are proposed by the museum or the contractors. Because of the special security concerns of museums, access by contractors' personnel needs to be closely supervised by the museum's security staff.

A major focus of the study team during this period should be the coordination of the education activities, special events, publicity, fund-raising, and plans for the opening. The parallel virtual exhibition on the museum's website may be launched in advance of the exhibition, since it will stimulate advance excitement about the show, in addition to being valuable in itself.

The construction and installation stage is likely to take anywhere from nine to eighteen months for most exhibition projects.

3.3.1.3.6 Commissioning

The completion of installation is a relatively short but critical stage in exhibition development. Prior to final approval of construction and installation, the task force, led by its chair and the project manager, should tour the exhibition and draw up a "*snag list*" of deficiencies that the contractor is required to correct. Some negotiation may ensue regarding which deficiencies legitimately fall under the original contract, and which are client changes, but in any case all problems identified on the snag list must be resolved before handover (commissioning) is complete. A similar screening of audiovisual components is needed before they are installed in their appropriate places.

The paint should be dry, the dust should be removed, and the contractors vacated from the site prior to the installation of the artifacts, works of art, or specimens, which is the responsibility of the curators and conservators. There should also be time reserved for a "soft opening" in which exhibit components can be pretested on school groups or other samples of visitors, with an allocation in the schedule for adjustments if needed. Then the visitor services and operations staff take over to arrange for the opening.

3.3.1.3.7 Evaluation

The exhausted project team still has one more job to do: evaluating the exhibition process. It is crucial, both for the museum and for the profession as a whole, to look back on a major exhibition project to identify aspects of the process that worked well and why, and to recommend changes to the process that will improve chances for success in the future. The task force itself should do this much.

In addition, a *summative evaluation* of the visitor experience of the exhibition should be conducted by the museum's evaluation specialist or by an outside contractor. This type of visitor evaluation is most effective if it goes back to the original interpretative plan to determine whether or not the exhibition actually communicates what it was planned to communicate. The evaluation should be submitted to the director and the exhibition department, which could use it to improve the museum's *exhibition procedures manual* based on the cumulative experience of many exhibition project teams over the years. This type of manual can be a vital document to facilitate the creativity of future exhibition project teams.

3.3.2 Interpretation

Interpretation is the term used to describe the ways that the museum *communicates* with the public about its collections and research activities. The term *interpretation* is somewhat misleading because it suggests that the "language" of museum objects is somehow "foreign" and needs to be "translated"—which is essentially one-way communication—whereas museums in the twenty-first century should be about two-way communication between the museum and the public. However, *interpretation* is the term generally used by the museum profession and includes:

- orientation (3.3.2.1);
- labels and text (3.3.2.2); and
- provision of information (3.3.2.3).

As with other public program areas, the museum should formulate a policy to express its approach to interpretation or communication. For example, most art museums used to have an almost universal philosophy of letting works of art speak for themselves, and therefore provided a minimum of labels in the galleries. Today, many go quite the other way because they believe that the more the visitor understands, the more the visitor will gain from the works of art. And there is every possible stop along a continuum between these two approaches. Indeed some museums have certain galleries devoted to an "art for art's sake" approach, and others that are heavily interpreted.

Among science and industry museums, some have a philosophy of "every exhibit must be hands-on in some way," while others prefer a more contextual approach with objects in cases and extensive graphic explanations. Again, there is every possible variant along the continuum. Science centers almost universally explain their interactive exhibits in terms of what is happening, why, and how it works.

The interpretation policy (which should also set out a language policy) provides a helpful framework for staff responsible for the museum's many forms of interpretation. Obviously it is the context within which interpretative plans (see 3.3.1.3.2) are written.

3.3.2.1 Orientation

Visitor orientation is of two types; unfortunately, museums tend to undervalue both of them:

- Physical orientation is informing visitors about where they are, the visitor services available and in what languages, what there is to see and do, and how and where to find those experiences.
- Intellectual orientation is clarifying what the museum is about and the many ways to explore it so that visitors are enabled to make informed choices about their visit. For example, should they follow the prescribed visitor route, or is there a quick highlights tour? A special family gallery? Is there a resource center for visitors who prefer to cover fewer subject areas in more depth?

Visitor studies and common sense indicate that visitors who spend most of their time lost or looking for the toilets or who are not sure what is on offer in the various galleries do not get as much from the exhibits as those who know their way around. Not surprisingly, being lost or uncertain increases the "I don't belong here" feeling and discourages repeat visits. Informing visitors at the outset about services such as cloakroom, rest areas, restaurant, shop, toilets, baby change areas, first aid, use of wheelchairs and strollers, and the role of guards and information desk staff helps first-time visitors especially to feel at ease.

The quality of orientation also impacts on the museum's revenue stream. If visitors are not aware at the beginning of the visit that there is a pleasant café on the roof, they may not make time for it. If they do not understand the full range of the museum's exhibits and programs, they may leave mistakenly thinking "We've done that," rather than, "There's so much more to see and do, we must come back."

Once the museum leadership and staff grasp the importance of orientation to the quality of the visitor experience, visitor orientation can be successfully addressed:

- If there is not enough room in the lobby, consider that posters outside the building can begin to communicate the museum's philosophy and what is inside.
- Use all possible means to communicate the visitor's choices, such as informational signage, interactive kiosks, the information desk, pamphlets, and floor maps.
- Develop a consistent way-finding system, starting outside and with directional signing throughout the museum's public spaces, and link signing with print and audiovisual materials.
- Train all front-line staff in the importance of helping visitors find their way and encourage staff to report back to management on the problems they learn from visitors—and then do something to solve the problems.
- Use the auditorium for intellectual orientation, where an audiovisual presentation of ten or twelve minutes can tell the core story of the museum. This is especially important for history or biographical museums.

3.3.2.2 Labels and Text

"Labels are the foot soldiers in the museum's wars," is how one curator described the centrality of labels in a staff workshop facilitated by one of the authors. "Wars" may be an apt description of the label-writing process in many museums. As with exhibition development (see section 3.3.1) each museum develops its own procedure for writing label and panel text. The museum's interpretation policy should guide:

- the names or themes of galleries;
- the size of label or text panel;

- the type of information to be provided (date, artist/inventor, provenance, accession number, gift, description, uses, donor, and the like);
- the tone (authoritative, Socratic, objective?); and
- the style (everyday language or technical terms?).

The museum's label-writing procedure establishes:

- the word limits;
- type size and color;
- placement; and
- writing and approval procedures.

The label text process generally starts with the curator responsible for a particular gallery or exhibit. Next the education department reviews it from the visitor perspective, and the publications department edits for style. The curator provides final sign-off on the text, while the director is usually the court of last resort. But the entire process should be controlled by the interpretation policy and a procedures manual determining length, style, tone, color, and placement. Too often an otherwise fascinating exhibition is marred by labels printed in type too small with insufficient color contrast placed in difficult locations, requiring visitors to stoop.

Tate and the Victoria and Albert Museum, among others, have had success in appointing a director of communications, a position that works with curators and educators to produce a wide range of interpretive materials, including labels, wall texts, broadsheets, gallery guides, and audio guides. When one considers that museums are in the communications business, but often pay insufficient attention to communications, this is a strategy that may be wholeheartedly recommended.

3.3.2.3 Provision of Information

We are living in an information age, and for museums this means that visitors seem to have an insatiable desire for more information, as almost every visitor survey will demonstrate. Information provision may include:

- the Information Desk, which is the front line for information. The staff or volunteers are prepared to respond to questions ranging from where to catch the bus to where a specific painting is to be found. Larger museums place information desks throughout the museum as well as at the entrances.
- information personnel (staff or volunteers), who may be positioned at desks, or who may roam the galleries wearing shirts that say "Ask Me." Science centers, which can provide these interpreters with white lab coats,

have been best at this type of information provision (which is, of course, labor intensive), but they are invaluable wherever they are employed, and whatever shirt or jacket they wear. This is an excellent role for well-trained volunteers.

- interactive information centers, which have been developed in many museums to provide visitors with a range and depth of information convenient to the galleries. These would be intrusive if located inside the galleries, but they are very helpful immediately adjacent—such as at the Rubin Museum of Art in New York, where the visitor can explore the subtleties of Himalayan art on monitors in study rooms at the back of each gallery floor. Some institutions, like the National Gallery in London, offer the visitor the opportunity to explore the entire collection on monitors and plan a personal visitor route based on them.

- the library, which may be fully accessible to the public or open at certain times or by appointment. Very often museum libraries are unnecessarily restricted to staff when they would be of great value to the limited number of visitors who wish to explore the subject matter of the museum in greater depth. A popular combination today is to link the library to the café, as the Thai Creative and Design Centre does in Bangkok, thereby attracting and holding the attention of the young people who visit it in great numbers; the risk of coffee stains on a library book is worth the great gain in visitor service.

- computers and multimedia terminals, installed in or near galleries to provide contextual information; access to some card catalog data on objects; or simulation exercises and games to explain processes, concepts, and principles. These are a valuable component of visible storage galleries, keyed to a number code shown on the shelves so that visitors can instantly access all the museum's catalog information (except for insurance or security data) for each individual object in a dense display, affording access to a large range of that part of the museum's collection.

- audio guides for both special exhibitions and permanent collections. These are currently evolving from the rentable wands still seen in many museums into systems linked to iPods or mobile phones. Audio systems are particularly important for highly popular exhibits like famous paintings, since they make it possible for large numbers of people to view them without crowding around to read a label. The content and tone of the scripts for these guides should, like the labels and graphics, reflect the interpretation policy of the museum.

- tours, lectures, and demonstrations. Because of their interpersonal quality, these tried and true methods continue to be the preferred way for many visitors and museum interpreters to communicate. Most museums offer a range of tours and lectures by docents (paid or volunteers), along with occasional lectures by specialists. In history, science, and children's museums, there may be demonstrators (sometimes costumed) and interpreters on hand to explain the exhibits.

3.3.2.4 Languages and "Universal Design"

The languages in which interpretation will be available, and *"universal design"* for the sight and hearing impaired are important considerations in the interpretation policy. In a globalized world, museums should communicate not only in the main languages spoken in the community, whether official or unofficial, but also in the main tourist languages. Where there are several official languages, as in Switzerland, Belgium, Wales, or Canada, many museums are required to provide all interpretation in multiple languages, including signage, labels, publications, and guided tours. In the many regions and communities that are culturally diverse, but where there is only one official language, the museum should provide leaflets, guidebooks, information paddles, and directional signs in the main minority languages. Label text may be made available on broadsheets in many languages as well as in large-print size for the visually impaired and for older visitors. Directional signs and floor plans in the minority languages are particularly important for reasons of public safety if they include emergency exit instructions. The museum should ensure that at least one member of its information staff who is able to communicate in the main languages spoken in the community is on duty at all times.

Tourism, particularly cultural tourism, has become such a major factor not only for museums but for their governments that museums that attract or hope to attract a high proportion of tourist visitors should consider providing services in the four or five main tourist languages. The main orientation, directional signs, and information leaflets should be prominently displayed in these languages, with translations of label text, guidebooks, and catalogs available for sale in the shop and for consultation at information desks and in study and rest areas. Guided tours should be available in various languages and for special-needs groups, including the visually impaired. Digital audio guides can be adjusted to meet the needs of the hearing impaired and can be made available in numerous languages.

Planning for physically, visually, or hearing impaired persons should affect all aspects of museum design, not only the toilets and circulation routes, which should be barrier-free and wide enough to accommodate wheelchairs. *Universal design* is the term that has been used to refer to ensuring that all aspects of a museum or an exhibition encourage access by all visitors, whatever their limitations. The museum's interpretative policy should include its commitment to these principles.

3.3.2.5 Management of Interpretation

Surprisingly, centralized management of the museum's interpretation services is rarely found in museums. Typically, Information Desks are managed by Visitor Services or the Communication Department, while tours and lectures are organized by the Education Department, and the Library is its own department; meanwhile, label writing, audio guide, and multimedia production are happening in many different places. Should there be one "Interpretation" or "Communications" department in the Public Programs or Operations Division, or is there a virtue in having a multiplicity of departments providing information? Since many departments communicate with the public, it may make the most sense to create an interdepartmental Interpretation (or Communication) Team that includes representatives from all departments, with a mandate to implement the museum's interpretation policy and coordinate the growing number of communication initiatives that will—as long as the museum staff is visitor responsive and creative—keep emerging everywhere.

3.3.3 Learning

Museums are redefining their role as public educational institutions. One of the signs of this realignment is a change in nomenclature from the generic "Education" to the more directed title, "Learning," which suggests not only that the interest is focused on the learner (rather than the educator), but also that the museum is a learning institution, and that there is learning on the part of the staff as much as on the part of the visitor. For a fuller treatment of this new approach to learning, see the book edited by Barry Lord, *The Manual of Museum Learning* (2007).

The mission statement of the Education Department of the Cleveland Museum of Art, a venerable one much influenced by the learning philosophy of John Dewey, summarizes the orientation of many museum education departments today:

> The Education Department staff serves as a catalyst between the works of art in the Museum's collection and visitors, young and old, from the Cleveland community and beyond. A passion for and understanding of art objects—as embodiments of aesthetic quality and of culture/history—is core to achieving this mission. Through programs and teaching, the Education Department staff strives to foster non-elitist perceptions of art and the Museum, strengthening the Museum's commitment to its community, and making the museum accessible to the widest possible audience.

In fulfilling such a mission, educators must remember four key factors about museum learning:

- Museums work best as *informal* rather than formal educational institutions.
- Informal education is most successful at *affective* learning—although some cognitive learning is also always involved.
- The outcome of affective learning is reflected in a change of attitude, valuation, or interest, rather than in the formal cognition of information or data.
- Affective learning works best when the experience is *fun.*

3.3.3.1 Provision for School Groups

School parties usually comprise from 15 to 25 percent of museum attendance, introducing many young people to museums and performing a valuable service for school systems. There is an increasing emphasis on relating the school museum visit to curriculum, to learning objectives and educational attainment targets. Cutbacks in school budgets have made museum bus trips harder to justify. Museum education departments are obliged to work more and more closely with teachers and curriculum advisors to integrate their programs with the needs of the schools. Some of the tools being developed include:

- Advisory committees: museum educators in some jurisdictions work with teachers and Community Advisory Committees to ensure that the themes, classes, and workshops they present are relevant, up-to-date, and meet the children's needs in the specific context of that museum's community. This is particularly important in disadvantaged communities.
- Teacher resource centers: many museums have established centers where teachers can borrow materials to use in the classroom to better prepare students for the visit and for follow-up activities. This Resource Center may also provide training workshops for teachers. Some museum training programs confer state accreditation for the teacher.
- Secondment to the museum of staff from the school system: this is a good way to facilitate close coordination and mutual understanding. A cross-appointment of a teacher who works half-time in the museum and half-time coordinating school visits is ideal.
- School–museum liaison officers: some museums have had success in appointing a teacher who is already enthusiastic about use of the museum for his or her class to serve as a liaison officer with all other teachers in that school, passing on information about new exhibitions or other programs that will be of interest to them. A semiannual meeting of these liaison

teachers at the beginning of each school term is an excellent way of ensuring that the museum's learning opportunities are not being missed.

- Youth advisory council: student volunteers, interns, and students on co-op or work-study programs provide invaluable training opportunities and keep the museum in touch with young people
- Website: the museum's website can create a more integral relationship between museums and schools. Students can access museum collections and information about them and even consult museum curators from their classroom. A judicious use of the Web should serve to whet the appetite of students for the real thing on a visit to the museum, and it has been demonstrated that students who have studied images of artifacts, specimens, or works of art prior to a museum visit learn much more readily from their actual visit.
- Museum schools: some museums have established partnerships with schools, whereby lessons are taught in the galleries, often with special attention to science, art, or whatever is the subject matter of the museum.

Many museums rely on volunteers to guide school visits and activities so that staff educators may focus on program development, training, and evaluation to ensure a growing level of quality. While a dedicated corps of volunteers is a tremendous asset for the museum, the challenge is in attracting volunteers who are able to respond to the interests of an increasingly diverse population, particularly in urban schools. Many museum Education Departments are working with Community Advisory Committees to develop strategies to meet this challenge.

To cover the costs of school programs museums may contract with school systems to receive an annual allocation for a specific service. Some museums have a per-student charge that varies with the cost of the program, depending on whether an educator has to accompany the class or not. Other museums offer school programs free of charge in recognition of their local, state, or national government grants, which may be conditional on such a service. Many museums are developing partnerships with the private sector to provide free or low-cost school visits, especially for areas where schools and families may not have sufficient means to pay.

3.3.3.2 Adult and Family Learning Programs

Museums offer informal education, which, with the exception of guided tours, consists of *self-directed learning*. The goal should be *affective* rather than cognitive learning, aimed at affecting visitors' interests, attitudes, or valuations rather than imparting information. This means that organized education programs should respond to people's interests and abilities and thus will vary widely, including workshops, courses, lectures, films, concerts, family activities, tours, seminars, symposia, and artists-in-residence. Some of these programs, such as a concert or film series, may be presented and perceived primarily as entertainment rather than as an educational program; again, the goal is informal affective learning, and that is most effective when the learning experience is fun. Programs intended for adults or families may be scheduled events such as a seminar in the auditorium for which a ticket must be booked in advance, or they may be a simple "drop-in" demonstration taking place in the gallery and open to all who happen to be visiting at that time.

Programs may be rather unusual, like the highly popular "sleepovers" at science centers or museums in Britain as well as the United States, wherein children participate in an overnight program of learning activities that includes sleeping in the galleries and breakfast in the cafe the next morning. Families with young children are particularly eager for learning opportunities near home, and this is a segment of the population that is growing in the early twenty-first century. Meeting the needs of this group is especially important because studies show that children who participate in cultural activities with their family are most likely to be participants as adults. Museum "Saturday Morning Classes" (some of which date to the early years of the twentieth century) are a good example: they are still going strong in many communities and being extended to summer and holiday museum camps.

Today, museum education departments are reaching an even wider family audience through special education galleries with a variety of exhibits and hands-on activities for school groups on weekdays and for families on weekends and holidays. Successful examples include the Royal Ontario Museum's pioneering Discovery Room in Toronto, the hands-on family gallery at the Frist Center for the Visual Arts in Nashville, and the Science Museum's Launch Pad in London.

The cost of providing public education activities, with or without nominal charges to the schools, is often covered by user fees, corporate sponsorship, and project grants from government agencies and private foundations. It is usually not possible for museums to recover all that they expend on their learning programs. These programs are, however, central to the mission statements of most museums.

3.3.4 Extension, Outreach, and Engagement

Extension refers to the programs museums offer outside the museum building to their traditional audiences; while *outreach* refers to museum activities that are designed for new or nontraditional audiences, whether offered in the museum or at another location. Just as the term *museum education* is being replaced by the more inclusive concept of *museum learning*, *outreach* is seen as a limiting idea implying a sense of "us and them." Increasingly museum program staff seek to engage audiences—both traditional and nontraditional.

Particularly for museums that have grasped their civil society role (see section 2.5), extension and engagement programs may be instrumental to asserting a stronger role in the community. Relatively intensive levels of staff effort are often involved in providing such programs. Recently, many museums have joined popular social networking sites and have experienced significant success engaging nontraditional audiences, especially young adults. There is now a need for young, technologically savvy museum program staff who in turn need management support in setting objectives and in facilitating their initiatives within the framework of the museum's mission. Eleanor Goldhar and her young colleagues at the Guggenheim Museum have contributed case study 3.4 that illuminates this approach.

Making museums engaging and accessible via the Web and more traditional ways to those who for reasons of limited education or economic or social class have not dared to enter their doors is increasingly important not only to fulfilling the museum's mission but to the sustainability of museums in society.

Whether public engagement is inviting local families to a special community evening at the museum, celebrating the Day of the Dead and other ethnic festivals, providing after-school study halls, or hosting monthly events for singles, the objectives cannot be accomplished in one event or one year. Museum program and marketing staff need to engage the entire museum to develop exhibitions and activities that will sustain the new audience interest over time.

SOCIAL NETWORKING
How the Guggenheim Got Started
By Eleanor Goldhar, Francesca Merlino, Ashley Prymas, and Laura Miller

The trend in the use of World Wide Web technology and Web design aims to enhance creativity, information sharing, and, most notably, collaboration among users. These concepts have led to the evolution of Web-based communities and hosted services, such as social networking sites and blogs—exciting opportunities for fostering meaningful engagement with new and prospective members, visitors or donors.

The exploding popularity of social networking includes audiences that are particularly attractive to museums: younger, educated, and both technologically and culturally savvy teens and adults. With over 130 million registered social network profiles, and each person averaging two to three social networks, these new channels represent an unparalleled opportunity to develop and maintain audiences in a much more cost-effective way than with traditional marketing techniques.

The most compelling aspect of Web 2.0 is that registered usage and interaction is free, and it operates on a different philosophy than traditional marketing. It is an environment where communication is democratized—where users shift from passive observer to author/creator, participant, and opinion-maker. The consumer is in command. Users can reach a global audience with no barriers and can customize their use in ways similar to TiVo and iPods.

In 2006 the Solomon R. Guggenheim Museum established a minimal presence as a placeholder on MySpace while exploring the potential of social networking channels. Competing New York City cultural organizations had successfully established a more active presence. Recognizing the opportunity, in August 2007, several younger marketing department staff (in their twenties and thirties) proposed a plan to introduce the Guggenheim into the social networking world. Allowing this process to grow organically—not through committees and procedures but with a simple "yes, let's try it"—has had a positive impact on the internal community (staff) and with our new audiences online.

The online proposal focused on five key social sites—MySpace, Facebook, Flickr, YouTube, and Delicious. Providing maximum content on a few key sites allows the Guggenheim to connect consistently with the target audience. Whether it's creating Facebook events, allowing users to view behind-the-scenes photos on Flickr, or posting exhibition news across MySpace, the Guggenheim is benefiting from social site activity through

Figure 3.4. Solomon R. Guggenheim Museum, New York

PHOTO BY DAVID HEALD

increased brand recognition, participation online, website traffic, and "viral" word-of-mouth publicity.

1. Best Practice

Before embarking on social networking, the museum's marketing department reviewed existing coverage of Web 2.0 best practice in press materials, surveyed other arts organizations sites, and talked with experienced colleagues from other New York City cultural organizations to learn dos and don'ts.

DO:
- A. Maintain brand identity and consistency with www.guggenheim.org.
- B. Utilize resources—collaborate with staff, manage digital assets, and take advantage of free Web 2.0 applications.
- C. Build web relationships—expand online audience.

D. Engage, inform, and interact—produce portable "viral" content, join/create groups.
E. Encourage reviews, comments, and discussion with online audience.
F. Schedule strategically—develop content to coincide with museum exhibitions, programs, and events that will appeal to the target audience, e.g., social or newsworthy events.
G. Tag, categorize, and link to www.guggenheim.org whenever possible; be easy to find and accessible to anyone, anywhere.
H. Track results—measure page views, friends/fans, subscriptions, and click-throughs.

DON'T:
A. Advertise or sell.
B. Censor commentary, unless it violates established boundaries.

2. Timeline

- January 2007: Information Services (one staff) creates a Guggenheim MySpace profile.
- August 2007: Marketing (two staff) begins work with Publications/Web (two staff) on implementation of new content in conjunction with Richard Prince exhibition.
- December 2007: Marketing relaunches the Guggenheim on MySpace with updated content.
- January 2008: Marketing launches the Guggenheim on Facebook.
- March 2008: The Social Net Team—Web, Publications, Education, Development, Curatorial and Legal staff—hold first brainstorming session; team created by staff who volunteer to participate.
- April 2008: All-staff memo sent outlining social network goals, inviting staff to become a friend on Myspace and Facebook.
- April 2008: Marketing launches the Guggenheim on Flickr and Delicious and adds these applications to the Facebook page.
- May 2008: "Bourgeois World Wide Web" Flickr group is created to stimulate preopening buzz for the Louise Bourgeois retrospective.
- June 2008: MySpace Friends campaign begins; Flickr and RSS application for podcasts added to the MySpace profile.

3. Social Networking Goals

A. Drive museum attendance and traffic to guggenheim.org.
B. Access new audiences and connect to current audiences.

C. Engage in peer-to-peer interaction and allow users to participate in the Guggenheim web space by networking, sharing images and video, subscribing to news feeds, blogging, and more when the new website launched in the fall of 2008.

D. Focus on brand recognition, convey value, and create consistent aesthetics among social networks and share sites linked with www.guggenheim.org.

4. Guggenheim Social Media Initiatives

Our initiatives encompass not only social networking, but also social multimedia.

4.1 Social Networking

Social networking sites allow users to share information, interact with friends, and engage with new audiences. The Guggenheim's Facebook and MySpace pages provide program information and dynamic content including photos of events and exhibition installations. Utilizing free web applications and RSS feeds, users are offered the latest museum press bookmarked on Delicious, podcasts, and select photos hosted on Flickr. YouTube videos will be directly streamed onto the Guggenheim's social networking sites. More importantly, users can offer reviews and comments, as well as invite the museum to participate in their own social spaces. The Guggenheim's social content is closely monitored by the marketing department, reviewed daily, and filtered for approval. Content is updated weekly, or as often as necessary.

Specific programs are as follows:

Facebook: To interact on www.Facebook.com in any capacity, a registered Facebook account is required. Facebook members can become a "fan" of the Guggenheim via the Guggenheim's museum/attraction Facebook page. Utilizing Facebook Insights, a free service offered with page registration, Guggenheim staff track "fan" usage, behavior, and demographic information. From its inception in late January 2007 to the summer of 2008, the Guggenheim built a Facebook fan base of over 5,400 unique users, 61 percent female, 70 percent between the ages of eighteen and thirty-four, growing at a rate of over 1,000 new "fans" per month.

MySpace: Anyone can view the Guggenheim's MySpace profile by visiting www.myspace.com/guggenheim_museum. To see items such as MySpace photo albums, videos, and calendar listings, or to message the

Guggenheim, one must become a MySpace member and a friend of the Guggenheim, either by request or invitation. Although MySpace does not provide a user tracking application, overall statistics are offered. From January 2007 to the summer of 2008, the Guggenheim accumulated over 7,800 MySpace friends, more than 25,000 profile views, and over 1,300 comments. In six months, the museum doubled its number of friends.

4.2 Social Multimedia

Audio, photo, and video sharing sites allow users to post, view, listen, and talk about shared content. Utilizing both archived and custom-produced materials, the Guggenheim recently began engaging users on social multimedia sites. The marketing department posts selected multimedia content as it becomes available. Guggenheim podcasts are made available on Facebook and MySpace, in addition to the following dedicated sites.

Flickr: In April 2008, the Guggenheim posted its first Flickr photo album of party images taken at a monthly event called Art After Dark: First Fridays, taken within the Cai Guo-Qiang exhibition. Within three months the museum's Flickr photostream received over one thousand views of the party taken by others, and now also contains images of a demonstration of jewelry production at the museum, and pictures from the museum members' opening reception for the Louise Bourgeois exhibition. Flickr users are invited to subscribe to the museum's photostream, comment on "favorite" photos, and message via Flickrmail. In May 2008, the Guggenheim's first Flickr group, called Bourgeois World Wide Web (www.flickr.com/groups/bourgeoisworldwideweb), was created to capitalize on the popularity of this artist's iconic spider sculptures and drawings to generate preopening buzz for the Louise Bourgeois retrospective. Facebook fans, MySpace friends, and select Flickr users were invited to join the group and submit photos of their favorite Louise Bourgeois outdoor sculpture. In a few months, fifty-six images were posted by twenty-three unique members of the group from around the world. A community photo-sharing project for the Catherine Opie exhibition was planned on the basis of this success.

YouTube: Given that the public has created and posted over three hundred Guggenheim videos, the museum is eagerly anticipating acquiring the ability to control content with the launch of its nonprofit YouTube channel. Inspired by the efforts of YouTube pioneers—MoMAvideos, the Asia Society, 92Y, and the Brooklyn Museum—the Guggenheim is developing an engaging lineup of video featuring the art of Cai Guo-Qiang and Louise

Bourgeois, as well as the museum's Eye to Eye tours of exhibitions with leading contemporary artists.

4.3 Other Social Applications

Delicious: This social bookmarking site allows users to save their favorite websites to one web location that can be accessed on any computer. If two or more users save the same website, they can then "speak" to one another about sites or articles of common interest. Bookmarks are recorded and tracked. On http://del.icio.us./guggenheim_museum, press reviews and other media relevant to the Guggenheim are posted for public view. Each post is labeled with keywords called "tags" for search optimization. The Guggenheim's eighty-plus bookmarked items are shared on Facebook and MySpace and are available by subscription.

5. Future Goals

As of the summer of 2008 we were aiming at the following future objectives:

1. Add staff to support creation, writing, distribution, management, and tracking of social media.
2. Build the museum's digital assets through closer collaboration with other departments.
3. Explore opportunities to create and store digital assets with external partners.
4. Develop increased internal support for social networking through staff-generated blogging.
5. Create a social media section on www.guggenheim.org to demonstrate institutional support, increase peer-to-peer interaction, and build international brand equity.
6. Create staff presentations to educate internal audiences about the value and impact of the social networking initiatives and the results achieved.

Social networking offers museums a wide range of audience development options—with immediate results—that we have just begun to explore.

3.3.5 Publications

The museum's publications program provides information about the museum collections, services, and research to visitors and to an expanded audience of the interested public that is not able to visit but may consult the museum's publications in libraries or purchase them in bookshops or over the Web. The range of publications may include exhibition catalogs, guidebooks, catalogs of the collection, books, children's books and games, teacher packs, leaflets and brochures, postcards, posters, and prints. Museums may publish scholarly journals, magazines, membership newsletters, and occasional research papers.

Museum publishing has entered the multimedia age with considerable imagination and creativity. Videos, CDs, DVDs, and other media are available from major museums, in some cases providing images of entire exhibitions or collections as well as information about them. The high cost of quality publication has led museums to forge partnerships with the private sector for both print and electronic media. While some museums have their own imprint, many publish books and catalogs with academic publishers; French museums routinely make agreements for special issues of commercial art and culture magazines on featured exhibitions.

Digital asset management is a major challenge for many museums, some of which have literally tens of thousands of images that are of value not only for their own publications and media, but also for film producers, advertising directors, or magazine editors—if they can only be systematically searched. Some museums have sold the rights to their images to private sector agencies, while many who prefer to keep control in their own hands have yet to apply the sophisticated digital asset management programs to the database of their images. As and when they do, this promises to be a new source of revenue as well as a creative use of a valuable museum asset.

3.3.6 Marketing and Branding

Museum marketing is closely connected to audience engagement that aims to create a broader visitor base while at the same time building a closer relationship with the museum's regular visitors. Thus, marketing is an integral part of the museum's communication with the public—and may indeed be a department within a communications division. Because it is focused on the public, museum marketing should be closely allied with public programs, but it is frequently found in the museum's administration division. Interestingly, many museums that have highly effective marketing programs do not have a "marketing department" at all—the marketing function is part of communications or development departments.

Wherever the marketing function lives on the museum's organisation chart, the management of marketing will be important to the entire institution:

curators are interested in how well an exhibition is attended, the visitor services staff welcomes the public through the doors, the development director knows that an increase in membership and donations accompanies high levels of public awareness, and the finance officer sees a substantial difference in the bottom line when attendance is up. This means that marketing projects are prime candidates for interdepartmental task forces (see section 2.3.2.3), especially for marketing major exhibitions and special events. This point is made very strongly by Isabel Cheng's case study 3.5 titled "Integrating Marketing Teamwork at the Singapore Zoo" in this section.

The management of museum marketing focuses on:

- identifying the museum's present and potential markets, and communicating effectively with them;
- advocating within the museum the continual improvement of the museum's services to meet the needs of people in these market segments so that they will visit the museum and return again (because an improved product is the most effective form of marketing); and
- increasing attendance and visitor-generated revenues.

INTEGRATING MARKETING TEAMWORK
AT THE SINGAPORE ZOO
By Isabel Cheng

The Singapore Zoo is well known for its open-concept zoo, where there are no visible cages and the animals are separated from the visitors only by wet or dry moats, giving the perception of a naturalistic setting for the animals. It has a strong unique proposition of being situated in a secondary rainforest in the urban nation of Singapore, thereby giving rise to its positioning as a *Rainforest Zoo*.

Over the four years 2005–2008, the zoo has successfully transformed itself from a viewing zoo to a learning zoo, attracting more than 150,000 students a year and 1.5 million visitors annually. The visitor profile, traditionally more residents than tourists, hovered at an 80:20 ratio for many years, but has since moved to 70:30, with visits by tourists gaining more popularity through intense advertising and marketing efforts. The strategy has also shifted to ensure focus on the three "pillars" of our mission, which are conservation, education, and recreation.

The Singapore Zoo takes a nontraditional approach to marketing, compared to other zoos. With a limited budget, yet with a commitment to educate visitors on conservation while at the same time trying to make the park self-sustaining, it is a continual challenge for the marketing team to ensure that the park is compelling enough to attract more visitors.

Over that four-year period, the zoo embarked on various marketing initiatives that resulted in an increase in total visitors year on year. The basic strategy is that since residents still form the core base of visitors, it is imperative that they be continually enticed to make repeat visits, while efforts are increased on all tourist fronts to bring in the more lucrative tourist segment, with its high potential to increase attendance.

To stretch every marketing dollar and get the biggest bang for the buck, the effort to target tourists remains within Singapore, directed at what we would call tourists' "touch points." Essentially this means that everywhere tourists go, such as visitor centers, airports, and popular tourist haunts, they will see the Singapore Zoo advertising. Attracting these tourists already in Singapore is like picking the "low-hanging fruit," compared to advertising in their home countries, where it would be extremely expensive, more fragmented, and less targeted. We also work very closely with inbound travel agents to ensure that the zoo is included as part of their tour program.

Getting residents to continue coming is yet another challenge. First we needed to understand the local visitor profile, which is mainly of families

Figure 3.5A. Orangutans in front of Singapore Zoo signboard

COURTESY OF SINGAPORE ZOO

with children under thirteen years of age. The peak periods for resident attendance are school holidays and public holidays. These are the periods for which we organize activities and events at the zoo. When the team organizes an event, the basic strategy is to have it focus on an inherent attraction of the zoo so that when the activity and advertising for that event ends, the brand equity built up for that property is not lost, especially if that attraction is a particular exhibit or animal that will always be in the park and has benefited from the exposure it has received.

To ensure synergy across all communication channels and to get "buy-in" from the other departments so that all will chip in from their respective areas to make the event big enough, the marketing team had to ensure that the various departments—zoology, operations, education, food and beverage (F&B), retail, and even horticulture—are all involved in the discussion from the very start. Brainstorming sessions are held and the respective departments are encouraged to come out with a related activity that will supplement the chosen theme.

As an example, last year when the theme was the orangutan, zoology offered orangutan enrichment programs, special feeding sessions, and commentary during the "promotion" period. Education ensured that the upcoming issue of their in-house publication that is sold to schools featured the orangutan on the cover, with part of the content dedicated to the plight of the orangutan, and even organized special talks on orangutan conservation for school children. Horticulture did orangutan topiaries for decoration at the entrance; retail had a rainforest theme with orangutan plush as the highlighted retail product; and Food and Beverage even created a special mango drink and named it "Ah Mengo," after a famous orangutan icon in Singapore Zoo called "Ah Meng." The marketing team brought in orangutan mascots and engaged artists to create face paintings and orangutan tattoos to entertain visitors. Orangutan bookmarks with conservation messages were given out to all visitors during this period.

All these activities were communicated via strategically placed newspaper advertising, electronic direct mailers, and in-park posters and banners. The corporate communication department worked with various publications to get free editorials on the activities by bartering entrance tickets as lucky draw prizes for readers of that publication. Ultimately it was a concerted effort by all departments focusing on the same key message and theme for the school holiday promotion event. And that concerted effort made the "promotional" event much bigger than it would have been if it had just been organized and planned by the marketing department alone.

A few years ago, in line with the shift from being a viewing zoo to a learning zoo, various initiatives were started that enabled the zoo to

Figure 3.5B. Singapore Zoo front entrance

increase its appeal to its visitors, one of the most important segments being families with children. One of the initiatives was to give a small memento at the point of exit to all children who leave the zoo with their parents. The memento, be it a bookmark or a sticker, has a simple conservation message on it pertaining to a particular animal. The idea is to have our most important guests, the children, leave with a smile on their faces when they get a free gift, as well as being educated on conservation in the process.

Other initiatives include ensuring that interpretative exhibits are more interactive and made to the height of an adult's knee so that children have easy access to them, and that the information in these exhibits is delivered in bite-sized chunks to make it easier for the children to understand.

The zoo map, printed on recycled paper, was made more colorful and interesting with lots more information. The investment was well worth it because instead of throwing the maps away after use, visitors are taking them home as a souvenir and showing them to family and friends.

These are but some of the initiatives that were launched. The total integrated marketing effort was only made possible with collaboration from all departments. This has, thus far, contributed to a 100,000 increase in attendance at the zoo year on year over this 4-year period.

3.3.6.1 Present and Potential Markets

Research on cultural participation and museum attendance in various countries tells us that between 27 and 35 percent of the adult population may normally be expected to attend a museum at some time. The frequency of attendance will vary greatly, from those who visit more than ten times a year and are likely to be members and supporters to those who visit occasionally, mostly as tourists. The typical characteristics of frequent museum visitors are that they have higher education and income than the general population (although education is a far more significant determinant than income), and that women attend more frequently than men. The prime age for attendance varies with museum type: for example, science centers and children's museums attract young families, while art galleries appeal to young singles and adults over forty-five. Attendance previously tended to decline after sixty, but this is changing as the population ages and museums become more attuned to improving facilities for the elderly and disabled.

Within these broad groups of visitors and nonvisitors, there are many specific *market segments*, relatively homogeneous sectors of the population that share common demographic, geographic, and behavioral or lifestyle patterns. Through its marketing strategy, the museum can influence their attendance patterns.

- The first step in museum marketing is to understand the museum's current visitors—the market segments they represent, the frequency of the visits, and their motivation. This may be accomplished by studying daily attendance records through observation and visitor surveys (see section 3.3.6.2). For a new museum project, it is usually valuable to undertake such studies of comparable museums, either within the same city or area, or of museums with similar collections or subject matter.
- The next step is to compare this reality with the demographics of the resident market (obtained from census data) and the tourists who visit the area (available from the local tourist board or chamber of commerce), and with visitor survey results from other museums or visitor attractions in the area that are willing to share that information. This should enable analysts to determine which market segments are underrepresented in the museum's visitor base.
- The third step is particularly challenging: to analyze what it all means, to set marketing priorities around *"target market segments,"* and to identify marketing strategies that will boost attendance from those market segments, consistent with the museum's mission, goals, and objectives. This stage constitutes a marketing plan for tasks ranging from advertising, promotion, and public relations to the creation of special events and

programs. These tasks may be carried out by museum staff—say, in the education department for the creation of learning programs, or in the graphics department to create posters—or they may be carried out by outside consultants, including public relations firms and advertising agencies. Whoever does them, it is important to note that marketing strategies based on the same data may aim at developing underrepresented markets or, on the contrary, may choose instead to serve current market segments better—and the choice must be made by the museum's senior management consistent with the museum's goals and objectives, not by marketing personnel alone.

- The fourth stage is implementation of the marketing plan. The role of the marketing manager is effectively to monitor the implementation of the plan or brief, coordinating completion of all the tasks on time, on budget and to an agreed level of quality.
- The final step is evaluation of the results, recording what should be changed and the production of a manual for ongoing marketing efforts.

3.3.6.2 Visitor Research

Visitor research is valuable not only to marketing managers. Visitor research collects up-to-date and reliable information about the museum's visitors to enable the museum to:

- improve its performance in its public role;
- focus on meeting public needs and expectations, and achieving outcomes related to visitor and general public interests; and
- demonstrate to current and potential funders and sponsors, whether in the public or private sectors, the degree to which the public is served and which sectors of the public are using the museum.

In order to meet these objectives, there needs to be a balance between *quantitative* analysis of demographics and behaviors, and *qualitative* methods that focus on feelings, attitudes, and motivations of visitors. This is particularly important because of these factors:

- Museums that thrive as civil society institutions will be those that are of real value to the community.
- Visitor data shows that "word of mouth" is often the most frequently cited motivation for a museum visit; this means that visitor satisfaction is likely to be the most significant generator of attendance.
- Museums have become more dependent on visitor-generated revenue and visitor spending in their gift shops and restaurants.

- The potential for converting visitors to become museum members and supporters is closely related to their level of satisfaction with the museum experience.

Attendance counts and visitor surveys are used to create a database of attendance, demographic, and lifestyle information, while methods such as in-gallery interviews, observation, workshops, and focus groups are used to understand visitor motivations and expectations and the quality of the visitor experience. This type of research is particularly important in addressing the needs of audiences such as visible minorities and low-income earners because these groups are underrepresented in traditional museum surveys and therefore relatively little is known about their attitudes, expectations, and experiences in the museum. Thus a focus group drawn from an underrepresented socioeconomic class may be of great interest, even if its members have visited the museum only once or not at all.

In surveying visitors, care must be taken to restrict questions to data that will really be of value. For instance, presenting a range of twenty occupation groups and asking visitors to indicate which one fits them most closely is of little value if the gradations between the occupation groups make no difference to the marketing strategy; broader classifications would be of greater value if they are the classifications on which decisions can be based.

The most effective and efficient approach to visitor research is to develop a comprehensive three- to five-year rolling program that focuses on quantitative research in some years and qualitative in others. The key is to involve representatives of all departments who work with the public in the audience research project team to ensure that all the museum's many evaluation activities (whether of education programs or from visitor comment cards) contribute to the visitor research database. The museum may have an evaluator on staff (a full-time or part-time position depending on the size of the museum) to design and implement research, or may contract outside consultants to do so, to analyze and disseminate the results through the project team, and to formulate recommendations for the director to take to the trustees if necessary. Again, the decision on whether to pursue underrepresented markets or to emphasize improved service to current markets is one for the museum's senior management and must be consistent with the museum's long-range mission, goals, and present objectives.

3.3.6.3 Target Markets

There are many potential market segments that a museum may seek to attract. Selecting *target markets* means choosing from among these segments to focus the museum's energy. The decision as to which markets to target will be based on many considerations, ranging from *affordability* (unless the market is saturated, it's less costly and risky to target more of the same kinds of people you are already attracting) to *responsibility* to engage a broader demographic to *creativity*, recognizing that new audiences will contribute new perspectives and new vitality to the museum. Five main factors need to be considered in selecting and prioritizing target markets:

- The size of the market and its growth potential.
- The importance of the market to the museum's mission and mandate. This applies particularly to the museum's role as a public educational institution in a culturally and economically diverse society.
- The capability of the market to contribute to visitor-generated revenues.
- The contribution of a particular segment to the tourism or economic development objectives of the city or region. There is a growing recognition of the central role of museums in attracting high-income cultural tourists, and in helping to increase the length of stay and visitor spending of all tourists. Communities also value museums because they are symbolic of the quality-of-life factors in attracting new industry and service companies to the area. And there is the vital contribution that museums and other cultural institutions make to attracting and retaining knowledge-industry workers, the group that economist Richard Florida has identified as "*the creative class*," which he observes is crucial to a thriving urban economy today.
- The negative factor of the costs associated with attracting each segment.

These policy decisions should involve senior management. The director should then present them to the board on the basis of recommendations from the marketing manager, resulting in quantitative goals to be set for each market segment in the context of three- to five-year attendance projections.

3.3.6.4 Marketing Strategies

Marketing strategies are the many ways in which the museum can improve its communications and service to target audiences with the objective of boosting attendance and visitor spending. The marketing strategy also aims to build a closer relationship with the museum's audiences, leading to repeat visits, membership, and donations. This is a continual process in which the manager of the museum's marketing activities must work closely with evaluation, curatorial, and public programming staff and development and visitor services departments, ideally through a task force project team.

Once the overall marketing strategy has been established, there may be as many as fifty specific marketing strategies to be implemented, such as new admission prices to appeal to local families, an advertising campaign packaging with hotels to attract summer tourists, evening openings targeted at the singles market, or seminars on contemporary art to appeal to collectors. Developing the right strategies requires expertise in museum marketing and knowledge of what has been successful elsewhere. Museums can benefit greatly from learning about the successes and failures of museums of comparable size and scope. This is called *comparables analysis* and consists of interviews with staff in the comparable institutions. Study of *best practice* examples is also helpful; this involves identifying examples of outstanding successes in institutions that may be much larger or smaller and carefully analyzing how their methods could be applied to this museum. In order to avoid taking the wrong lessons from comparables, or imitating failures that look like successes, both types of research should be facilitated by staff or external consultants who have considerable experience in museum marketing and managing organizational change.

Marketing strategies should be implemented in a deliberate way, with opportunities for evaluation planned as part of the strategy. Regular reports to the interdepartmental task force on progress in their implementation, evaluating each step in the process, are necessary.

3.3.6.5 Branding

As the saying goes, "If you don't decide on your brand, others will do it for you." Every institution and corporation has a brand, whether they consciously control it or not. A museum's *brand* is what all the people who are aware of the museum think of it. By more closely determining the brand, museum management can sharpen that perception, position it to advantage, and enhance appreciation of the museum in the public sphere. Of course, it ultimately depends on the product—the quality of service that the museum is providing—but public awareness of a good museum may still be diffuse and uncertain, whereas with closer attention to branding, that awareness may be focused, consciousness of the value of the museum can be heightened, and interest in participating in the museum can be increased among people, governments, and the private sector.

The past decade has seen intensive activity by some of the world's leading museums to build their brands. The Solomon R. Guggenheim Foundation was foremost, extending its brand from its signature Frank Lloyd Wright landmark building in New York to the equally remarkable architecture of Frank Gehry in Bilbao and in other branches elsewhere, currently extending the brand still farther to plan another Gehry building, the Guggenheim Abu Dhabi. The Louvre started later but has caught up, building on a brand developed over two hundred years that it has now extended through recurring loan agreements with the High Museum in Atlanta, building a branch for northern France at Lens, and leading the consortium of French museums into long-term loan agreements for an institution that is to be called the Louvre Abu Dhabi. In Britain, the single name "Tate" has been focused as the brand not only of the prodigiously successful Tate Modern and Tate Britain in London as well as its branches in Liverpool and St. Ives, but also now of an art magazine, a boat along the Thames, and a television service.

These major museums have learned to "valorize" their brands. The motivation is certainly at least partly to enhance their capacity to generate both earned and especially contributed income. Donations, sponsorship, annual giving agreements, and even government subsidies are so much easier to attract when negotiations for these contributions are preceded by a strong and positive brand awareness, the more widespread the better.

Branding is really about strengthening public awareness of the contributions that the institution is making to society. Awareness can be enhanced by various means, such as:

- marketing campaigns, specifically "awareness campaigns";
- website—and Web presence outside of the museum's own site;
- advertising;
- public relations;
- festivals and events.

Awareness campaigns are commonplace in NGOs (nongovernmental organizations) concerned with such issues as animal rights or the removal of land mines. They are not aimed at getting the listener or viewer to do anything, but rather are simply raising awareness of the issues involved. They may not even attempt to convince the recipient to believe in the cause, but simply try to stimulate an awareness of it. For a museum, a brand awareness campaign would be directed at stimulating awareness of the contribution the museum is making to society. Paid advertising is relatively unimportant in such a campaign, but a good public relations program, a strong brand on the Web, and specific events or festivals can stimulate this positive awareness.

Of course it is ultimately the quality of the actual service being delivered and the values behind the exhibitions, educational programs, and activities that the museum is providing at home and abroad that are the true motors driving its brand. The museum logo, wordmark, tagline graphics, and the control of its presentation, the images associated with it, and the ways in which it is used in various media and events are *in support of* the brand. They are *not* the brand. The successful museum managers of institutions of all kinds and sizes in the twenty-first century are likely to be developing better and more conscious control of their museum's brand.

theater, retail) and other key departments such as education, exhibitions, special events, marketing, and membership. It was crucial first to understand fully the programs and promotions that frontline workers were expected to promote, accommodate, and even deliver. This meant creating task force working groups and comprehensive tools to ensure communication and align planning.

The visitor services department led the way by revamping the lobby operation and ticketing system to move people faster and ensure that members and visitors with special needs had the level of service they required. Visitor services also took over the operational interface with the education department, including group sales and scheduling, and public program ticketing and crowd control. These areas had been historically fuzzy in terms of responsibility, and therefore had never functioned properly. As programs became increasingly popular, many were sold out or oversold, resulting in a level of mayhem not generally seen on the "Museum Mile." Education agreed that they were the originators of content and programs, while visitor services should assume all operational elements. This meant that education trained visitor services personnel in how to promote school tours and adult programs. However, when it came to scheduling, coordinating with security and tour guides, ticketing, and collecting revenue, the visitor services department was responsible. Most importantly, this centralized the schedule, checking in, and tracking of attendance and revenue, all of which had previously required a baroque system of coordination, which failed more often than not.

Additional initiatives included:

- working with marketing and development departments to ensure accurate attendance reporting around specific promotions and initiatives;
- coordinating operational policy and training with the security, food service, and retail departments to create consistency among the frontline staff;
- addressing priorities with the maintenance and cleaning staff; and
- ensuring that visitor services staff could provide more curatorial information to visitors through training and reference materials.

Finally, an *operations committee* was established to mirror the type of communication that had been long in place around exhibition development. This committee reported to the deputy director of finance and administration, and met biweekly to plan for upcoming exhibitions and events of note. The committee was comprised of the heads of the visitor services,

3.3.7 Visitor Services

Visitor services, including admissions, retail and food services, rentals, and general visitor care, greatly influence the quality of the visitor experience and communicate the museum's attitude toward the public. Like marketing, visitor services have been included in this section of the chapter because they have so much to do with the public, even though they are usually part of an operations department or administration. These services are often managed by administrative departments, although the staff, whether full- or part-time, salaried, contract, or voluntary, have more personal involvement and communication with visitors than most other museum workers. They offer a wealth of frequently untapped information about the museum's visitors and their needs. And to do their job well, they need extensive training, monitoring, and evaluation.

Museums that are truly visitor-responsive have redefined the role of front-line staff from being vaguely "administrative" to asserting a very conscious approach to "visitor services," creating a new working environment that integrates visitor services staff fully into the museum profession. Where this has been done, as it has at many of the larger museums, great improvements have been achieved in the level of visitor satisfaction. Where it has not yet been accomplished, visitors often suffer from ill-informed admission clerks, bored security guards, and undistinguished food services. Amy Kaufman's case study 3.6 in this section demonstrates the importance of establishing visitor services as part of an operations division, as well as the power of all museum departments working together to improve services to the public.

IMPROVING VISITOR SERVICE BY FOCUSING ON OPERATIONS
By Amy Kaufman

In 1998, attendance soared at the Solomon R. Guggenheim Museum in New York with the opening of the groundbreaking and controversial exhibition, *The Art of the Motorcycle*. The museum saw attendance grow from an average that hovered around 15,000 per week to nearly 24,000 visitors per week. Although the institution had always aspired to attract more visitors, it was not actually prepared to serve this number of people. Cracks started showing in visitor service, internal systems, and wear and tear on the building itself.

These lapses were reflected in lower-than-desired visitor satisfaction. Queues formed around the block, elderly people waited in the rain, dust bunnies rolled down the famous ramps to greet the crowds, restrooms required a level of supplies and cleaning that no one had anticipated, and many museum members did not fare much better due to an antiquated tracking system that involved a ten-pound three-ring binder.

So it was no surprise when visitor complaint forms—which we in visitor services were committed to answering in writing—soared in number, detail, and vitriol. The crowds often resulted in a poor experience for all. If you were fortunate enough to get off the ground floor in a good mood, you were still faced with crowds on the ramps and single-occupancy restrooms.

Serendipitously, the decision had already been made to strengthen the visitor services department by taking it out from under the umbrella of the marketing department, where it had lived for many years. Prior to this decision, visitor services had been seen primarily as a public face and customer service provider, therefore the marketing designation made sense. However, the reality was that visitor services was, in partnership with security, running the daily operation of the museum. Each day, it was these two departments that opened the doors, monitored the public flow, addressed issues as they arose, protected the artwork, and acted as the primary interface with all other departments. It was these two departments that received and processed adult and school groups and ran after-hours public programs. Although "operations" was not in the museum's vocabulary at the time, the importance of centralizing and better controlling all operational elements emerged as a necessity.

Improving the *operation* included creating stronger links among the operational departments (visitor services, security, facilities, food service,

security, facilities, theater, retail, and human relations departments, with others such as exhibitions and special events personnel being invited as needed. The central goal of the committee was to improve the visitor experience, the staff experience, and the safety of the building and collections. New systems and controls were enacted over time to promote better coordination of operational elements in purely operational departments as well as with departments not centered on operations. Over time, the committee saw a marked increase in visitor satisfaction and, internally, a level of efficiency and morale that had not previously existed.

In the end, those responsible for running the operation gained a voice, assumed new levels of responsibility, and effected significant change; these internal successes were reflected in the quality of service that visitors experienced.

the awareness campaign, because it reflects the museum's brand in the eyes of all those who attend. Sensitivity must also be exercised toward regular visitors when rental events are being set up. If setup occurs early in the day, visitors may feel that the museum is not open for them. That is why many museums are careful to plan special places for rentals.

3.3.7.5 Food Services

The main reason for utilizing museum space for a restaurant or café is to enhance the visitor experience by providing visitors with rest and refreshment and a place to socialize or meet friends. The results of good food service can be to extend the time the visitor spends in the galleries and to encourage repeat visits. Poor quality and poor service may have the opposite effect. When food services are privately contracted, the museum's standards and requirements should be incorporated into the contract with the restaurant operator.

These standards and requirements can only be developed on the basis of understanding the museum's visitors and their needs, balancing these with the café operator's need to generate sufficient revenue (see section 3.5.2.1.3). Young families want simple, healthy, inexpensive food served in an atmosphere where spills and cries will not be too embarrassing; older visitors prefer a quiet environment with inexpensive refreshment, served at the table; and there may or may not be a market for white tablecloths and elegant cuisine or a casual cappuccino bar.

Separate facilities for school lunches are recommended wherever school visits require them, since it is well advised to spare other visitors the relative havoc of a spirited group of school children excited by their visit to the museum and enjoying the relaxing time over lunch. Vending machines may be sufficient to supply their needs.

An important consideration for both food services and retail shops in many museums is to position them so that they can serve the general public as well as museum visitors. The shop should be visible at the entry and almost inescapable upon exit. The café may wish to take advantage of a rooftop view, and in many larger museums there is a case for several levels of service, one designed for quick service (if not fast food), and the other for evenings or full dining service. For smaller museums and galleries, an attractive bistro with natural food and a fine assortment of coffees and teas is often the best approach. Careful determination of the location of the shop and the right level of service for the museum's market is needed, along with a business plan by experienced restaurant operators.

In most cases the operator who holds the concession is likely to ask for the catering contract for museum rentals as well. In order to improve his or her chances of success, museum managers should offer this service as an option to renting parties, but should allow them the option to bring in their own caterers, possibly at a small additional cost, since some events will wish to have their own dedicated catering.

The staff who work in the café, like those in the shop, have the opportunity to serve visitors and communicate with them personally. It is important that they understand that their job is *serving visitors*, not just serving food. This means training, monitoring, and evaluating contract as well as salaried staff. Quality control must be built into the management contract with the food service provider, including provisions as to actions the museum management may take to warn, suspend, or end the contract if the quality of food or service is no longer appropriate.

3.3.7.6 Visitor Services as a Responsibility of All Museum Staff

To achieve the goals of visitor responsiveness, museum management and public program personnel especially need to get closer to the visitors than surveys, reports, and comment cards. It is difficult to create a visitor service orientation for the museum if management, curators, educators, and programmers are not even at work during those times when most visitors are in the building—on weekends and holidays. Part of the institutional change required to focus the museum on its public role involves management rethinking its role, which could start with something as simple as a roster so all museum personnel take time in rotation to work in the galleries on some weekends. This is an excellent practice observed in many leading museums.

3.4   FACILITY PLANNING AND MANAGEMENT

Museum sites range from a university campus to a city park, from a busy downtown street to a historic battlefield or a heritage village. Museum buildings range from contemporary creations by today's leading architects to heritage structures painstakingly preserved. There is a widespread myth that old buildings make good museums, and a widespread belief that great architects make great museums. Neither is necessarily true, although either may be made so by careful planning. Planning the development of space and facilities for museums and managing them well are the subjects of this section.

3.4.1 Facility Planning

In many cases, museums grow beyond their bounds as a result of one of their essential activities—collecting. Museum buildings are also continuously being expanded or upgraded because of growing audience expectations and technological change: tourists join community residents with ever higher expectations of the museum experience, intensified by their common acquaintance with the world's leading attractions via television and other media, as well as international travel. Multimedia imaging technologies are only one of a series of technological breakthroughs that have affected the nature of the museum experience, as well as the research and knowledge base underlying it.

All of these factors result in a constant, ongoing process of growth in the number, size, and complexity of museums around the world. In fact, museum buildings are among the most complex of building types, and among the most costly. As a result, they are inevitably products of compromise, as budget and technical limitations must be mutually adjusted. Yet museum projects around the world in a distressing number of cases have not fulfilled the expectations of those responsible for them. Buildings that are too small or too large, elevators that open onto corridors with lower ceilings or inadequate turning space, and lost opportunities that could have rewarded visitors with a far richer museum experience are observed around the globe.

The planning of museum buildings, their extension, relocation, or renovation, is a process that must be executed carefully in order to ensure that it meets the needs of the museum profession to care for the collection, serves the museum's visitors as creatively as possible, and fulfills the requirements of the community. This is the subject of a previous book that we have written and edited, with contributions from other specialists around the world, entitled *The Manual of Museum Planning,* originally published in 1991, with an updated edition from HMSO Books, London, and AltaMira Press in 1999.

One of the fundamental issues at the outset of a facility planning process is to determine the *design year*, which may be defined as the last year for which the facilities being planned are to be adequate. It may seem paradoxical to begin by determining the year in which the plans being made will be insufficient, but in fact it is necessary in order to draw a horizon or limit on the extent of collection growth, exhibition space expansion, attendance increases, or other factors that may determine the size and character of the additional space needed. For many projects, the design year is set at twenty or twenty-five years—since opening day of the new or expanded facility is usually five years after the planning period, and since growth of collections and other resources can be reasonably projected for that length of time.

3.4.1.1 The Role of the Architect

Facility planning for museums is a field in which several disciplines have an interest. Many museum professionals, and trustees, assume that planning a museum is "a building problem," and therefore can only be solved by an architect. There is no question that the architect has an important role to play—

but the architect cannot know how a museum works. Determining the functional requirements of a museum is a job that is best done by museum professionals, before the architect begins work. Calling the architect too soon is the most common error in the museum facility planning process.

Architects have six favorite words that most museum directors and curators who have been involved in museum planning projects will recognize. The first three are: *"It's too early."*

This is said when the museum director or curator attends a meeting at which he or she sees architectural concepts but does not see certain features that as a museum professional he or she knows to be vital to a successful museum. When the director or curator asks about these features, the architect assures everyone that these are concept sketches, and that it's too early to get into the kind of detail implied by these questions.

So the museum director or curator waits. Some months or even years later, depending on the speed of the project, he or she goes to another meeting, at which much more detailed plans are shown by the architect. The museum requirements are still not in evidence. When he or she repeats these concerns, the museum professional hears the architect's other three favorite words: *"It's too late."*

The museum requirements now can be met, the architect assures us, only at considerable expense. The museum requirements should have been stated earlier!

Such a frustrating experience is by no means solely the architect's fault. Very often it is the museum professionals who do not or cannot articulate their needs in ways that the architect can use.

The same is true of exhibition designers, market analysts, management consultants or others who may be consulted in the museum planning process. Each of them can make a useful contribution only to the extent that museum planners make the museum's needs known to them. Taking the time to plan the facility before consulting architects, designers, or others is the first step toward building, expanding, renovating, or relocating a museum successfully. This type of planning is often called briefing or programming, and its result is termed a *functional brief* (in Britain) or a *functional program* (in the United States). A preliminary but also very valuable document in the planning process may be termed a *facility strategy*.

In his case study 3.7 in this section, entitled "Planning Tate Modern," Peter Wilson, a veteran of that project among many others, relates the very successful story of the planning and design of that remarkable structure at Bankside, London, which is already undergoing a major expansion to accommodate the great crowds it has attracted since opening. Peter shows how the careful preparation for the competition, which was directed at selecting an architect, not a design, led to an intensive planning process in which senior Tate personnel (including Peter) made their requirements known to the architects, thereby evolving a final functional brief.

PLANNING TATE MODERN
By Peter Wilson

The Tate Gallery (Tate) is one of Britain's national museums. It was established at Millbank in London as a branch of the National Gallery in 1897 to house Sir Henry Tate's collection of British paintings. Within a few years it had become the repository for the modern art that the National Gallery did not wish to accommodate at Trafalgar Square. It struggled for decades with its dual identity as the national collection of British art and the national "museum of modern art."

By the 1980s, and despite a large extension suitable for the display of contemporary art having opened in 1979, the issue was perceived to be soluble only by providing identifiably separate "containers" for the two collections. Tate had acquired sufficient land adjacent to its original site to extend the existing museum substantially, had a master plan in place to achieve this, and had built one extension, the Clore Gallery (for the Turner Collection) on the extended site. There was a perception that the further development required a stage-by-stage approach to funding, and the master plan called for a group of individual museums on the site, including a sculpture museum, a contemporary art museum, and a library and archive center. This strategy had yielded neither public nor private funding. When Nicholas Serota became director in 1988 it was a time for a reappraisal of Tate's strategy. The Tate had just opened a successful northern outpost in Liverpool dedicated to modern art, and the time was ripe for a solution involving a separate museum of modern art in London to be examined.

The first task was to demonstrate how much space was required to create an effective display of Tate's collection of modern and contemporary art. A very straightforward space-planning methodology was used. It was based on the thirty-by-thirty-foot (nine-by-nine-meter) square gallery module of Tate Britain's 1979 extension. These modular spaces could be combined to replicate the square-, double-square, and triple-square floor plans of the prewar Tate rooms. The advantage of this approach was that curatorial staff had familiarly shaped and sized spaces to work with. They were able to construct a series of hypothetical "rooms" to display the whole modern collection. The rooms were assembled into a notional museum building diagram that was overlaid on the expansion space available at Millbank. It was a clear visual demonstration that an adequate national museum of modern art could not be accommodated there.

Having established that the ideal space requirement for the new museum of modern art, which was given the provisional title Tate Gallery

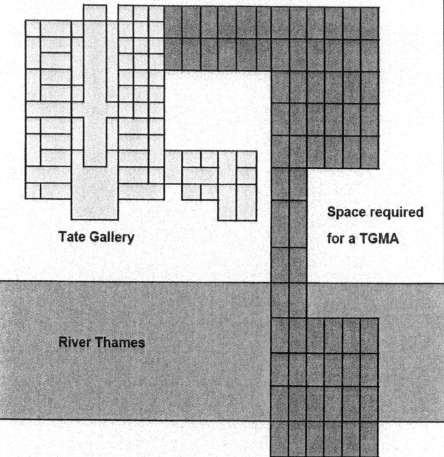

Figure 3.6A. The space requirement for a museum of modern art at Millbank: the building required, assumed to be a single storey top-lit gallery like the existing Tate Gallery, would have needed to bridge the Thames!

Tate Gallery

Space required for a TGMA

River Thames

PETER WILSON

of Modern Art (TGMA), was for a display area slightly bigger than the original Tate (see figure 3.5A), it was decided to look for a suitable site before developing the functional brief further. The process that led to the choice of the former Bankside Power station is well documented (see Karl Sabbagh's *Power into Art: Creating Tate Modern*, Bankside, 2000). A fundamental requirement was that TGMA needed a more central and better-frequented location than the original Tate on Millbank. Tate Gallery Liverpool, located within a historic dockside complex, had vastly exceeded its visitor targets, and at this time (1993–1994) a further out-post of Tate had opened at St. Ives in Cornwall. Its seaside location provided a ready-made footfall that was clearly a factor in its success. Bankside's much-frequented location adjacent to London's Southbank cultural complex with spectacular vistas of St. Paul's Cathedral—a major tourist attraction—across the Thames was ideal.

The choice of an existing building, however large and however capable of alteration, provided a set of opportunities and constraints that were used to develop a simplified brief for the *Competition to Select an Architect*, published in 1994. Tate deliberately chose to provide only a very basic and outline brief, including a schedule of areas, a diagram indicating possibilities for the conversion of the power station (see figure 3.6B), and a series of flow charts indicating relationships between major spaces.

The competition was emphatically to select an architect, not a design, so the second stage concentrated on discovering the short-listed architects'

Figure 3.6B. Opportunities Diagram from Tate Gallery of Modern Art: Competition to Select an Architect

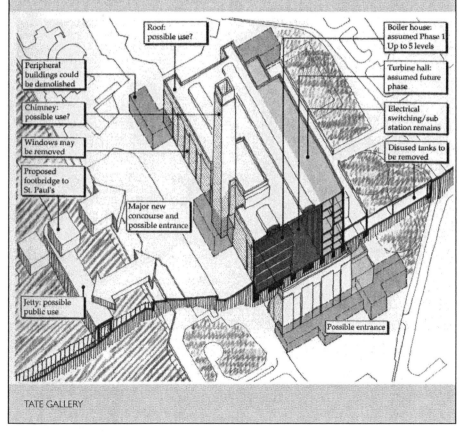

Roof: possible use?

Boiler house: assumed Phase 1 Up to 5 levels

Peripheral buildings could be demolished

Turbine hall: assumed future phase

Chimney: possible use?

Electrical switching/sub station remains

Windows may be removed

Disused tanks to be removed

Proposed footbridge to St. Paul's

Major new concourse and possible entrance

Jetty: possible public use

Possible entrance

TATE GALLERY

Figure 3.6C. Harry Gugger of Herzog & de Meuron and Ron German of Stanhope, Tate's project managers, examine a large scale model of the turbine hall in the architect's studio in Basel.

PETER WILSON

collaborative strengths through interaction with Tate's experienced client team. Herzog & de Meuron of Basel, Switzerland was chosen as the firm demonstrated a truly collaborative approach. In addition they made two original interventions:

- The first was an architectural addition signaling the change of use (called by them "the light beam"), which admitted light into the upper-most gallery level while allowing a rooftop restaurant to sit above it.
- The second was a ramped western entrance starting outside of the former turbine hall and continuing within it for one-third of the length of the building, which significantly reduces the impression that the lowest floor is below street level, preventing any of the available volume from feeling like inferior basement accommodation.

Having deliberately chosen an architect rather than a design, the challenge facing the Tate team was to build on the early rapport established through the competition workshops. Herzog and de Meuron had not previously encountered a client who wished to develop the brief through dialogue, and Tate's consciously iterative style was quite demanding. An initial period when the architects visited London monthly to report progress and receive comments and then returned to Basel to develop their designs in isolation did not suit the Tate team. For the rest of the design development period and beyond, a core Tate team made regular workshop visits to Switzerland with other London-based design team members.

These sessions were punctuated with visits to other sites of interest: to Tate St. Ives, Tate Liverpool, the Louvre, the Musée d'Orsay, the Bonnefanten Museum in Maastricht, and a number of the architects' recent projects. The relationship that built up and the spirit of debate and constructive comment led to an excellent working relationship. The wide range of sites visited ensured that there were always opportunities to discuss contentious issues openly and without fear of offending the sensibilities of either party. Specific outcomes included the choice of untreated wooden flooring that arose from the trip to Maastricht and the generous retention of the original power station windows, which arose from an appreciation of the approach that had been taken at Tate St. Ives.

Figure 3.6D. Tate Modern from across the Thames on June 10, 2008

One clear principle that grew from Tate's experience of the historical development of its original home at Millbank was that the new TGMA would be *adaptable* rather than *flexible*. Flexibility requires a definition of what may be accommodated in the future, whereas adaptability is achieved through dialogue between client and designer, leading to a shared appreciation of what makes a good range of spaces and why and how that is so. Already Tate Modern (which is what TGMA became when it opened in 2000) has been adapted a number of times—indeed the project budget anticipated that this might happen from the outset by providing a fund to spend one year after completion. This had the double benefit of allowing lessons to be learned and of persuading newly appointed operational staff to "wait and see" rather than demanding changes during the project's lifetime.

The success of Tate Modern owes a great deal to the shared vision of a successful public building that grew from the friendly and productive collaboration between the client team and the whole project team. Tate Modern achieves visitor numbers of around five million per year—more than twice its design capacity—and a second phase, once again designed by Herzog and de Meuron, has received planning permission and is expected to be completed by 2012.

3.4.1.2 Factors Affecting Facility Planning

Six areas affecting the museum's requirements need to be studied in order to develop a museum facility strategy that can lead toward a successful functional program or brief:

1. Visitor analysis: Both qualitative and quantitative analysis of the museum's present visitors (if the museum is already open) helps to determine visitor needs in the facility. Surveys and tracking studies may be helpful in developing this analysis, remembering to consult physically challenged visitors, teachers with school groups, tour bus providers, and other specialized interest groups as well as general visitors.

2. Market analysis: Still more important, it is necessary to analyze the potential market, again both quantitatively and qualitatively, so that the new facility might reach out beyond the present attendance group to serve a broader public. The analysis may aim at identifying target markets for a new facility, or the different markets attainable after an expansion, renovation, or relocation. The decision to take advantage of such opportunities or not is, of course, dependent on the museum's mission, which should be considered or may be reconsidered at this time.

3. Collection analysis and development strategy: The heart of the museum is its collection of works of art, artifacts, or specimens. A thorough analysis, not only of its present size and character, but especially of its anticipated growth, along with decisions about the amount we wish to display and the ways we wish to display it, is essential. Provisions for adequate storage, security, and collection care are also vital considerations in the museum facility planning process.

4. Public programs evaluation: Museums appear to be about objects, but are really about people. What do we plan to do in the museum? For what activities must we provide? The museum's exhibitions, its approach to the interpretation of its collections, with all the technological potential now available; its education program; its publications and media productions; its extension and outreach programs; and the amenities to be provided to the visitor, including shops and food services, all have important implications for the museum plan. Often neglected but most important—the unseen heart of the museum's public programs—is scholarly *research* within the museum: staff, space, and facilities must be provided for the research activity that is the museum's lifeline, and the research conducted in the museum must be planned to meet the museum's public programming needs.

5. Institutional context: A much neglected but very important sector of museum planning is the determination of the museum's relationship with government, educational institutions, other museums, the tourist industry,

and potential donors or sponsors in the private sector. Although these issues are usually considered more in the context of strategic or master planning, they are equally important for facility planning because the needs that they generate require space and facilities. If, for example, the museum is to become more independent of government, or more responsible for generating its own funds (as has happened at the Louvre in Paris, for example), it is likely to require more and better-located retail space, food services, and function rooms. If it is to offer programs in partnership with the school district, it may require additional facilities to be designed and built with input from the schools.

6. Institutional Plan: Another often-neglected area is the most fundamental one of determining or reconsidering the museum's mission, its mandate, and its purpose, as well as its mode of governance and the structures through which it is administered. Although these again are often thought to be part of a strategic or master plan rather than an accommodations plan, in fact they directly affect the priorities that must be decided as it becomes apparent that not all the space and facilities that are desired can be provided.

These six areas of analysis point to conclusions about the museum's needs in these areas:

- Staff: How many people will be needed to provide the intended public programs with the projected collection? Where will they work? Are there sufficient staff rooms and support facilities?
- Space: Galleries, storage areas, and the public and nonpublic support spaces need to be listed and associated in terms of their required adjacencies and grouped in zones that meet engineering requirements and cost categories. The result is usually termed a *space program*.
- Facilities: An exhibition plan may form part of the facilities plan, as will facilities and equipment requirements for conservation, documentation, and the many other specialized museum activities.

Planning for staff, space, and facilities is sometimes approached, especially by engineers, primarily in terms of meeting relevant *building code* requirements for fire protection, health, safety, and the needs of the physically challenged. Compliance with code is of course important, but facilities planning should also be seized by museum planners and trustees as an opportunity to fulfill the museum's mission more fully than before—or perhaps even to reconsider that mission. Meeting internationally accepted museum standards of environmental control, lighting, and security may for example be instrumental in enabling the museum to organize or borrow major exhibitions.

In particular, museum managers need to consider the fundamental question of the degree of visual *access* that they wish to provide to the public. Again and again, unplanned museum building projects proceed without examination of this basic issue. Many museums exhibit only 5 to 15 percent of their collections, and there have been numerous instances of museums concluding capital expansion projects with a *lower* percentage of their collections on display. This would be acceptable if it was intended; but very often, the key questions have not even been asked, such as:

- What is the current display/storage ratio?
- Is it satisfactory?
- If not, what ratio would be acceptable?
- How can we achieve it?

The answers to these questions very often lie in changing the density of objects on display by introducing new methods of display, or increasing the space given to certain modes. Possible modes of display (as described in section 3.3.1.1) include:

- *aesthetic or contemplative display*, usually found in art museums, typically with the lowest display density (for example, 30 pictures in a gallery of 150 square meters or 1,500 square feet);
- *contextual, thematic or didactic display*, with objects placed in the context of each other so that they may be understood, usually allowing a higher density (more objects per square meter or square foot) than the aesthetic approach;
- *room settings*, that is, grouping objects as they would have been found in their original setting, often allowing an even higher density than contextual display, especially if the collection allows the room to be well furnished;
- *visible storage*, sometimes called *study storage*, in which objects are grouped by type as they would be in storage, except that they are intended for visual inspection and comparison, allowing the highest level of density and often the highest density of information as well, especially if the objects are keyed to an adjacent computer offering public access to the catalog information about them.

Considering such options is the first responsibility of the museum professional planning exhibition galleries. In calculating their effect on the number of objects that can be provided for public viewing, and the space required to do so, museum planners must begin with the existing display densities, past and projected collection growth rates, and the museum's policies toward improving visual access and the visitor experience.

In some museums, the problem may rather be one of overcrowding of galleries, insufficient space for interpretation, or the deterioration of collection objects due to prolonged display over many years. Conservation of the collection must always claim priority in planning for display, and the facility planning process may provide the first opportunity for decades to facilitate a rotation plan replacing overexposed or particularly delicate materials with other examples in order to give them a much-needed rest from the accumulation of lux hours (footcandle hours) of exposure. Planning for lower density displays may also enable the museum to tell the stories associated with the objects more effectively to a wider audience.

Once all possibilities have been considered, the museum's requirements for staff, space, and facilities can be translated into monetary needs—anticipated expenditures for both capital and operating costs—and into opportunities for revenues. If the result is beyond the museum's fund-raising means, then it may be necessary to reconsider. But at least all the options will now be known, and choices can be made with a clear understanding of the opportunities being lost, and the priorities decided.

VISIBLE STORAGE AT THE SMITHSONIAN AMERICAN ART MUSEUM
By Georgina Bath

The Luce Foundation Center for American Art is a study center and visible storage facility that displays objects from the collections of the Smithsonian American Art Museum (SAAM) in Washington, D.C. SAAM is located in the U.S. government's historic Patent Office building, and the exhibition gallery that is now home to the Luce Foundation Center was originally built to display patent models in floor-to-ceiling glass cases. When the Smithsonian Institution acquired the building in 1958 (and opened it to the public a decade later), the space was used as the museum's library, and the public could visit only by appointment. One of the museum's goals for its recent renovation was increasing gallery and public spaces. The area that once housed the patent models and later the museum's library was ideally suited to its new function as *visible storage*.

Development began in 2000 when the museum secured a $10 million grant from the Henry Luce Foundation to create the center. Over the following six years, staff planned, researched, and designed the installation, which opened in 2006. More than 3,300 objects are on view in 64 glass cases, complemented by 10 interactive computer kiosks, 6 special installations, and an information desk.

Response to the Luce Foundation Center has been positive. The Luce Center has become a lively destination where visitors discover and make connections with our collection. Visitor comments convey the spirit of the center:

- "This visible storage is such a wonderful idea. Everyone should come here to see some of the museum's usually hidden treasures. The kiosks are such a valuable tool—and I love the artists' videos and interviews."
- "Your scavenger hunt is great. I have a ten-year-old son who has had just about enough of museums today. Then he got hold of your scavenger hunt and he's running around looking at everything! Thank you, thank you!"
- "It's great that you have staff in here. You have the answers to our questions and all the background stories, too."
- "I love how this is organized; you get to see so much art. I like the way the cases are organized, so each type of object has its own space and they are densely packed, but not crowded. It allows you to look at the pieces without getting overwhelmed."

Figure 3.7A. Luce Foundation Center Display Cases, Smithsonian American Art Museum, Washington, D.C.

PHOTOGRAPH BY KEN RAHAIM, COURTESY SMITHSONIAN AMERICAN ART MUSEUM

The Luce Foundation Center ties directly into the museum's mission by providing a state-of-the-art facility for the general public to understand, appreciate, and enjoy our collection. In particular, it allows SAAM to exhibit an extremely broad sampling of American art. Instead of focusing on a few popular artists or genres in the collection, we cater to a vast number of niche markets, by showcasing both the depth and breadth of our collection. All visitors to the Luce Foundation Center discover something that captures their interest, whether it's a century-old fish decoy, a painting of the post office in their hometown, or a model of a public sculpture that they walk past every day.

In conceiving the center, we wanted to provide visitors with a genuine behind-the-scenes experience—an opportunity to walk through art storage and see thousands of artworks that are normally kept off-site. To help visitors navigate the space, we organized the objects into broad categories:

- nineteenth- and twentieth-century paintings
- nineteenth- and twentieth-century sculpture
- folk art
- contemporary craft

Large colored graphics on the ends of the cases clearly indicate the different sections. Within the categories, each case side has a contextual theme. Sometimes the theme is obvious—in contemporary craft we divided the objects by medium—but occasionally a case's design was determined more by the size and shape of the available objects than by content.

In addition to the cases, the Luce Foundation Center displays three collections in drawers: portrait miniatures, medals and medallions, and craft jewelry. These pneumatic drawers were designed and manufactured specifically for the Luce Foundation Center, and the portrait miniatures in particular benefit from this manner of storage. Miniatures were usually executed in watercolor on ivory, and as a result are extremely sensitive to light, vibration, and humidity. For these reasons, the miniatures could be on view only for a few months if displayed in a typical gallery setting. The drawers allow us to safely display over four hundred portrait miniatures, giving SAAM the unique ability to provide permanent access to a large collection in its entirety.

Didactic interpretation is limited to make room for as many objects as possible in the cases. Paintings are identified by a small label including the artist's name, the picture's title, and its accession number, while objects are identified by accession number only. Extended information on every

Figure 3.7B. Luce Foundation Center Display Drawers

PHOTOGRAPH BY MILDRED BALDWIN, COURTESY SMITHSONIAN AMERICAN ART MUSEUM

work of art is available through ten interactive touch-screen computer kiosks. For over four years, museum staff researched and wrote interpretive text labels for each of the 3,300 objects, and detailed biographies for 1,100 artists. In addition, we produced over one hundred video and audio clips, including interviews with contemporary American artists and narrated slideshows. The computer kiosks also offer a way for people to extend their visit outside the bricks and mortar of the museum. As visitors browse the digital collection, they can "collect" their favorite artworks into a virtual scrapbook and e-mail it to themselves. Once at home they can peruse the objects they collected in the museum, visit the museum's website to collect more, create themed scrapbooks, write their own labels, and share their scrapbooks with others.

Staff is available at the information desk in the Luce Foundation Center seven days a week to answer questions on the museum's collections, exhibitions, programs, and activities. Since the facility opened, it has become a lively and vibrant part of the museum, with a variety of ongoing programs that range from family scavenger hunts and sketching workshops to gallery talks and guided tours. The Luce staff members have collected a wealth of statistical data and anecdotal feedback, providing valuable information about the visitor experience throughout the museum.

The Luce Foundation Center is continually evolving as we discover and develop new ways to serve our audiences. Upcoming plans include:

- offering audio content over cell phones;
- developing additional media for the computer kiosks;
- promoting the free Wi-Fi available in the center; and
- running a multimedia mystery game in which participants work in teams to solve a series of clues using cell phones, computers, and live-action dialogue.

By experimenting with new techniques for engaging our visitors, we can ensure that the Luce Foundation Center for American Art will remain a vital part of the museum now and into the future.

3.4.1.3 Site Selection

Site selection is sometimes part of the planning of suitable accommodations. Lists of factors affecting the decision are usually drawn up, including:

- availability;
- access;
- audience development potential;
- cost of acquisition and development, balanced by funding opportunities;
- security considerations;
- building type (if it is a question of renovation of an existing structure);
- size and layout of site or existing structures;
- parking;
- visibility;
- compatibility of neighbouring facilities; and
- contribution to local development plans.

Each factor should be weighted before it is evaluated—that is, each factor is given a "weight" value in terms of its importance, and this is multiplied by its evaluation to give a total rating for that factor. The same weighting applies to all sites under consideration, whereas each site is assigned a specific value for that factor. For instance, a site with excellent access by public transportation and other means might rate a value of +3, whereas a site with limited public access might be valued at −2 for that factor. If the importance of access has been weighted at 2, then the site with excellent access would gain a total of 6 points for this factor, whereas the one with poor access would lose a total of 4 points (−4). A plus and minus evaluation system is useful, since for each component some sites will have positive advantages rating a plus evaluation, while others will not only be deficient but may even have negative connotations for that factor, rating a minus evaluation.

The weighting of site selection factors should be done in relation to fundamental issues of the museum's mission, its policies, and its institutional character. If, for example, it has been a government, corporate, or university museum but is now being encouraged to become more self-sufficient, the site selection criteria related to audience development should be very heavily weighted indeed; sometimes a difference of a few hundred yards or meters is crucial in relation to the resultant building's public image and the museum's ability to function effectively as a public attraction. If funding is possible only for some sites, but is crucial to the enterprise, then that factor must be given heavy weight. On the other hand, a security issue may be so alarming that it outweighs all other factors, so security must be assigned an appropriate weight.

A question frequently asked is whether renovation of a historic building is preferable to a new purpose-built structure, or vice versa. The answer must always be specific to the particular comparison being made. Renovation is often less expensive, sometimes by as much as one third of the capital cost. But the governing body of the museum may find themselves paying this difference many times over in higher operating costs, while the staff may be regretting the decision to renovate daily, as they try to cope with inadequate spaces, awkward corridors, multiple floor levels, and insufficient turning room outside lifts or elevators.

Very often the preservation of a historic building for which no other use is feasible may be given as justification for preferring renovated space. This may be praiseworthy from the viewpoint of architectural preservation—and that preservation may indeed be part of the museum's own mission—but the justification should be recognized as unrelated to the functional requirements of the museum, so that the costs in both capital outlay and operations may be considered as well.

3.4.1.4 Organizing the Facility Planning Teams

Who is to undertake facility planning? The governing body usually establishes a *building committee* to guide the process by establishing and monitoring the policy and budgetary framework for the project, often in relation to a fundraising campaign. The museum's director must provide leadership. And it is essential for the museum to name a *project manager*. He or she may be already on staff—but if so, must be relieved of other duties while assuming the project management role; alternatively, project management skills may be contracted for the life of the capital project only. The process of museum facility planning and programming (US) or briefing (UK) is often facilitated by specialized museum planning consultants (like the authors), who work with all of the above personnel to achieve the optimal result. Even with professional museum planners and an experienced project manager, it is vital to involve the staff—all those who will have to provide services to the collection and to the public—in the new facility. Museum facility planning is very much a team effort.

The most important step in organizing the museum's forces to address a capital project is therefore to establish both a museum project team and a building team, which usually includes a building design team.

- The museum project team comprises museum personnel who address the various museum functions affected by the capital development—curatorial concerns, conservation, security, revenue generation, and many more. This team should be led by the museum planner, whether a professional consultant specializing in this area or an appointed member of the museum staff. The museum project team's task is to ensure that the museum's requirements are clearly stated, and that those requirements are met by the architects, engineers, and contractors. The cost consultant (or quantity surveyor) should also meet with this team, to ensure that the cost implications of their requirements are made clear.

- The building team includes the architect, engineers, landscape architects, and other technical specialists needed, along with the contractor and the construction manager. Their task is to answer the requirements of the museum project team with technical drawings and specifications. The museum planner directing the museum planning team should also meet with the building team, to ensure that the requirements of the museum project team are understood and met within the limits of the budget and schedule. The cost consultant or quantity surveyor also meets with the building team to estimate cost implications of its designs and specifications; he or she is also on both teams.

- Before the contractor is engaged, the architect, engineers and other specialists constitute what may be called the *building design team*. The museum planner should also be part of this group, in order to ensure that the requirements of the museum project team are met, along with the cost consultant.

Note that the museum project team is fundamental to the planning, design, and construction process; its work should be addressed before the others. Yet time and again the process begins with the formation of a design team only. At a recent conference on building museums, a session on the planning process featured and discussed only the work of the building design team! Other design professions cannot be faulted if the museum profession itself fails to do the necessary planning for its own buildings.

This relationship is evident in the results of the planning process as well. It is to be hoped that the architect's response and that of the rest of the building team will be inspired, and the resultant building will be memorable. But the concern of the museum project team is simply that the building should do the job that the museum requires of it.

The project manager meets with all of these teams, and from time to time convenes a meeting of the combined teams that brings them together. The museum's director should attend those combined team meetings, and can then report back to the building committee of the museum's governing body. The building committee should not normally attend the team meetings of the concerned professionals.

3.4.1.5 The Functional Program or Brief

The sequence of events in the facility planning process for museums should begin from a strategic or master plan, which should be agreed or updated as required, in order to place the capital project in context, in relation to the museum's mission, mandate, and objectives. Beyond a strategic plan, a capital project requires the collection analysis and development strategy, public programming plan, market analysis, and marketing strategy that are part of a master plan. If it is a new museum, this may be called a feasibility study, culminating in a conclusion about the relative feasibility of a museum or other facility. (Section 3.1.1 describes these preliminary planning steps in more detail.)

With the strategic and master plan establishing the institutional goals and the collection, programming, and marketing objectives, it is finally possible, preferably with the aid of experienced museum planners or programmers, to draft the key document that is known in Britain and many other countries as a *functional brief*, but in the United States is called a *functional program*—a statement of the museum's functional requirements of space and facilities. It is called "functional" because it describes spaces in terms of the functions they must perform.

A functional brief or program is written in language that the museum's trustees and management can understand (because it provides requirements, not specifications), and usually includes:

1. planning and design principles (not expected to change for the life of the project) and assumptions (which may be changed, but if so will affect the planning and design);
2. site characteristics and requirements for access, signage, security, and the like;
3. a list of all spaces in the building with their dimensions, organized by zone, as outlined subsequently in this section;
4. functional area descriptions, sometimes combining spaces from different zones if they are associated in one of the museum's functions, such as exhibitions, education, retail, or food service;
5. space adjacencies critical to the effective functioning of the museum;
6. building access, egress, and circulation patterns for visitors, staff, suppliers, and VIPs, and for collections, supplies, food, and garbage, all of which may be shown along with space adjacencies in access, adjacency, and circulation diagrams;
7. building systems and standards required throughout the building, or by zone, with specific standards for the collection or parts of it, as well as human comfort standards;
8. detailed functional requirements of every room in the building, again grouped by zone, often presented as a spreadsheet correlating many factors to each space in the building so that it functions as a checklist for the architect, engineers, contractor, and the museum itself at the time of *commissioning* (handing over to the owner) the building.

A *facility strategy* usually includes some or all of the first seven of the foregoing list, but not the detailed functional requirements for every room. Often a facility strategy will be produced for fund-raising as well as planning purposes, and the museum will proceed to a full functional program only after sufficient funds have been raised to justify this more detailed level of planning; or a facility strategy can be the basis for an architectural competition, with the functional program being produced for the selected architect.

The analysis of circulation patterns should be done in consultation with the building manager or building engineers, as well as with the chief of security. It is crucial, for example, to ensure that food supplies can be delivered and garbage removed without crossing or duplicating collection circulation paths if at all possible. Similarly, access of service personnel for repair and replacement to plant rooms should be made possible without passing through or by collection zones. Provisions should be made for visitors of all kinds, including children, toddlers, the physically challenged, and for "very important persons" (VIPs), as well as visitors to offices who may arrive during closed hours. VIPs, such as politicians, experts, artists, or musicians, who attend the museum to open an exhibition or give a performance or lecture, may need a separate discreet entrance, a small lounge while awaiting the event, and access to and from the galleries or theater where they are to present, without passing through general public areas.

Building systems and standards for the entire building or for zones of it, and the detailed functional requirements that apply these standards, as appropriate, to every room in the structure, systematically record the variables for:

- architectural issues, i.e., floor, wall, and ceiling surfaces; doors, windows, glazing types, and insulation levels required;
- atmospheric functions, i.e., air-conditioning, humidity control, outside air controls, room pressure, heat gain, and environmental control standards;
- mechanical specifications, i.e., hot and cold water; steam, gas, or compressed air requirements; floor drains, exhausts, and room controls;
- visual requirements, i.e., focal contrast levels, daylight or blackout provisions, views in or out of the room, privacy requirements, light fixtures, direct or indirect lighting recommendations, *color rendering index*, and *color temperature*;
- electrical functions, i.e., intercom, telephone, audio, video, cinematic, power and emergency requirements, clocks or other applications, computer needs, surge protection, and other power security functions;
- acoustical functions, i.e., ambient sound and speech privacy levels;
- security levels, motion sensors, closed-circuit television, panic hardware, locks, hinge pins, and glass-breakage detector requirements;
- fire safety issues, i.e., fire ratings for structure, doors and dampers, smoke density and flame spread numbers, fuel-contributed levels, fire detectors, extinguishers, and sprinklers;

- special functions such as vibration and load-bearing levels and hazard controls;
- a matrix of all functions related to spaces, grouped in zones of public/non-public and collection/noncollection (four in all) that are most useful for both engineering and costing purposes (see section 3.4.1.8 later in this chapter).

In addition to listing the requirements for the above factors, a functional program or brief ensures that the building:

- meets relevant building codes;
- fulfills the requirements of standard-setting authorities, which may be related to eligibility for government or private foundation grants;
- satisfies the expectations of national and international lenders of individual objects and of whole exhibitions; and
- and operates as efficiently as possible, with energy-saving and other "green" sustainability requirements, as far as possible, given the special requirements of a museum.

The drafting of this functional program or brief should not be assigned to architects or engineers. Their expertise does not lie in the statement of museum *requirements*. The architects and engineers provide the *answers*, with their drawings and specifications; but the purpose of the functional program or brief is to get the *questions* right, to state the museum's *requirements* that the architect and engineers must meet in their work. The development of the museum planner as a specialized role within the museum profession has been very much in response to this demand for experienced museum professionals who have learned the language of the facility strategy and functional program or brief.

THE NEED FOR A FUNCTIONAL
PROGRAM OR BRIEF
By Barry Lord

I was invited with a group of museum professionals to review three sets of architectural drawings and models for the expansion of a venerable museum in continental Europe. The collection featured medieval and Renaissance oak and other wood furniture and carvings, housed in a 1950s structure with a massive floor-to-ceiling window wall along all of the galleries. With that much glass, environmental controls were quite impossible: the curator told me that on a humid summer afternoon one could hear a concert in the galleries—the squeaking of the joints of furniture!

The three sets of short-listed architectural plans and models (for which the museum had paid) all provided a mixture of temporary exhibition galleries, a members' lounge, a pedagogical center, a restaurant, and many other attractions. But what was to be done with the permanent collection? I was advised that the plan was to build all these new facilities, and then to renovate the existing building with whatever funds remained. But in fact, this was the only time in twenty years when the museum would have the funds to accomplish any substantial physical improvement, and their money would all be spent by the time they completed the addition, so that nothing would be left for the permanent collection galleries.

When the time came to make comments on the architects' plans, I had to say that I chose none of the three. The architects were all disappointed, but I reassured them that it was not their fault. No one had asked the right questions, so none of the architects could give the right answer. No one had recognized that the museum's highest priority had to be the preservation of its collection and that this need should have been at the center of the brief given to the competing architects. I could only recommend that the museum reconsider its brief before beginning over again with the architects—which I understand was subsequently done. Such a functional brief was what was needed.

3.4.1.6 From Architectural Concept to Evaluation

Whereas the functional program or brief asks questions—sets the requirements—the work of the architects and engineers is to provide answers. Their drawings and specifications are called *architectural documentation*; in Britain sometimes it is called a *technical brief*. The museum project team and the building team should meet together to resolve issues that arise as the functional program or brief is translated first into an *architectural concept* or *design concept*, and then into progressive stages of *schematic design* and *detailed design* or *design development*, along with technical *specifications* by the engineers as well as the architects, in response to the requirements of the functional program. If museum planning professionals have been engaged in developing the program, they should also be commissioned to review the designs and specifications as they are produced in order to advise on the degree of compliance with the requirements or to suggest compromises as needed.

For many museum projects there is both a *design architect*, who may do only the concept or may proceed only as far as schematic design, and an *architect of record*, usually a local architect licensed to practice in that jurisdiction, who may be responsible for continuing the process through detailed design and for issuing *construction drawings* as the basis for the documentation to be issued to contractors to bid on building or renovating the structure. An exhibition designer may also be part of the design team, especially for natural history, science and technology, or history museums involving complex, large-scale exhibits.

Computer modeling as well as three-dimensional models may be employed at various junctures throughout this process to aid in visualizing the result, as well as to assist in fund-raising. *Building imagery modeling* (BIM) is increasingly used as a critical part of design development, facilitating the identification of potential conflicts between the various design and engineering components.

Throughout this process compromise is inevitable, and welcome—but should always be made with an eye to ensuring the optimal achievement of the museum's functional requirements within the limitations of budget, time, and technology. Consideration must be given to the usually inverse relationship of capital and operating costs—a savings in the former often leading to an increase in the latter, and vice versa. The design stage concludes with *bid (or tender) documents* on the basis of which contractors prepare their proposals, and the consequent contract negotiations after bids are opened. The cost consultant (or quantity surveyor) should have provided estimates at each stage, possibly beginning with very rough order-of-magnitude projections after the master plan, refining the estimates through the programming process, and costing each set of designs. The opening of bids or tenders proves how accurate the process has been. It is important to include a review of the competing bids in terms of their compliance with the functional program or brief, as a prominent part of their evaluation. The selection should certainly not be made on the basis of lowest price alone.

The construction of new or renovated museum space proceeds toward *commissioning* (handing over the building to the client), as do most building projects, but it is important that the project manager, the museum project team, and/or the museum planners should be able to review the project at various stages of its completion to ensure that the museum's needs are being met. And the final stage of the process should not be forgotten—*evaluation* of the building's performance, again measured against the requirements of the functional brief or functional program.

3.4.1.7 Cost of Facility Planning

The cost of facility planning is often considered to be high, but this is usually because it has not yet been put in the perspective of the cost of the capital project as a whole. Many museums are cash-poor, even at the beginning of major capital projects, and are often reluctant to allocate money to planning, when it could be used to "get on with the job." Yet the entire planning and programming process usually costs no more than 1 percent of the total project value. Even taken together with the cost of the ongoing review of the architects' and engineers' drawings and specifications throughout the design process, total costs are likely to reach only 1.5 percent. The costs should be seen as the initial 1.5 percent spent to ensure that the remaining 98.5 percent is well used. The costs of the architect's or contractor's change orders may be much more substantial if not guided by good planning.

The cost of the entire period throughout which the museum planners should be meeting with the architects and engineers to review their schematic and detailed designs and specifications will vary according to architectural billing practices throughout the world, but is usually only about 12.5 percent of the total project value, including the 1.5 percent for planning and programming. It is during this planning and design phase that the opportunities to make changes are still relatively inexpensive—before we hear *"It's too late!"*

3.4.1.8 Zoning

Throughout the facility planning process, the best way to control costs, as well as to understand the complex spaces found in a museum and to organize their engineering requirements, is to group the museum's spaces into four zones, labeled A, B, C, and D:

A. Public Noncollection Zone: Spaces such as lobbies, theaters, shops, and restaurants, which require a high level of finish for the public, but do not require the high security and environmental controls requisite to protection of the collection.

B. Public Collection Zone: Permanent collection and temporary exhibition galleries and any other areas where both the public and the collections may be together. These are the most expensive and demanding areas in the museum, since they combine high levels of finish for the public with museum standards of environmental controls, lighting, and security for the collection.

C. Nonpublic Collection Zone: Permanent collection and temporary exhibition storage, conservation laboratories, curatorial workrooms, all exhibition handling and work areas, and other support areas where objects from the collection will be found. This zone requires the collection-sensitive environmental controls and high levels of security, but not the high levels of finish requisite for the public. Note that "collection" here refers to objects on loan as well as those owned by the museum.

D. Nonpublic Noncollection Zone: Support areas behind the scenes where collections will not be permitted—such as the mechanical rooms, noncollection storage areas, and the offices. These areas require neither the sophisticated environmental controls and security nor the high levels of finish requisite for the public, and are therefore the least expensive spaces in the museum building.

The analysis of the museum's space into these four categories is of immeasurable help to the architect and engineer in planning efficient adjacencies, as well as to the cost consultant (or quantity surveyor) and the construction manager in determining where and how to cut costs if that should become necessary in what is called a *value engineering* process. This four-zone analysis also allows us to see most clearly how efficient the building is, or could be made. The norm is for most museum buildings to be about 60 percent public (Zones A and B), with about 60 percent of their space holding collections (Zones B and C). About 40 percent is usually gallery space (Zone B), with about 20 percent in each of the other three zones (see figure 3.8.).

Zoning of the building is also instrumental in planning for operating efficiencies or for planning to enhance "green" sustainability. These are usually challenging in a museum, since its requirements for environmental controls and security may necessitate equipment or facilities that could be more efficient if standards were lower. Proper zoning of spaces allows engineers to work with museum planners to mitigate these effects wherever possible, and it at least permits the identification of those factors where cost savings and compromises can or must be made.

Figure 3.8. Normative Space Distribution by Zone

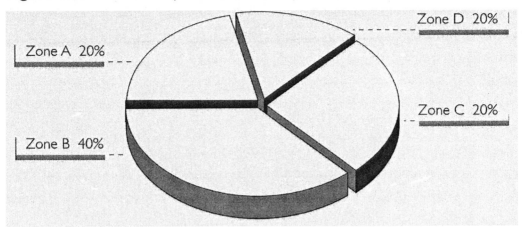

3.4.2 Site and Building Operation

The operation of museum sites and buildings involves three functions:

- managing daily operations;
- maintenance and repair; and
- security.

Following a discussion of these three functions, this section will conclude with a consideration of the ways in which museums can put an environmental consciousness to work—how museums can be at least somewhat "green."

3.4.2.1 Managing Daily Operations

Managing the operations of a museum site and building requires the correlation of six major factors, usually prioritized as follows:

1. health and safety of visitors, staff, and others;
2. security and preservation of the collection;
3. comfort and convenience of visitors;
4. facilitation of staff requirements;
5. preservation of the building; and
6. sustainability, environmental conservation, and energy savings.

If the building is a historic structure, the fifth priority is likely to become the third, ahead of visitors and staff. If the historic building is more important than the collection it contains, the fifth priority may even be second, ahead of the collection as well. The operation of a museum site and building may be seen as an art of balancing all these concerns, some of which will be mutually exclusive at times. It is helpful if the operations manager or building engineer makes clear the priorities, not only in general, but also with reference to specific directives or practices.

Both *monitoring* and *control* functions are required to manage these five factors. In addition to the operations manager the conservators and those responsible for public programming should have input to the standards to be achieved and should receive regular reports on actual conditions. The cooperation of those responsible for building operations with those responsible for the collections and those concerned with visitor services is vital to the smooth functioning of the museum, and may require the intervention of senior staff from time to time to ensure efficient collaboration. Regular meetings, perhaps monthly, are well advised.

The inherent conflict that is often observed between preservation of the collection and preservation of the building should be acknowledged, with priorities clearly understood by all. The collection manager's goal of maintaining a constant relative humidity (RH), in temperate zones usually at 50 percent, plus or minus 3 percent at 20–21°C (68–70°F), with as little variation as possible, may present a difficult challenge to the building engineer, especially in historic structures, if the external RH is varying widely, from 90 percent in midsummer to 20 percent in midwinter, for example. Air barriers to stop conditioned air from entering the structural envelope, and vapor barriers of 4 ml polyethylene with a permeability rating of 0.04–0.08 perms to stop water vapor from dampening the insulation must be carefully designed and installed, with overlapping sheets and stapling of both sheets to each stud. Failure to do so can harm the building fabric, and may be signaled by such symptoms as efflorescence on the museum walls.

Air circulation is a function where the needs of the collection and the public must sometimes be adjusted. Since it is expensive to condition air in order to prolong the life of the collection, it is foolish to replace that air with large volumes of unconditioned outside air that requires reconditioning. The outside air dampers should be of fixed volume design, controlled by a timer set to admit the minimum acceptable volume of fresh air during public hours, and to close at other times. Carbon dioxide (CO_2) monitors that adjust the volume of outside air to the human use of the space are expensive, but repay their costs many times over in day-to-day operating efficiencies—given the particular concerns of the museum for conditioning the air in its buildings.

Nowhere is the collection/public conflict more apparent than in questions of *fenestration*. People like windows, and both architects and many museum professionals believe that skylights are attractive features in a museum gallery, due to a preference among many for natural light, especially in art museums. Entire walls of glass are common in contemporary architecture. Windows in galleries are *not* recommended, and in historic structures are usually blocked (in such a way as to ensure that the window blocks are not visible on a historic facade.) But skylights over galleries are commonly found in both historic and new structures; Louis Kahn's central skylights at the Kimbell Art Museum in Fort Worth and Renzo Piano's raked roof over the galleries of the De Menil Collection in Houston are often cited as models to emulate. Glass walls provide an even greater challenge.

All these openings in the museum wall and ceiling challenge the ability of the best building engineers; some have been heard to say that there is no such thing as a skylight that doesn't leak, only one that hasn't leaked yet! Others find that solutions that work in temperate climates, such as the ingenious arrangement of louvers and computerized environmental controls in the area under the skylights above the *Neuepinakothek* galleries in Munich, do not work nearly as well in harsher climates of greater extremes. One very expensive new art museum in a northern climate had buckets collecting drops on its carpeted and cathedral-ceilinged, skylit gallery floors only a few weeks after it had opened.

All fenestration should be triple-paned, with at least 0.5 inch (1.3 cm) between panes; laminated glass or Plexiglas should be used with an ultraviolet filtration capability of reducing UV rays to less than ten microwatts per lumen, and with a polycarbonate outer layer for security. Louvers, operated by hand or photocell, are needed to ensure that the sun's rays enter the gallery indirectly, and the area below the skylight may have to be housed separately from the gallery (with another layer of glass as its floor and the gallery's ceiling) to provide a "halfway house" in which the difference between the outside and internal environments can be equilibrated to prevent condensation along the edges of the panes.

Museums in tropical climates have the added problem that most of the professional literature is focused on temperate zone conditions. Artifacts or specimens of tropical origin have a different hydroscopic capacity. The surfaces of some fine furniture in one tropical setting were inadvertently sacrificed in the attempt to meet inappropriate temperate conditions. In Singapore and elsewhere we have recommended 65 percent instead of 50 percent as the relative humidity (RH) set point for collections of tropical origin.

Energy-saving approaches using lower-technology methods to control the environment, with the added attraction of cost saving, should be adopted wherever possible, but with a cautionary note about their effect on the collections or on the museum's ability to borrow exhibitions. Conservators may prescribe greater ranges of fluctuation in conditions affecting the collections. For instance, the engineer may be advised to allow a 5–10 percent variation from the RH standard for about 5 percent or more of the museum's operating hours. This may be done seasonally, with a 5 percent step-up in the set point in each of three spring months, and a 5 percent step-down in the corresponding fall months.

The effect of such variations is limited, however, by the fact that museum buildings must meet not merely the requirements of the institution itself, but also those of actual or potential *lenders*. The need to maintain the highest standards in the temporary exhibition galleries twenty-four hours per day year-round—or at least to maintain the capability to achieve these standards when needed to meet the demands of lenders—is the ultimate criterion determining the provision or the upgrading of many museum heating, ventilating, and air-conditioning systems. And if that capability must be provided for the temporary exhibition gallery, it is often more cost effective to provide it for all the collection zones.

Maintaining the standard 50 percent, plus or minus 3 percent RH at 20–21°C (68–70°F), year-round should not present a major problem in a well-designed new building constructed to accommodate that capability, especially in a maritime temperate climate. In a historic structure, or in any building not constructed to maintain such a standard, it may be difficult or impossible, especially in a continental climate. A 55 percent RH standard may be the best compromise possible, and even then it may be necessary in a historic structure to adjust the humidity settings by 5 percent RH each month for three months each spring and fall, allowing a fluctuation from 40 percent RH in the winter to 55 percent in the summer, and a temperature swing from 21 to 24°C (70–75°F). and back during the same three months. In any event, metals and paper collections require a drier store, kept closer to 40 percent RH if possible.

Whatever standards are required by the museum's chief conservator, it is important for those responsible for the building's operation to insist that they can and must be attained. Engineers themselves are often resistant, or point to the consequent high cost of building operations, so the museum manager needs to be sure of the conditions required, and to insist on them. Some years ago, a survey of a series of Florida museums found that only one had a perfect record of maintaining the humidity and temperature levels that the managers of all the museums surveyed said they wanted, but did not think they could achieve. The director of the one successful museum observed that the difference was simply his unrelenting quest over a two-year period with his consulting engineers—reinforced by his refusal to pay them the last 10 percent of their fees until the desired results were obtained!

The control systems and the equipment provided to the museum can be decisive in facilitating achievement of the desired standards. Electronic humidistats with a low drift factor and a short operating span should be used, connected to a *direct digital control* (DDC) computer-operated electronic control system. The control humidistat should be mounted on a wall of the room with the tightest specifications. Ducted electronic electrode disposable-cylinder steam humidifiers are recommended for small- to medium-size museums, although larger institutions may utilize central steam humidification.

Redundancy is an important consideration in planning and operating a museum building system. By "redundancy" we mean the capability for building systems to sustain operation despite malfunction or power outage to the regularly operating equipment. This need not mean that the museum must maintain 200 percent of its heating, ventilating, and air-conditioning equipment requirements; it may be sufficient to have about 130–140 percent, since normal usage is likely to require only about 65–70 percent of capacity at any one time. Redundant power capability and dedicated and supervised security telephone lines are also important for security as well as preventive conservation purposes.

Once the standards for both regular operations and redundancy capacity have been determined and the equipment installed, much of the site and building operations schedule can be regularized in procedures manuals. Although initial operating manuals may be the last product required of the contractors, the museum director and the conservators especially should ensure that these manuals and the priorities they manifest are consistent with museum policies. Simple procedural errors, such as leaving the front doors of the building open to waft outside air through a foyer directly into expensively conditioned galleries, have been observed even in otherwise sophisticated institutions—the reason being that no one had explained the museum's requirements and the reasons for them to the attendants or shop clerks who opened the doors for human comfort.

The loading dock and the shipping and receiving bay are areas where staff procedures sometimes transgress not only museum policy but also the reasons why expensive equipment was provided in the first place. One useful way of ensuring that roll-up loading doors are not left open too long is to install two interrelated locking mechanisms on the two sets of roll-up doors, one at the outside vehicular access to the museum, and the other at the interior access from the shipping and receiving bay to the area where crating and uncrating will take place, such that if one door is open the other must be locked. A separate personnel door beside the shipping door is also important, with a security station controlling access to both, hopefully with the help of closed-circuit television and a sound system, so that delivery personnel can be identified before either door is opened. Viewing panels 3 inches (75 mm) wide by 18 inches (450 mm) high should be provided at 4 feet 6 inches (1.4 m) above the floor in all doors through which collections are to move, and doors, corridors, and lifts should maintain at least an 8-foot (2.44 m) width and 10-foot (3 m) height from the loading dock through to the galleries and stores.

Cooperation between security staff and building operations personnel is crucial to the well-managed museum. Both should be fully familiar with the policies and procedures of the other, and regular (perhaps weekly) meetings between the chief of security and the operations manager or building engineer can be rewarded by greater efficiencies in operation as well as assured security. It is particularly important that both departments are fully informed of such events as the delivery of incoming exhibitions or the shipment of outgoing collections. The operations manager should also have a sign-off arrangement with the registrar or curators to ensure that no artifacts, specimens, or works of art enter or leave the building unless authorized.

Computerized *building management systems (BMS)*, with screens on which conditions in each room can be observed and printed out if required, have made building operations far more efficient in museums. No new museum and no major renovation should be undertaken without including a BMS room. These should incorporate relative humidity (RH) readings for each room where they are required, including the inside conditions of display or storage cases, which should be recorded on a chart (not simply as lists of numbers). Conservators' hygrothermographs, with their styluses recording temperature and RH on graph paper drums in the corners of galleries, are increasingly being replaced by less cumbersome and more easily monitored computerized instruments integrated with the BMS display.

The sixth and last priority, environmental sustainability and energy savings, is usually challenging for museums, which are inherently an energy-inefficient building type. However, natural history and science museums in particular often wish to set an example, and other museum types should do what they can to enhance energy efficiency and sustainability.

The California Academy of Science in San Francisco is perhaps the most obviously environmentally conscious building, with its literally green roof of grass. In the early twenty-first century, environmental conservation, global warming, and increasing energy costs are all combining to encourage the development of green strategies for the construction and operation of museums.

Green strategies may be of two kinds:

- strategies to promote sustainable environments; and
- strategies to promote energy savings.

Sometimes these goals may be combined, but in each case higher capital costs must be balanced against operational savings. Energy-saving options that do not compromise the collection's environment should be encouraged, but each strategy should be considered in a cost-benefit analysis, weighing the potential for operating savings against the certainty of higher capital cost.

Managing relative humidity and temperature levels to "precision control" tolerances twenty-four hours per day year-round is the main reason why museum buildings are seldom exemplary green buildings. In addition, the reliance on electric light instead of daylight, and on incandescent lamps instead of less energy-consuming lamps such as the discharge or light-emitting diode (LED) types, mean that museum electrical and heating loads are bound to be high. Preservation of the collections must always take priority over energy saving.

All aspects and impacts of any proposed energy-saving devices or practices must be considered in deciding whether to introduce them. For example, energy-saving measures such as "free cooling" or airside economizers that are often used in other building types to lower energy consumption may not work for museums because the money saved in cooling costs may be lost due to the increased load on the particulate and gaseous filters and the humidifiers. It is also very difficult to provide a stable RH when utilizing free cooling.

Some other energy-saving measures that *are* recommended for consideration by cultural building consultant Murray Frost include the following:

- Waterside economizers, which have proven effective for museum use despite the initial higher capital investment.
- Multiple types of chillers, such as a high-efficiency standard chiller for the most economic production of chilled water, combined with a double bundle heat recovery chiller for the provision of "free" reheat energy for RH control, combined with a reversible cycle chiller (heat pump) for heat production in the winter and additional cooling capacity during the summer.
- Air exhausted from the building via the heating, ventilation, and air-conditioning (HVAC) system (but not via exhaust systems from restrooms or other spaces) could be put through a heat recovery device to capture sensible and latent heat for the tempering of the outdoor air being brought into the building.
- A dedicated HVAC unit in the outdoor air duct could further temper this makeup air before being distributed to HVAC units serving specific spaces throughout the institution, thereby lessening the load on each of these units and allowing them to be more efficiently sized.
- The use of carbon dioxide (CO_2) sensors to control the quantity of outdoor air being brought into the building, instead of purging the space with a fixed amount of outdoor air all the time, has already been recommended. The sensor minimizes the exchange of the relatively expensive conditioned air when the galleries are empty during closed hours, or scantily attended during slack times, but responds to crowds at an exhibition opening or other event by increasing the frequency and volume of air exchange. Such a sensor requires an additional capital cost but one that earns its keep in subsequent energy savings.

- The provision of airlocks at entrances either as vestibules or as revolving doors is energy efficient and can help to prevent the entry of dust, gaseous pollutants, and pests into the building. The two airlock doors of the vestibule should be at least 10 feet (3 m) apart, so that the one door closes before the other can be opened.
- With the high reliance on electricity in many museums to provide cooling, air movement, lighting, and vertical circulation, and since a significant portion of this load is present twenty-four hours per day, it may be possible to use *cogeneration*; this would involve providing an electrical generator to produce electricity for the operation of chillers and other electrical equipment, with the heat from the generator engine used for controlling RH by providing reheat energy and for winter heating.
- In the near future, fuel cells (hydrogen and oxygen combined to produce electricity, heat, and water) may be commercially available.
- Building materials have a finite life, with known time spans for each material used, after which replacement will be necessary. The *recyclability* of each material could be used as a criterion in making the choice of materials during construction or renovation. For example, linoleum with a linseed oil base would score higher in the recyclability category than vinyl or tile flooring.

Museums can be designed to last for a century, with materials and equipment designed for replacement at defined times, such as every twenty-five or fifty years. *Life-cycle costing* of the building during its planning and design will help to make the museum itself, as well as its community, more sustainable.

3.4.2.2 Maintenance and Repair

The cleaning of museum buildings is another area where building operations come into contact with the needs of both collections and the visiting public. Clear lines of demarcation must be drawn between building maintenance and collection care responsibilities, especially if there are open displays or large artifacts or specimens that are easily accessible to cleaners. This is particularly important if cleaning staff are on contract and so do not report directly to museum management. A cleaning manual should be strictly enforced, including details of materials and equipment to be used, degrees of access to and within areas holding collections, and so on.

Museum concrete should include a hardening agent, and all surfaces should be *sealed*, including those above false ceilings. This is not only to prevent concrete dust from falling but especially to prevent it from entering the air circulation system. All other surfaces should be painted.

Vacuums should be central systems vented to the outdoors, or may be portable *high-efficiency particulate air filter* (HEPA) vacuums, which boast a dust-capture efficiency of 99.97 percent. Carpentry workshops and any other dust-producing workrooms should be vented outdoors, and care should be taken in planning the air-circulation system to ensure that dusty air from such work stations is not recirculated.

The correct replacement of air filters is another task that requires a carefully drafted procedures manual. The bank of filters, measured by the American Society of Heating, Refrigerating and Air-Conditioning Engineers' atmospheric dust spot efficiency test section of ASHRAE test 52-76, should provide 25–30 percent prefilter capacity, 40–85 percent medium-efficiency filters, and 90–95 percent after-filters. Activated charcoal filters are recommended for the filtration of gaseous pollutants. Each filter should be provided with its own manometer to indicate any drop in pressure, and these should be monitored individually, with each filter changed as necessary.

Cleaning materials and techniques should be reviewed and approved by conservators, and maintenance personnel should be included in training sessions aimed at familiarizing them with the requirements of the collection. Similarly, public expectations and those of the staff providing visitor services should be made clear so that performance evaluation of cleaners can be based on compliance with museum procedures manuals and specific public needs.

The replacement of lamps is a routine but critically necessary activity that requires a procedures manual written in consultation with the curators and conservators. There is little use in a museum policy requiring a low level of ultraviolet radiation (under ten microwatts per lumen) if the maintenance worker replaces the lamps in the gallery with fluorescent tubes that do not have the built-in levels of UV protection, or discards the sleeves that were supposed to control the UV emission levels along with the first generation of tubes. Similarly, the maintenance worker needs to know precisely which lamps are needed in which orientation in each display, or the effects contrived by lighting consultants may be lost after the first change of lamps.

An important principle of museum facilities planning is to provide access for repair personnel that does not require them to pass through or past collection zones. Much repair may be done after hours, so it is a simple security precaution (and puts far less responsibility on the shoulders of the repair workers) if replacements or repairs can be done without walking through or past galleries or collection stores. If the layout of the building makes such a provision impossible, it is necessary to accompany repair and replacement personnel at all times.

Deferral of maintenance and repair is a chronic problem in museums. Budgets for upkeep or improvements always appear to be easier to postpone than others, with the result that relatively minor maintenance requirements become progressively more serious until they result in major capital costs for complete replacement. Such deferrals may also weaken the security system. An assiduous management should seek to avoid such long-run inefficiencies by maintaining regular budget commitments for maintenance and repairs. A *preventive maintenance* program is also critical to enhancing sustainability.

The repair and replacement of exhibits provides an interesting question for museum managers: how much should the museum undertake directly, and how much should be contracted out? Some museums, particularly in continental Europe, traditionally have had exhibit designers or even architects on staff, as well as extensive workshops where new exhibits could be built and old ones repaired or replaced. The result in some cases was a "house style" of exhibits—for better or worse. Today, many museum managers prefer to contract exhibit design, choosing a different designer for each project, thereby reducing their workshop needs to the minimum. Even framing may be seen to be more cost-effective if done on contract, rather than dedicating space, facilities, and trained staff to a function that is required only intermittently; however, insurance implications of having to send works outside the building for even minor work should also be considered. For many museums the solution is to provide both a "clean workshop" (in Zone C) for framing, mount making, and routine cleaning of objects in the collection or on loan, and a "dirty workshop" (in Zone D) for carpentry, spray painting, or other exhibition preparation work without collections present.

The advent of electronic, video, and computerized exhibition components, especially in science centers or children's museums, points to another need: the requirement for relatively quick and easy replacement parts on hand, with weekend as well as weekday staff trained to fix exhibits before too much "down time" accumulates. Failure to provide for such replacements results in too many of the "Sorry, this exhibit is not working today" signs that frustrate the museum public, especially those who are one-time visitors. Admission charges have been one important factor in stimulating museums to ensure that malfunctioning exhibits are quickly repaired or replaced. It has also led many to calculate the anticipated "life span" of exhibits, and the projected cost of their upkeep, when preparing an exhibition plan. Video art and other time-based media art are the challenges for art museums, especially when the technology of the period in which the artwork was produced is no longer manufactured.

3.4.2.3 Security

Planning and managing security for museums is an undertaking of primary importance and should be the museum manager's first concern in a new posting. "Security" here refers to the entire range of activities concerned with the protection of the public, staff, and others in the museum, and the protection of the collections from all threats to them.

Like building operations, security affects and is affected by both the collections and public activities aspects of the museum, so that the chief of security should meet regularly with those responsible for these functions, as well as with the operations manager, to ensure that security provisions are effectively in place at all times. The security chief should also meet regularly (at least annually) with local police, fire, and hospital officials to ensure that the museum is up-to-date with current practices in these jurisdictions and to acquaint them with the museum building's layout and recent or proposed changes to it.

Security is an area where policy and procedures manuals should be utilized fully and updated regularly. The management of security includes an ongoing process of recurrent planning and policy formulation and review of procedures manuals to update them to accord with present realities. A security policy should include:

- risk analysis;
- health and safety precautions;
- insurance coverage and valuation procedures (see 3.5.4);
- security equipment, present and recommended; and
- emergency procedures manual.

A *risk analysis* involves answers to four basic questions:

1. *What is to be protected?* The collection should be analyzed in terms of monetary value—classified by value categories of over or under certain monetary levels—and in terms of interest to thieves or vandals. Famous works of art or artifacts may be particularly vulnerable, and objects made of precious metals are always of interest to thieves because they can be melted down. Some artifacts are politically controversial or involve religious values that may attract attacks. Others may be of lower monetary value but may be of great value to the museum and the community for other reasons. Although the same high level of security should be maintained throughout the collection zones, it may be useful to classify the collections into categories A through C, strictly from the viewpoint of their value to be secured so that special attention may be given to category A objects.
2. *What are the threats?* An explicit identification of the risks will help to focus the security plan on reducing or eliminating them.
3. *What level of risk is acceptable?* Many threats cannot be eliminated entirely but may be reduced to the level that the museum's security policy can accept. Purely from a security viewpoint, the museum could remain closed to the public to maximize the safety of its collections, but since the museum is a public institution, its management must determine the degree

of risk that is acceptable. There might, for example, be a policy against open displays of objects in Category A (those with the highest monetary value).

4. *What countermeasures are appropriate?* Again, museum policy must determine acceptable standards among security options. One very busy museum in Manhattan, for instance, encourages its warders to be strict and even officious with the public, because it prefers to err on the side of security, rather than putting its emphasis on a visitor-friendly atmosphere. Another museum might make exactly the opposite priorities.

The threats to be evaluated in a risk analysis include:

*   *natural disasters*, such as earthquakes, hurricanes, tornadoes, floods, forest fires, or simple power outages;
*   *building faults*, such as electrical or heating system deficiencies, or structural weaknesses;
*   *theft*: art theft in particular is said to be second only to the drug trade as a source of revenue to criminals, and a distressingly high proportion of museum thefts are said to be "inside jobs" connected with or committed by a person who has joined the staff for that very purpose;
*   *fire*;
*   *vandalism*;
*   *accidents* of staff or visitors; and
*   *social or political hazards*, such as bomb threats, strikes, or demonstrations.

Risks may be evaluated in terms of their:

*   *probability*, from least to most likely to occur;
*   likely *frequency* of occurrence; and
*   seriousness of *consequences* for the museum.

Risks may be:

*   *eliminated*, for example, by changing staff procedures to stop causing or allowing a hazard;
*   *reduced*, by installing detection or response equipment;
*   *transferred* to an insurer; and
*   *accepted* as necessary to the fulfilment of the museum's public mission.

All four of these responses may be utilized in regard to a particular collection or exhibition, or indeed in protecting a single valuable object. Certain risks may be eliminated and others reduced with protective equipment for an insured object in the collection, but since the museum is dedicated to providing public access to it, some degree of risk will be accepted.

The museum's security policy should accordingly identify the following range of countermeasures (the famous "four Ds"):

- *Detection*: Methods of determining whether a threat is occurring, include surveillance by guards or warders, intrusion alarms, smoke detectors, display case alarms, and closed-circuit television.
- *Deterrence*: Methods of reducing the likelihood of threats may range from perimeter fences to case locks. The perception of deterrence may be just as important as the reality: most museums now recognize the value of making security obvious—so that visitors can see closed-circuit television screens near the entrance, for example.
- *Delay*: If a threat arises, the intention of security is to retard its progress. Two-hour firewalls around collection areas (with one-hour walls elsewhere) are a typical example, as is the practice of restricting egress from the building to one guarded exit, rather than permitting multiple means of getaway.
- *Defense*: An *emergency procedures manual* should detail appropriate staff response in the event of a threat. All staff and volunteers should be provided with this manual—not just security staff—and there should be regular drills and rehearsals. In addition to fire drills, vandalism, theft, visitor illness, and accident scenarios should be enacted, with staff being tested on their ability to respond in accordance with the museum's security policy as detailed in the emergency procedures manual. All staff should know when and how to call for an ambulance or fire or police protection, and all should understand the legal implications of liability for actions taken or not taken, for the museum or for themselves (with legal advice consulted in preparing the manual). After-hours response should also be covered, especially for those who are to receive telephone calls if the intrusion alarm or the fire alarm should be activated. An *emergency measures team* of those employees empowered to coordinate responses to emergencies should be identified in the manual, and the team should meet regularly (at least semiannually) to review the museum's readiness.

It is possible to develop a risk analysis for individual objects, groups of objects, or an entire collection. An arbitrary scale of 1 to 10 for degrees of *criticality* and *vulnerability* may be devised, with "criticality" defined as how important the object is to the museum, and "vulnerability" measuring the extent to which it is at risk. Then:

Risk = Criticality × Vulnerability

Thus if a category A object of prime importance to the museum (high criticality) is moved from inside a case to an open exhibit, its risk factor would be greatly increased—so that the chief of security might suggest to the curators or the director that the relocation might be reconsidered.

The museum's security policy should define three levels of security for exhibition galleries:

- *high security*, for exhibitions of highly valuable items, with special provisions, possibly including constant surveillance during open hours;
- *moderate security*, for exhibitions of original works of art, artifacts, specimens, or original archival material, for which the museum's routine security patrols and surveillance should be maintained;
- *limited security*, for exhibitions that do not contain original works of art, artifacts, specimens, or original archival material; these might be supervised by a person with duties other than those of a guard (such as an educator or even a volunteer) and might be mounted in a corridor or foyer.

Seven levels of security may be distinguished for collection storage rooms, all of which should have two-hour fire protection on all walls and doors:

- Alarmed vaults: with all-interior masonry-reinforced walls, ceilings, and floors and heavy metal doors on a combination lock. All visits must be accompanied by authorized staff and recorded. Vaults may be required for gems, stamps, coins, precious metals, jewelery, and other relatively small items of high value.
- High security collection storage: also with all-interior masonry walls, ceilings, and floors, but with steel doors and frames with a minimum six-pin tumbler lock and key control. This would be required for works of art, weapons, furs, and other objects of high value.
- Permanent collection storage: the museum's main storage rooms, of solid construction with solid doors under key control, required for the main body of the museum's permanent collection. Storage should be organized by medium to facilitate specific environmental control set points; that is, separate storage rooms for metals, textiles, costumes, and works on paper, all of which may be set at 40 percent plus or minus 5 percent relative humidity, and separate rooms for painting racks, ceramics, glass, bronze, and so on, all at 50 percent plus or minus 5 percent RH.
- Temporary exhibition storage (often called *transit store* in Britain): solid walls and doors under key control in a nonpublic area adjacent to the crating/uncrating area, required for temporary loans to the museum or other works of art, artifacts, specimens, or archival materials in transit. This area must have conditions approximating those of the permanent

collection storage, since it is likely to be visited by couriers accompanying loans from other museums.

- Storage cabinets: these may be located in nonpublic areas, or under or above exhibit cases in the galleries. Key control is critical, and objects stored should not be of high value.

- Off-site storage: key control, alarm response, and patrols of these areas present particular challenges and should be appropriate for the nature of the collections in such storage; often required for larger items, such as vehicles or military equipment. An environmentally controlled van may be needed if there is to be frequent movement of objects in the collection to and from off-site storage.

- Hazardous materials storage: nonflammable and fire retardant materials (at least a lockable metal cabinet with key control) should be used to store hazardous materials used in the museum (such as some conservation laboratory supplies). Occasionally some collection materials are themselves hazardous, such as certain types of photographic negatives in archival collections, and so require the same conditions.

In considering security planning for the museum site and building as a whole, it is useful to think of it as a series of concentric circles of protection, with the collection at the center and the following layers of protection, from the outside inward:

- *Museum grounds*: Landscaping can enhance security by eliminating trees overhanging or shrubbery near buildings. Parking areas should be separated from the building by an access area subject to surveillance. Exterior lighting is an important consideration. Closed-circuit television (CCTV) systems should be in operation here, as well as inside the building.

- *Building fabric*: Walls and roofing materials should resist intrusion; fire ratings should in general meet building code requirements, but for walls surrounding collection zones should be at least two hours. Doors and door frames are a particular concern, with fire rating required to be equal to the walls and with a solid core; doors in historic structures may require discreet reinforcement. Hinges should be interior, secured by nonremovable pins. Exterior openings should be protected with magnetic switches and glass breakage detectors, with doors secured by 6-pin tumbler deadbolt locks with a minimum throw of 1 inch (25 mm). Windows, especially ground floor windows, present a major challenge: interior blocks (not visible on the exterior), bars, or shutters that descend over the openings when the museum is closed may all be considered. Roofs should be examined carefully, since entry is very often gained through skylights or service doors there. Basement or half-basement windows or doors must also be reinforced.

- *Perimeter alarms*: Intrusion alarms should be installed at all entrances and on all windows, including any skylights or other roof access points, with direct telephone connection via dedicated lines to either a police station or the security company, whose response to an alarm should be detailed in the emergency procedures manual. A verified passive infrared detector system should extend to all interior spaces, with the same telephone connections. The closed-circuit television system should utilize *close coupled discharge* (CCD) color cameras, which should be positioned to record the faces of persons both entering and exiting the building at all points; computer software programs are available that combine CCTV cameras with computerized plans of the building so that security personnel observing them can actively select or record images of interest and store them in computer memory. Pressure alarms on the roof should also be provided, especially in buildings where the architect has made the roof publicly accessible at some points.

- *Security stations*: Many museums have two security stations, where guards operate and observe CCTV systems and monitor alarms. One is usually visible to entering visitors, providing access for guards (or warders in the U.K.) to intercept anyone attempting to enter or leave. The other is usually adjacent to the loading bay and the shipping and receiving door, with control over the personnel door through which all delivery personnel must approach the museum; CCTV and a sound system should be provided at this door, so that guards may interrogate delivery personnel before allowing them access even to the controlled area within the personnel door. The personnel door should lead only to a foyer, from which further ingress into the museum is also controlled by the guard within the protected security station. This personnel door for delivery personnel may also function as the staff entrance; if not, a similar arrangement must be provided at the staff entrance. Some staff must enter before opening hours, while others leave after public hours, in both cases presenting some risk, unless their entry and exit is via such a security station.

- *Guards* or *warders*: This force makes up the largest single group of employees in many museums. They are also the people with whom the public has the most frequent and sustained contact. It is therefore crucial that they be well trained and well motivated, especially since they are seldom well paid. They are traditionally uniformed, although this need not be paramilitary but can be simply an official but not unfriendly jacket and pants or skirt.

Attempts to mix education or interpretation functions with security have generally not been successful: guards must focus their attention on security. But they should be trained in the nature and value of the collection, and in museum visitor service policy.

Security guards' operations manuals should include:

- their postings schedule;
- routines for opening and closing the museum to the public;
- after-hours patrol practices (possibly with punch clocks at various points within the museum);
- instructions for handling deliveries and other property control procedures;
- key control measures, today usually referring to control of access cards;
- locking and lock-checking routines;
- exhibition gallery surveillance requirements;
- crowd control measures;
- instructions on maintaining security during construction or exhibition replacement
- instructions for monitoring building systems during nonpublic hours; and
- emergency measures procedures for all risks.

Procedures for removing objects from exhibitions, and the use of a card notifying the public that an object has been temporarily removed, should be controlled and recorded. Curatorial and conservation personnel must maintain close communication with security officers each time an object is removed from or added into a display. Especially when new permanent collection exhibitions are being planned, security officers should be notified, consulted, and given an opportunity to comment on designs from a security standpoint. Some years ago in the Australian Museum in Sydney a security guard participating in a planning meeting for a new permanent collection exhibition pointed out that the design of one gallery would require two surveillance personnel; with a few deft changes in the layout, the exhibition designer cheerfully reorganized the vitrines so that only one surveillance guard would be needed—thereby saving the museum thousands of dollars over the years that the exhibition has subsequently been on view.

An important management principle is a determination to consider security guards as members of the museum staff who can in some cases develop into other positions, rather than isolating them from other functions; this approach, which was implemented with success at the Kelvingrove museum in Glasgow, for instance, leads to security personnel who are likely to be far more involved in and aware of customer care as well as security issues. Requiring higher educational qualifications (and compensating accordingly), providing training and offering personal development opportunities are all well advised policies for encouraging a security guard staff to be engaged with the museum, its visitors, and its collections. The opposite but lamentably common approach of subcontracting these functions to an outside professional security company with little or no interest in the content of the museum is not recommended.

- *Interior alarms:* The system should include alarms to alert security personnel if visitors approach exhibits too closely, as well as intrusion alarms that activate to any movement after hours, connected to the police station or security company in the same way as the perimeter alarms.
- *Display cases:* Case design is an issue not only for the exhibition designer, the conservator, and the curators, but also for the chief of security, who should be consulted when display cases are being planned. Their location should be examined to ensure that they do not block emergency escape routes and that they do not offer too easy an exit for a smash-and-grab thief. Proximity to fire exit doors is a serious concern. Polycarbonate glass or plastic should be used, and can be laminated to include clear ultra-violet light filters. Small, freestanding cases should be avoided; by preference display cases should be substantial and well anchored to the floor or wall, and their locks should be tamper-proof. Sliding glass panels are ill advised, since they are difficult to protect from intrusion; lockable access panels should be hinged, preferably horizontally, with nonremovable pins. Corners and joints should be tight. Display materials, in cases or without, should be fire resistant; the security department (as well as conservators) should routinely test any new materials proposed. Works of art, artifacts, or specimens should be discreetly but securely fastened within the case; the Asian Art Museum of San Francisco has gone much further in developing support systems to protect its collections from earthquake, both in display cases and in storage.
- *Security screws:* Pictures are sometimes suspended by chains or rods from hanging rails, with the security concern being to anchor both the chain or rod and the point of attachment of the picture to the chain or rod. Far preferable—and often required by lenders—are security screws, which pin a "fishplate" to the wall behind the picture and to its stretcher (rather than the frame). Security screws can be turned only by specially fitted screwdrivers, more complex than the usual slots or squares. Unfortunately the best-equipped of thieves stock a wide selection of security screwdrivers, so the security screw is not foolproof, but it is a substantial deterrent, since circumventing a security screw takes a considerable period of time unobserved.

Three "concentric circles" form three levels of security for the building as a whole, which incorporate the security levels described above for exhibition galleries and collection storage:

- Outer Level 1: comprising the perimeter, exterior lighting, locks, the intrusion alarm system, and interior-space surveillance of public zones A and B, most of which is inactive during public hours and in use only when the museum is closed;

- Median Level 2: comprising the nonpublic noncollection zone D and some nonpublic collection work areas (zone C), which should always be alarmed when the museum is closed, and may be alarmed during public but nonworking hours;
- Inner Level 3: comprising nonpublic collection zone C areas, such as collection storage rooms, which are always protected by alarms that can be deactivated only by authorized personnel or on their instruction. Security personnel ordinarily should control access to these spaces and maintain a log of all entrances and exits to these rooms.

Fire safety presents another range of concerns that must be addressed by the museum's security policy. The world over, fire presents the most serious threat to museums, not only in those housed in historic wooden structures but in many more recent structures as well. Although theft or vandalism may remove or damage specific items, fire can ravage whole collections, and may destroy them completely.

Smoke detectors are the preferred means of detection of fire, except in kitchens where heat detectors should be used. Ionization, photoelectric, or projected beam photoelectric smoke detectors may be used.

Sprinklers used to be resisted by museum managers, due to the risk of water damage, but widespread experience with fire response times, along with technical advances in sprinkler design, have rendered such fears outmoded, especially when compared with the very real destruction that even a few seconds' fire can cause. Individual-action on-off sprinkler heads (that turn off when the heat level drops), with copper, thermoplastic, or internally galvanized iron pipes and water cleaned to potable or boiler water standards, should be specified. Dry pipe sprinklers, although commonly found in museums, are actually problematic due to the delayed reaction time and the risk of corrosion products being spewed out with the water when activated; however, some lenders may not allow their objects to be displayed under water in pipes, so that if the preferable wet pipe sprinklers are used (with the foregoing specifications) a supervised valve may be needed on the pipe serving the temporary exhibition gallery so that the pipe may be drained during the period of the loan if that is allowed by local fire officials. Mist sprinklers are now being authorized for heritage buildings (such as those of the State of New York) and offer a positive alternative, since their fine mist suppresses flames yet does not have the negative effects of a deluge.

Halon systems and halon fire extinguishers are no longer legal in many jurisdictions, for environmental reasons. The best remaining options for fire extinguishers appear to be a combination of pressurised water (for nonelectrical fires) and CO_2. All staff should be regularly (at least annually) tested in their ability to utilize the museum's fire extinguishers, and the tags signifying that extinguishers have been successfully tested should be examined regularly (at least quarterly) for the dated initials of authorized inspectors.

Museum facility planning should include provision for *firewalls* (two hours for collection zones, to code elsewhere), doors to match these *fire ratings*, and *fire compartmentalization*, especially in collection storage. This means that large storage rooms should be compartmentalised by firewalls at regular intervals, rather than designed as one continuous area—a practice that may facilitate provision of separate storage rooms for each medium, with environmental control set points adjusted accordingly. Atriums and stairwells are danger areas, especially where they must be retained as an authentic feature of a historic building; they usually require enclosure on the landings, with fire doors for access. Renovation projects should be utilized by the chief of security as opportunities for provision of additional fire walls or doors, and museum facilities planners should include security consultation as part of the planning process.

There is an inherent conflict between two aspects of security—the desire to control egress from an area, and the need to provide fire or other emergency exits. The latter requirement usually dictates panic hardware ("break bars") on fire doors that must allow the user to access the outdoors directly. Yet these fire exits may provide a thief a convenient exit from a gallery, sometimes directly to a parking lot. All fire exits should be audibly alarmed, and in some jurisdictions delays of some seconds are permitted on lower-level access doors allowing egress from fire escape stairwells. The chief of security needs to meet with fire and police officials, and to balance fire safety requirements against the museum's concern to prevent theft.

Finally, it should be noted that good security depends on good housekeeping. Good cleaning and maintenance procedures, good signage (including "No Smoking" and a discreet but firm "Do Not Touch" for open exhibits), sound preventive conservation practices, and an alert and informed staff of guards will contribute to both the appearance and the reality of improved security for the collection and enhanced safety for visitors.

3.5   FINANCIAL MANAGEMENT

As the organization chart developed in chapter 2 and the job descriptions provided in the appendix to this book indicate, the administration division of a museum is responsible for a wide range of functions, including financial management, which is the subject of this final section.

For museums operated by independent not-for-profit associations, financial management has always been a central concern. In the past few decades, with governments around the world emphasising increased self-reliance, even for museums that are wholly integrated with their own line departments, ensuring the financial well-being of the museum has become a major responsibility for museum management. The status of the Louvre, for example, has been completely transformed in the past two decades, so that today it is responsible for its funding for both operations and capital projects. The job descriptions and qualifications of museum directors increasingly focus on their capability to manage the finances of the institution, especially their fund-raising abilities.

For museum directors especially, the challenge is to provide for the institution's financial needs while maintaining its creativity and scholarship. Finance officers should view their positions as facilitating research and public service, while development officers should see their roles as providing the means for building the collection and furnishing the facilities for people to enjoy and learn from it. As long as the mission of the museum is kept in view, financial management should aim to support it. Directors and trustees must ensure that the mission is paramount and that the museum's financial arrangements support it, not the other way around. For this reason, this section on financial management follows all others, rather than preceding them. The appearance of losing sight of these priorities was what disturbed many people about the famous Victoria and Albert Museum advertisement of some years ago, "An ace caf', with a rather nice museum attached."

This section begins with a consideration of the annual cycle of drafting and monitoring museum budgets (3.5.1) as the primary method of financial control. Revenue generation (3.5.2) follows, being the most urgent requirement for many museums today, although controlling expenditures (3.5.3) can also be critically important. Risk management (3.5.4), adequately insuring the museum's assets, is the indispensable method of protecting the institution against loss, while financial planning and development (3.5.5) can ensure a positive future in the long term.

3.5.1 Budgets

A budget is a plan with money attached. An annual budget attaches monetary values to the year's goals, which are the quantified short-term applications to the budget year of the museum's longer-range qualitative objectives. There should be a discernible continuity from the goals and objectives of the museum's long-range strategic plan through the objectives of this year's action plan to the amounts allocated in this year's budget. In recommending the budget to the museum's governing body, the director should be able to demonstrate this continuity.

Specifically the director should point to *variances*, the fluctuations in allocations due to the influence of the museum's current action plan goals. Some governments require "*zero-base budgeting*," which requires museum managers within their line departments to justify each allocation in relation to the programs it makes possible, as if it had no history. In most museums, however, many allocations are assumed to continue because those functions must be sustained, and it is only the variances—the increases or reductions in these amounts—that are of interest.

In practice, budgeting is usually done departmentally, but budgets may also be organized by program, objective, or function:

- The *departmental* approach is the most common: each department is asked to review its past year's allocations, adjust for current objectives and tasks, and recommend next year's figures.
- Alternatively or additionally, budgeting can be by *program*: each department identifies the programs or services it is providing and allocates funds to each in accordance with the priority or emphasis given to that activity in the current year's plans.
- Budgeting by *objective* can be a useful review process, in which fluctuations in the current year's proposed allocations are evaluated in relation to the objectives identified in the museum's strategic plan and the outcomes they are intended to achieve.
- *Goals* of the current action plan should be reflected in the fluctuations of allocations; checking budget changes against agreed goals or longer-range objectives should be a part of every budgeting process.
- It is also useful to review allocations in terms of the fundamental museum *functions* (as illustrated by the triangle of essential museum functions in fig. 1.2). How much of the museum's financial resources is dedicated to collecting (the acquisitions budget)? How much to documentation, preservation, research, display, or interpretation? How much is going to administration? The answers can be revealing, and can point to a need for changes in the balance of allocations, in view of the museum's mission and strategic plan.

Museums may budget for various funds and purposes:

- operating budget: the annual revenue and expenditure for the museum's collection care, public activities program, and operation of its site and building;
- acquisition funds: the amount retained for purchasing objects for the collection, or for the expenses associated with acquisitions;
- endowment funds: usually donated moneys that are invested, with all or only a portion of the interest earned being spent, either on operations (in the case of "unrestricted funds") or for specific purposes such as acquisitions, exhibitions, or a lecture series ("restricted funds");

- capital budget: an amount retained for planned development of the museum's site or buildings, such as renovation, relocation, new construction or exhibition renewal;
- grant projects: government or foundation grants often require separate accounting of the projects their contribution is meant to support;
- reserves: amounts retained for contingencies, or for future development projects.

The operating budget should be the end result of an annual budgeting process. This should be a constant cycle, with the progression to next year's budget beginning immediately after this year's has been approved. Figure 3.9 suggests a year-round approach to budget generation by quarter:

Figure 3.9. The Budget Cycle

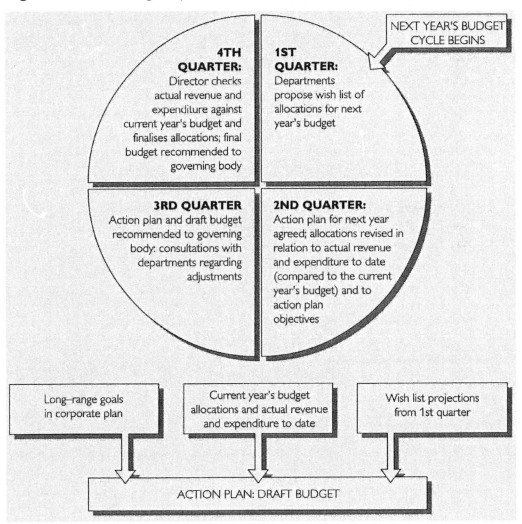

The annual budget cycle proceeds in the following way.

First Quarter: During the first three months after the passage of the previous year's budget, it is important to encourage those responsible for each department to "dream anew"—to project a wish list of all desirable (but reasonable) programs and activities that the museum should undertake, in order that new ideas and projects may be given full consideration. The director and the finance officer should be concerned to *stimulate creativity* and to resist cynicism during this phase. Although many of the ideas and projects may not be realized in the immediate future, it is vital that the museum's management should be challenged by new ideas, taking full account of them before budget limitations are addressed.

These "blue sky" budgets should not, however, be irresponsible: each activity or project should be costed with reasonable order-of-magnitude estimates, with all attendant revenues projected; if possible, projects should be phased so that consideration can be given to entering into at least the first phase of projects, programs, or activities that are subsequently approved. It is also valuable to keep these projections ready to respond to grant-aid opportunities as they arise; many of the projects may be suitable for grant funding.

Second Quarter: During the second three-month period the director, the finance officer, the relevant divisional deputy director, and the officer responsible for each department should meet to develop next year's action plan. The *action plan*, as shown in figure 3.9, aims to reconcile the input from three documents:

- the long-range qualitative objectives relevant to this department in the museum's corporate plan;
- the current year's budget allocations for both revenue and expenditures compared with actual figures to date; and
- each department's "blue sky" budget proposals of the first quarter.

Variances from last year's allocations (increases or reductions) should be drafted to reflect the agreed action plan for that department.

Third Quarter: During the following three-month period it is the responsibility of the finance officer and the director to recommend the action plan and its accompanying budget implications to the museum's governing body, generally through the finance committee. The governing level of the museum's administration or the trustees should review this draft budget and action plan in relation to the museum's long-range interests and should ensure that the museum's mission and all of its functions are being adequately served. For example, an overcommitment to exhibitions or other public activities might reflect a director's priorities, but the interests of the institution may require more balanced funding of research or collection care. Another consideration is the extent to which revenue-generating activities may not only pay for themselves, but may also generate funds that can be dedicated to other functions, thereby justifying allocations to revenue-generating activities.

The governing body or the trustees have the responsibility to raise additional money to fill the gap between income and expenditures if they agree with the recommendations of the director that the expenditures are required to fulfil the museum's mission and goals in the time period under consideration. Following on the governing body's reaction to the proposed action plan and draft budget, the director and the finance officer should return to the departmental level, and work out the requisite adjustments to the departmental allocations.

Fourth Quarter: The finance officer should report to the director on the comparison of actual revenues and expenditures to the expiring fiscal year's budget figures after three quarters (nine months) of activity, and both should issue any instructions requisite to keeping the museum on budget or as close to it as possible. The director should then determine the final allocations for the coming year's budget, making adjustments to the action plan and its draft budget in view of anticipated shortfalls or overages, and return to the governing body for approval of the final budget.

Monitoring the current year's actual revenues and expenditures in relation to budget allocations is important both as a means of control within the present year and as a vital part of the preparation of the coming year's budget. Figures should be refined in accuracy as the budget cycle proceeds, and as one cycle succeeds another, reflecting the museum's experience of the current year's figures and any deficits or overages to be carried forward. As soon as the budget is approved, of course, it becomes the subject of that ongoing monitoring, as the next budget preparation cycle begins.

3.5.2 Revenue Generation

Many museum administrations used to be considered, and used to consider themselves, primarily as cost centers, expending government funds to provide public services. Although a few in some parts of the world remain in this position (not always comfortably), a very large number of museums in the past few decades have been obliged—or have wished to—focus much more on their potential to generate nongovernmental revenue. This section on revenue generation therefore precedes the consideration of operating expenses that follows.

In recent years much attention has been paid to museums' capacity for generating funds from their operations. This section examines the potential of earned revenue (3.5.2.1), but it also considers the proportionately far more important subject of contributed funds (3.5.2.2) and ends with a brief discussion of the management of fund-raising campaigns (3.5.2.3).

REVENUE GENERATION AND COST CONTROL AT THE CANADIAN MUSEUM OF CIVILIZATION
By David Loye

The Canadian Museum of Civilization Corporation is what Canadians call a "crown corporation." The museum corporation, established in 1990, fulfills a unique national role in:

- collecting and preserving key aspects of Canada's social, military, and human history;
- expanding knowledge through research focused on singular artifacts, communities, personalities, and sites;
- transmitting knowledge across Canada and the world through exhibitions, a major website, publications, shared materials, and special events.

The museum corporation is responsible for the management of Canada's national museum of human history, the Canadian Museum of Civilization (CMC), as well as the Canadian War Museum, the national museum of military history. Together, the two museums attract close to 1.8 million people a year, making them the most visited museums in Canada. About one half of those visitors are Canadians from outside the National Capital Region, where the two museums are located (the War Museum is in Ottawa, Canada's capital, while the CMC is across the Ottawa River in Gatineau). A further 25 percent of these visitors are from outside Canada, thus enhancing tourism and Canada's image in the world.

The annual cost of operating the museum corporation is approximately Can$77 million, consisting of $60 million in annual federal government support, with the remaining $17 million, or 22 percent, derived from self-generated revenues.

A study conducted in 2007 for the Department of Canadian Heritage by Lord Cultural Resources, titled "Assessment of Revenue Generation Capacity of the National Museums of Canada," provided a detailed review and assessment of all Canadian national museum revenues. The study concluded that Canada's national museums derive the same general range of earned and contributed income combined relative to national museums in other countries. The CMC and the War Museum combined had the highest earned revenues of any Canadian national museum, and covered the highest percentage of relevant operating costs. The CMC and the War Museum also exceeded the benchmark established by comparing major international museums.

Figure 3.10.

CANADIAN MUSEUM OF CIVILIZATION, GATINEAU

Although revenues now cover over 20 percent of total museum spending, this has not always been the case. In 1990–1991, the first year of the newly instituted museum corporation, revenues were Can$4.2 million and represented just over 5 percent of the costs of running the two museums. Revenues in the early 1990s were derived mainly from the IMAX theater, boutiques, and general admission. Revenues in 2006–2007 totaled Can$17 million and were derived from increasing the traditional sources noted above, as well as developing new areas that contribute to the increase in overall revenue performance.

New revenue streams have been developed for facility rentals and related catering services, mobile boutique kiosks, parking, sponsorships, and affinity membership programs. In addition to these new revenue streams, traditional areas, such as general admission, cafeteria, boutiques, and IMAX are subject to ongoing reviews of pricing and marketing approaches. These ongoing reviews by management take into account significant visitor feedback and result in ensuring that competitive market pricing is in place and that opportunities are seized upon as they arise.

In 2007–2008 the museum corporation revamped its overall admission pricing model and introduced a "mix and save" approach. The primary objectives of the new model are to streamline an overly complicated pricing model, introduce incentives for the visitor to buy and select more museum programs, create more flexibility in choices, and increase the sales of combination packages between the corporation's two museum sites.

Early results from this new model have shown an increase in combination purchases that include the two museum sites and reduced box office wait times resulting from a pricing model that is easier to understand. However, the up-sell model also reduced the overall average ticket price to the IMAX theater, resulting in lower gross margins. As a result, the museum introduced an additional fee for IMAX combinations while maintaining the original "mix and save" concept. This change highlights the importance of continually reviewing commercial performance and adjusting strategies to respond to market or financial conditions.

While revenue performance has played a critical role in enabling the museums to maintain and fund their programs since the early 1990s, so has expenditure containment. Museum expenditures have grown at less than the rate of inflation, while the museum now offers more permanent collection exhibition space than ever before. In the early 1990s, the total cost of running the museums, including building costs and property taxes, was estimated at approximately Can$65 million. For 2007–2008, the total cost is estimated at Can$77 million, an increase of $12 million, or 18 percent, over almost eighteen years, while the consumer price index for this region rose by 46 percent over the same period of time. It should be noted that the museum corporation also constructed a new facility for the Canadian War Museum, which opened in 2005.

To achieve effective expenditure management, the museum corporation has implemented a detailed annual budget process that follows the "zero-base" approach: every activity must justify its base as part of a three-year planning horizon. Faced with significant financial constraints and the requirement to fund increases to fixed building costs from new revenues or existing government funding, the museum has worked diligently to reduce expenses, increase efficiencies, and where necessary reallocate resources. These reallocations have included staff layoffs; outsourcing of functions; and, as noted earlier, the increase of revenues to support programs.

The museum also participates in benchmarking exercises to validate its internal operations in several key areas. These exercises are critical to identifying areas for improvement and go hand in hand with the management approach of ongoing reviews of revenue opportunities. Two key areas that are benchmarked on a regular basis are facility management and information technology (IT). These two areas account for significant museum spending and are critical to the operation of the corporation. Both areas rely heavily on outsourcing, and the museum maintains very positive relationships with key private sector companies that are primarily responsible for many of the day-to-day operations of these two areas. Results from the annual International Association of Museum Facility Administrators (IAMFA) benchmark exercise and the museum's commissioned study of IT indicate that the museum ranks near the top of its peer groups in these two critical areas.

The Canadian Museum of Civilization Corporation has maintained its market leading position for close to two decades. This corporation's ability to deliver its mandate and attract ever increasing numbers of visitors to its two sites are a result of having the management processes and approach to grow the business, while keeping a constant eye on the bottom line.

3.5.2.1 Earned Revenue

Earned revenue refers to the museum's capacity to generate revenue from its operations, in contrast with government funding, endowments, sponsorship, or donations, all of which may be termed *contributed revenue*. Earned revenue includes the following sources of funding, most of which derive from services to visitors, which is why these categories of revenue are often referred to as visitor-generated revenue:

- admissions;
- retail sales;
- food services;
- memberships;
- rentals;
- films, performances, and special events;
- educational programs;
- publications and media; and
- contracted services.

3.5.2.1.1 Admissions

Charging for admission to public museums has been and remains an issue of controversy. The argument put by opponents to charging is that museums are a public service and should be financed by taxes; advocates of charging observe that the quality of museum service often improves when staff and visitors know that admission is being charged, and that relatively affluent tourists who often account for half of museum visitors do not contribute to the cost of free museums, which are borne by the taxes imposed on residents of their host communities. The imposition of admission charges on formerly free museums generally results in an immediate decline in attendance of approximately one-third, which is sometimes (but by no means always) recovered over the following five to ten years, depending on the extent to which the museum follows up their introduction of charges with exhibitions and other programming of wider appeal, enhanced marketing and other strategies to boost attendance levels. Conversely, the experience of going free after having had admission charges has resulted in attendance increases of 50 percent or more in both Britain and America, as noted in Kate Markert's case study 3.11 of the Walters Art Museum experience in this section.

There has been much research and debate on the impact of charging on the demographic characteristics of visitors, with some studies demonstrating that low-income and minority visitors value the visit more when there is a charge; and others indicating the opposite—that these populations attend less when they hear that there is a charge. There are so many variables in the museum attendance equation that it is impossible to isolate the admission charge and its impact on various market segments. One such variable is the type of museum: many art museums have had greater difficulty than other museum types in attracting children and persons in lower education and income categories; accordingly it is more common for art museums to offer free admission overall or to children, or at least to offer free admission days. Science museums tend to be of wider appeal to a variety of market segments and thus are less likely to be motivated to offer free admission.

Free or low-cost admission in and of itself does not guarantee broad public participation in the museum—therefore *both* charging and noncharging museums must examine how they communicate with the public, whether they are welcoming to the diversity of people in the community, and what their programs have to offer to their residents and tourists. Further, since there are many ways to charge and many ways not to charge—as will be seen—what is needed is an *admission strategy* appropriate to the specific situation of each museum.

It is sometimes said that admission revenues do not justify the cost of collecting them, but most museums that charge find that 10–20 percent of their total net revenue can be derived from this source. Admission rates must be appropriately comparable to those for other attractions in the area, and are usually scaled for adults, seniors, children, families, and groups. There are numerous ways to reduce the cost for frequent visitors such as offering free entry to members or free or discounted entry for everyone on particular days or evenings.

Some museums have been concerned that offering a free admission day in order to increase diversity of visitation encourages people who could easily afford the cost of admission to wait for the free day. An alternative approach, which may be equally or even more effective in attracting attendance from cultural minorities and low-income groups is to extend invitations offering free or reduced admission through these groups' own community and social organizations, religious institutions, or schools. This approach avoids offering free admission to those who can easily afford to pay, and helps to build partnerships between the museum and the community or social organizations. Sponsorships may also be sought to compensate the museum for the lost income. Whatever approach is used, it is preferable that the free admission tickets should not look different from those that are charged, in order to avoid stigmatizing those who arrive with the free tickets.

In 2001 Britain's Labour government, committed to optimizing access to museums for all through free admission to the permanent collection, agreed to a funding formula with the national museums to compensate them for the loss of revenue and the cost of serving greater numbers. The result has been a 50 percent increase in attendance at the national museums, although the diversity of that increased audience continues to depend on the individual museum's programs and their marketing of them. In 2006 the Baltimore Museum of Art and the Walters Art Museum in the same city introduced free admission, as reported by Walters' associate director, Kate Markert, in her case study 3.11 in this chapter. Overall the Baltimore experience has been successful, suggesting that a similar approach would work elsewhere, as long as government officials are supportive enough to augment government funding sources to offset the loss of admissions revenue.

Another admission strategy is to charge only for special exhibitions and events, but to offer free admission to the exhibition of the permanent collection. This has proven successful in many jurisdictions around the world, both in maintaining revenue and in providing a free basic level of museum service to both tourists and residents. In some circumstances, this strategy may result in higher levels of income from the retail shop, programs, and food services as a result of higher attendance levels than if there were a general admission charge and fewer visitors. Kate Markert comments on the challenges and the effects of this strategy in her case study in this chapter on the introduction of free admission with charged admission for special exhibitions at Baltimore's museums.

Museums in major metropolitan areas with a large attendance base of over 1 million visits have been successful in introducing a "discretionary admission charge," by which is meant that there is a "recommended" admission charge but visitors may pay what they wish so long as they pay something. This approach may be distinguished from a truly "voluntary admission charge," where a donation box is located near entrances and exits but may be ignored if the visitor so chooses.

Museums charging admission may benefit from the application of computers to ticketing. The combination of such software programs with visitors using charge cards for ticket purchases has resulted in a growth of mailing lists of patrons of those museums that retain the names and addresses of ticket purchasers. Membership recruitment programs (by mail or by telephone) may be targeted at these visitors. These ticketing records can also be used to facilitate visitor surveys, which may be based on postal code prefixes cross-referenced to demographic data. Of course, any such usage must comply with data protection laws and should also be consistent with the museum's code of ethics, reflecting the museum's commitment to respect its visitors' privacy.

GOING FREE
The Experience of Baltimore's Museums
By Kate Markert

Baltimore enjoys the good fortune of having two major art museums with wonderfully complementary permanent collections:

- The Baltimore Museum of Art, well known for its Cone Collection of nineteenth-century and early modern art and its great contemporary, American decorative, and African and Oceanic art collections;
- The Walters Art Museum, with strengths in Ancient Egyptian, Greek, and Roman art, Medieval art, European decorative arts, Asian art, illuminated manuscripts, and old-master paintings.

Together, these museums form one of the great encyclopedic repositories of the entire history of world art in the United States.

The two institutions have struggled with their location in a city whose population has been declining over the past few decades. The flight of the middle class from the city, failing schools, drugs, and crime all contribute to the problems of aging American cities and the erosion of the potential local audience base.

The Strategy

In early 2005, the two museums banded together to approach the City of Baltimore and adjacent Baltimore County for three years of support for going free—offering free admission to their visitors. These funds would cover lost admissions revenue, allow for a promotional budget to announce the initiative, and fill in for lost membership revenue, an inevitable by-product of going free, as other museums, such as the Cincinnati Art Museum (carefully studied as the closest comparable) had experienced. It was a time of surplus government budgets (due to higher than expected real estate transfer taxes primarily, a positive outcome of the housing bubble of that time) and an election year. The initiative was quickly adopted by Baltimore County Executive Jim Smith and then-mayor of Baltimore (later governor of Maryland) Martin O'Malley. Another local county executive, several foundations, and a corporation also contributed to this initial funding effort.

Museum advocates argued that making the two museums free would encourage many more locals to visit them—increasing both the number of attendees and the diversity of those visiting. Mayor O'Malley said in the

Figure 3.11. Free Admission Announcement

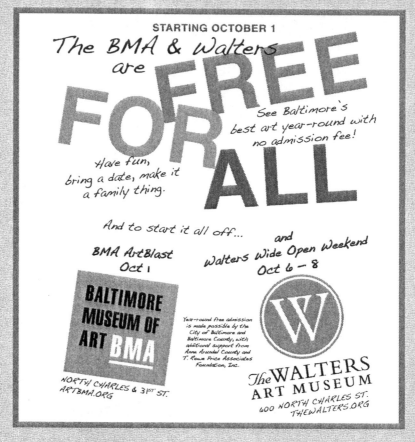

COURTESY OF LAPLACA COHEN ADVERTISING
KATE MARKERT

press release, "This significant investment will provide many more people with the opportunity to experience the beauty, creativity and significance of art in our lives." The initiative was also welcomed by the Baltimore Area Convention and Visitors Association as a way to differentiate Baltimore in the regional cultural tourism market, making the city more competitive with the many free national museums in nearby Washington, D.C. It was also seen as a way to broaden Baltimore's reputation as a creative and welcoming place to live. Baltimore County Executive Jim Smith called it "an investment in the future of the entire metropolitan area."

First Year Results

Results surprised even the most enthusiastic supporters of the initiative. In the initial proposal to the city and county governments, the museums projected a 15 percent increase in attendance, more first-time visitors, and greater audience diversity. Both museums experienced much greater total attendance, and even more diversity than was expected. Both also experienced losses in membership revenues, but not greater than had been predicted. And both experienced exuberant increases in philanthropic donations from upper-level members and major donors, some of whom even ensured that the initiative would continue with their endowment gifts.

The Walters Art Museum's 55 percent increase in overall yearly number of visitors (from 126,000 to 195,000) correlates to the 50 percent increase reported in Great Britain when their major museums dropped admission charges. Even more heartening was the dramatic increase in first-time visitors (46 percent) and family program participation (150 percent). Educators found themselves with five-, six-, and eightfold increases in uses of the museum's "Art Cart" and other educational materials. On weekends especially, the museum buzzed with the voices of families happily dragging "Discovery Quilts," puzzles, and games throughout the museum, talking about the treasures they found there. Repeat visits were encouraged through "passports" in which children could collect stamps indicating that they had completed activities in each of the many different museum collection areas.

Challenges

One of the biggest difficulties with free admission in a formerly charged admission environment is that it removes one of the major reasons for which people become members. The Walters saw its membership drop by 25 percent, stabilizing and starting to increase only when a special exhibition with an admission fee was added to the museum calendar. Museum staff worked to offer members other benefits—special member days, early admission into exhibitions, and discounts on programs and store merchandise—and that effort continues.

Another challenge is to require visitors to pay for special exhibitions, once they are accustomed to entering the rest of the museum at no charge. Attendance at both museums' first paid special exhibition after going free was disappointing. At the Walters, discounted special exhibition tickets on Fridays didn't bring the hoped-for increase in traffic. Another marketing challenge is to communicate that visiting the permanent collection is still free, even with a paid special exhibition.

Another misconception is that people who come in free will then spend more money in the museum store. That has *not* tended to be true, a trend borne out by other museums' experiences during free times. A notable exception for the Walters was the tremendous response to the Gee's Bend exhibition merchandise, a free exhibition of popular art that drew crowds buying everything from mugs to rugs.

The Future

Overall, the experience of going free has been enormously positive, with the increases in numbers of visitors and their diversity generally holding up as we advance into year two of the experiment. We have not seen a continued increase above the original jump from paid to free—but we have sustained a leveling of attendance at the higher attendance number. More marketing efforts need to continue to create an even greater awareness that the museums are free. Although there was a huge ($200,000) campaign in October 2006, encompassing bus ads, billboards, print, and events, the "free" message needs to be constantly reemphasized to bring in more new visitors.

The number of basic-level members is now almost completely dependent on the strength of the special exhibition schedule, although membership and marketing staffs continue to test various offers and strategies in addition to the obvious economic incentive provided by free entry into a popular ticketed and charged exhibition. The number of upper-level members at the Walters has grown about 10 percent, and is on track to continue growing in year two. These members are motivated by philanthropy and many wish to support the museum staying free.

Both museums wish to institutionalize being free, and have begun undertaking endowment campaigns to secure the financial wherewithal to support it beyond the three-year government grants that initiated the program. Success with the endowment campaigns is critical to the long-term viability of the museums continuing their free admission policy.

3.5.2.1.2 Retail Sales

While admission charges may remain debatable, little controversy attends the almost universal provision of museum retail shops. Visitor surveys in recent years indicate that growing numbers among the museum-going public expects a high-quality museum shop, and complain when they feel that the range and quality of stock, its presentation, or customer service are inadequate. The shop offers visitors an opportunity to take home a product that will remind them of their museum visit and, if it is a book, catalog, reproduction, poster, CD, or DVD, will provide further opportunity for study and entertainment after the museum visit: therefore the quality and educational value of the retail offerings should be consistent with the mission and goals of the museum.

Smaller museums make their shops cost-effective by combining volunteer retail clerks with paid retail managers. Some larger institutions, such as the Victoria and Albert Museum, are not only totally professional in the operation of their shops, but have also been successful in extending their profitable on-site operations into mail-order sales via catalogs and a parcel delivery service around the world. The V&A has also copyrighted patterns from its collection (such as William Morris wallpaper), and licensed them for reproduction. In the past decade online sales have contributed significant additional income to museum retail receipts.

To reduce crowding and improve service, it is sometimes worthwhile to separate children's shops and bookshops from the general retail offerings. Prices in all shops may range from relatively expensive items for credit-card purchase to low-cost souvenirs, including some items intended for purchase by children—or their grandparents. Markup may be only 40 percent for books or museum postcards, but is usually 100 percent or may be even more for other items.

Spending per visitor varies widely by the size of the shop and the type of museum. A larger shop usually results in higher sales per visitor but often in lower sales per square foot or square meter; but a shop that is too small in a well-attended museum will actually result in lower revenue at the busiest times because visitors will perceive it to be too crowded and so will avoid it. Sales at art museums tend to be far more substantial than at most science or children's museums. Revenues in all museum types can be much higher if the stock is well matched to the market and the attraction (preferably changed for each major temporary exhibition), and if the shop is well located and advertised.

Location is critical to museum shops, as in all retailing. Facility planning should provide for a shop that is visible to visitors entering the museum and *inescapable* to those leaving. If possible, the shop should also be visible to passers-by, and accessible to shoppers who are not even visiting the museum (if this can be arranged while respecting museum security). The ideal museum shop is positioned so that it can open and close independently of the museum, maintaining additional hours to those of the museum if necessary in order to meet market demand—especially at holiday shopping seasons.

Most museum shops combine a site-specific line of publications, media products, reproductions, and souvenirs with a more generic stock of books, toys, jewelry, crafts and other gifts that are more or less unique in that community, and may provide an important sales outlet for local artists or artisans. The production of special lines of merchandise for major exhibitions (so-called blockbusters) is a means of both increasing retail revenues and promoting the exhibition. All new stock should be submitted to curators for approval, on aesthetic as well as intellectual grounds, and to the marketing manager for the perspective of likely appeal to various market segments. The curators and the director should approve all reproductions or replicas made of objects in the collection.

Some museum shops have made themselves far more effective by changing their stock significantly for each temporary exhibition, keeping the stock relevant to the current exhibitions. To do so, of course, the retail manager must be a part of the exhibition planning process. Even more common now are shops specific to temporary exhibitions, usually located immediately at the end of the temporary exhibition galleries. Specialized shops dedicated to particular permanent collection exhibitions, such as the one adjacent to the U-boat exhibition gallery at the Chicago Museum of Science and Industry, have also become commonly accepted practice in many museums. New museums or expansions are now designed with provision for such ancillary retail spaces.

Picture rentals, usually operated by volunteers but directed by museum staff, are often combined with museum shops or may be adjacent to them. They serve both artists and the public by circulating works of art on monthly rental to homes and offices, often with option to buy.

"*Production for sale*" by museum demonstrators on industrial heritage properties—such as ceramics produced at a historic pottery—can be an attractive addition to interpretation at a living-history site, but attempts to combine it with wider distribution and truly industrial levels of production have proven problematic. The museum's priority to interpret the heritage slows production, in most cases to a pace that is not cost-effective in industrial terms.

With a few such exceptions, most museum shop initiatives have proven successful, so that retail sales remain one of the most promising of the museum's revenue options. Cost of sales is generally in the range of 50–60 percent of total sales, leaving a gross margin of 40–50 percent. Taking staffing and other overhead into account leaves a net profit of 10–20 percent of gross sales. Gift shop operations often contribute 5–10 percent of total museum revenues. Museums are increasingly extending their retail operations, with varying degrees of success, through such means as:

- catalog sales;
- satellite shops (in other cities or countries as well as elsewhere in the same city, often in airports);
- placement of the museum product line in other museum shops and in suitable commercial outlets;
- sales on television shopping channels; and
- online sales, a major growth area.

Most museums continue to operate their shops directly, in order to maximize income, maintain quality control, and provide an individually different retail character associated with their institution. However, in recent years a number of agencies have developed to operate museum retail shops. These agencies are able to achieve cost savings by bulk ordering of stock and supplies, and they can service online and catalog orders directly, while undertaking to allow for the individual differentiation that is important to a successful museum shop specific to the character of its host institution. One such agency in the United States is paying a commission of 27 percent of gross sales to the institution involved—certainly as high an earning percentage as could be expected if the institution were operating its shop itself.

3.5.2.1.3 Food Services

Unlike shops, museum-operated cafeterias and restaurants generally do not produce high levels of income for the museum. The museum director and the food services manager must understand the objectives of the food service (visitor comfort, extending the length of stay) and attempt to ensure that it does not lose money (although many museum-operated food services do lose money when all relevant staffing and overhead costs are attributed to them).

While many museums operate their shops directly, most prefer to contract or "concession" food services, and to receive either a share of proceeds from the contractor (concessionaire) or a rental fee or both. The reason is that food service is a business type with a high rate of failure or bankruptcy, requiring a particular expertise and economies of scale that are generally not achievable in museums. Accordingly, many food service companies will bargain for a very low (or even no) rate of return to the museum, with the condition that they must be the exclusive or preferred caterers for special events and rentals in the museum.

Thus the contractors or concessionaires aim to achieve economies of scale by operating several food services throughout the building or the campus (if the museum is part of a larger cultural complex) and especially by catering for special events and rentals. This can be a satisfactory arrangement as long as the museum maintains a quality-control provision in the contract, whereby the museum may cancel the contract, after appropriate notice, if quality does not meet the museum's standards over a stated period of time. This is a crucial contract provision, since a poor or overpriced lunch or an unsatisfactory snack can outweigh an otherwise outstanding museum experience or event in the minds of many museum visitors and supporters. This quality control provision should address not only cooking, ambience, and customer service, but also nutrition and the use of natural food, as opposed to a strictly market-driven reliance on artificial and junk food. The contractor and the museum should agree in the contract on policy regarding the type of food to be offered.

Many food service contractors will aim to provide catering for rentals of museum facilities by outside agencies as well as for special events. However, the museum may be in a more flexible and accessible position for rentals if it allows outside caterers to bring in their own caterers for rental events. In most situations the museum offers the contractor's catering service as an option, possibly at a discount, but also allows those renting their facilities to bring in their own caterers if they prefer.

Design quality of the museum restaurant or cafe is important, especially if the museum opts to have the dining area themed to a period style. The contractors' compliance with the theme may extend to uniforms and should be maintained in detail if it is adopted at all, since visitors may judge the museum's authenticity by the consistency of theme in the cafe. However, authenticity and theme can be carried too far in museum food services: attempts to cook and serve food in historic settings are often problematic, due not only to concerns about the preservation of the heritage building and its furnishings, but also because of the need to use modern equipment to meet contemporary health and safety codes as well as customer expectations.

In museums with a high visitor footfall, either year-round or seasonally, reasonably quick food service in the main dining area without long waiting times is highly desirable. The Museum of Modern Art in New York has devised an ordering system that allows visitors to register their requests against a number at a counter, then go sit down with the number displayed, allowing service staff to bring them their meals. This results in a far more pleasant experience than a cafeteria queue.

Most smaller museums find that a good-quality cafe with a light-snack service, with or without a warming kitchen to heat precooked meals, is sufficient for their visitors and for after-hours rentals. Larger institutions may offer a full restaurant as well. Some very busy museums have evolved three levels of service—a franchised fast food service, a cafe for light refreshments, and a full-service dining room, with the latter two appropriately designed. The Metropolitan Museum of Art in New York often features live music in both its cafe and fine dining areas during its very successful evening hours.

As with the museum shop, the location of the museum cafe dramatically affects its profitability. Many art museums like to include a courtyard, where sculpture can be enjoyed by diners seated outdoors in temperate weather, or at least viewed from behind glass during the winter. More important commercially is a location that facilitates access after museum hours, if there is a market for that level of food service in that location. The museum's lavatories, or a separate set of washroom facilities for diners, must also be accessible if the cafe is to be open after the museum's public hours.

If a museum is located in a commercial area with convenient access to food services, it may choose not to invest its capital resources in a food service area but to develop admission policies that encourage visitors to use neighbouring restaurants and cafes and to reenter the museum as often as they wish on the day. Tickets and posters could reassure visitors that they can return as often as they like and provide a map of nearby food facilities. This is often helpful in establishing good relations with nearby restaurants and retailers and may help to justify needed governmental support, since the museum's policy promotes economic development and income from tax-paying private businesses. The nearby restaurants and their operators may then be encouraged to become corporate or individual members or sponsors.

The museum must also provide for its other food service needs:

- refreshments for exhibition openings and other special events;
- food services for a multipurpose hall or party room (especially if rentals are involved);
- a school lunch area for school groups; and
- light refreshments for the staffroom and the members' lounge.

As noted above, the first two of these activities may or may not be included in the food service contract.

In providing all of these services, care must be taken to ensure that food supplies and garbage circulation routes do not cross areas or use corridors in which the collection is normally held or moved. Refreshments for exhibition openings should not be served in the galleries themselves, but in an adjacent multipurpose function room that does not hold artifacts, specimens, or works of art—if such space is available; space planners should have such an area on their priority list if it is not.

Still another space provision that is often found advisable is a *school lunchroom* for school parties who bring boxed or bagged lunches. Many museums find that a dedicated space for this purpose frees their cafes from large numbers of low-spending school children whose drinks or other refreshments can be adequately served by automatic dispensing machines—although again the concern for nutrition and natural food should be borne in mind. The area allocated for school lunchrooms need not be left empty on weekends or evenings—instead, it can become a revenue earner through rentals for children's birthday parties.

3.5.2.1.4 Memberships

Museums that are line departments of governments, universities, or corporations usually do not offer memberships, although some have established "Friends" organizations. Memberships are most common among independent nonprofit institutions, where they serve more importantly as a means of organizing and retaining loyal support groups, in contrast to their function as a secondary source of revenue. Nevertheless, building and sustaining a strong membership sinks healthy roots into the community for any cultural institution, so that even governmental museums would do well to consider such a program.

In the not so distant past many museum directors expected membership fees to cover only the cost of providing services to members. Today many museums are becoming much more ambitious about their membership programs, both as a source of revenue and as a means of extending their support from the traditional base of high-income individuals to one that reflects the social, economic, and cultural diversity of the community.

There are two types of museum members:

- the relatively small number who join out of loyalty to the institution or interest in its specialization; and
- the much larger group who are attracted to join by the advertised advantages of belonging.

Membership of the latter group is built and maintained by offering tangible benefits geared to the interests of frequent visitors, supporters, and donors such as:

- free admission to museums that otherwise charge for admission;
- free or reduced admission to major charged exhibitions;
- discounts at the museum shop, for charged programs or for rentals;
- a regular newsletter;
- invitations to exhibition openings or other events;
- priority access to museum activities and programs; and
- special activities like travel expeditions guided by museum experts and behind-the-scenes tours of the museum by curators.

When the direct and indirect costs of these value-for-money memberships are calculated relative to the revenues earned, many museums find that they actually do not make money from them. Moreover, memberships motivated solely by value for money often end once the perceived benefits cease and are harder to retain. Children's museum memberships, for instance, are usually discontinued once the children in the family reach an age at which they are no longer interested in attending. Nevertheless, it may be very worthwhile for the museum to maintain such a membership program in order to demonstrate to funding governments or grant-giving foundations the extent of the museum's support base in the community.

For the first mentioned group, those who join in order to support the mission of the institution or to participate in its specialized field of interest, the membership is seen more as a form of philanthropy, civic pride, or personal interest, and these motivations should also be recognized and appreciated. Charges for upper-level memberships in this category may be higher, but the costs of serving these members, paradoxically, may be relatively lower.

In order to attract both types of motivation, categories of membership should include individual adults, couples, seniors, students, and families, but they should also provide several donor and corporate membership levels on a graduated scale of increasing support with attendant benefits or exclusivity privileges. Corporate membership at higher cost levels should include benefits (such as free or reduced admission) for the member company's employees, both as a means of creating a closer relationship with the corporation and as a means of expanding the museum's audience. Corporate or donor memberships at the higher cost levels may also rate invitations to exclusive events and reduced rental costs for corporate hospitality or opportunities to sponsor exhibitions or events.

3.5.2.1.5 Rentals

The rental of museum space—lobbies, theaters, meeting rooms, multipurpose party rooms, or even some galleries—to groups or companies who wish to associate their event or their image with the museum has become another source of self-generated revenue. This practice depends upon well-located multipurpose spaces for rental with access outside the museum's open hours as well as during visiting times, usually with movable chairs and tables stored nearby and with handy food services.

Since museums require a multipurpose space for exhibition openings, special events, or receptions, it becomes attractive for them to rent these rooms as well. For this reason this multipurpose space, which may also be called a function room or a party room, is usually equipped with video and projection facilities and with movable chairs and tables (kept in an adjacent storage room). It may also be adjacent to the museum's lobby or to the theater or auditorium facilities, which will usually have fixed seating and lecture room facilities; all of these facilities, individually or together, may be made available for rent. Food services and refreshments of adequate quality are crucial, as is access to the museum's public toilets. To enable it to be used for exhibition openings, the multipurpose function room or party room should also be adjacent to the galleries.

Some museums, especially those that are government supported, provide such facilities to specialist groups or community organizations primarily as a public service. However, the cost of security, and possibly other personnel, can be significant, so even where this is sometimes done there is considerable interest in converting this area into a revenue center. Once this is agreed, museums should not charge below the going rate for comparable rentals in their communities, since this would be effectively providing a subsidy and undercutting commercial operators in that area. On the contrary, museum rentals should be priced at the high end of the market, at "carriage trade" rates, since their competitive advantage is to offer the prestige of association with a leading cultural institution.

Corporate hospitality is a common source of customers for museum rentals. Especially for institutions with attractive gardens or heritage buildings and grounds on-site, weddings can be a lucrative source of revenue. Birthday parties are another valuable service, especially for children's museums, and can provide a good use of a school lunchroom as well. Of course the museum must provide clearly defined guidelines that respect its conservation and security principles in its rental contracts. The volume of rentals may need to be restrained if the museum is housed in a historic structure, where wear and tear on the fabric of the heritage resource itself is threatened by overuse.

3.5.2.1.6 Films, Performances and Special Events

Film programs and performing arts presentations, such as dance and theater, can complement a museum's exhibitions. Special events may be of any kind, including festivals during holidays. Some smaller museums welcome half their visitors on a dozen special-event days during the year, for which special admission rates may be charged.

The capacity to offer such attractions is, of course, dependent on the provision of adequate facilities. For many museums, a lecture auditorium with digital projection equipment is sufficient. Again, access after the museum galleries' opening hours is important to make such facilities cost-effective, including access to the museum's public toilets. If evening programs of two and a half hours or more are planned, it is best to provide the comfort of fixed seating to theater standard on a raked floor, rather than just movable chairs on a flat floor.

A significant planning decision affecting museum operations is whether the auditorium or lecture theater is also to be used for the museum's orientation program or other regular attractions. Trying to combine both functions in one space can lead to operational problems, so in many cases consideration must be given to providing two facilities—a specialized theater for the orientation or other regular presentations, and a separate lecture theater for film or lecture programs.

On the other hand, some museums have observed that their theaters are the most underutilized spaces in their buildings. Particularly today, when audiovisual programs are available in many media and formats accessible at home, it can be more difficult to attract an audience to a film series, for example. As a result, in some instances these spaces have been removed or have not been planned in from the beginning. This may be shortsighted, however, since usage of the theater may be simply a function of mounting attractive and successful programs.

Some larger museums and science centers have had success with large-screen theaters, such as IMAX or IMAX DOME. However, the "wow" effect of these big-screen showings has somewhat diminished over the past decade, partly as a result of the availability of large-screen home entertainment systems with surround sound and partly due to the adaptation of these formats to regular Hollywood films and the ubiquity of the large-screen theaters, especially since the digitalization of the formerly cumbersome film format.

Simulators have added another dimension to museum exhibitions, which can form yet another revenue center if an additional fee is charged for their use. This adaptation of technology (originally developed for aviation training) to the needs of the leisure industry has been successfully used in science centers and in military and aviation museums. Some try to make do with archival footage (such as a World War I dogfight), but the experience is vastly improved if the funds are raised to develop a new "dedicated" program directly related to the story line of the museum or the exhibition.

Still other entertainment formats are available to museums. Digitally programmed planetaria are attractive features at science centers and may be utilized for presenting laser shows with popular music as well. Multimedia theater programs, including such features as moving screens and computerized lighting effects, with or without live actors or animatronic figures, can be developed—sometimes called "4D theater" if they incorporate such special effects as misting, smoke, scents, and simulator chair movements. These are usually part of the "destination experience," specific to the story the museum has to tell.

An adaptation that is particularly relevant to history museums is the *object theater*, in which a few outstanding selections from the museum's collections, or replicas of them, appear as "stars" in the spotlight while a voice-over and/or projected imagery brings them to life. The effect is to concentrate the visitors' attention on the original artifacts or replicas that are featured and to communicate very effectively their meaning and relevance to the story the museum is telling. In addition to serving the museum's mission, this can be a far more effective way of communicating the essential meaning of some "star" artifacts, rather than featuring them in a display case.

Another option is live theater, which may be attractive for a summer season, when student actors are available, or as part of an employment grant scheme. Historic sites may opt for first-person interpretation, in which costumed actors play their parts in period and answer visitors' questions from within the time and space limitations of the historic setting.

If possible, in institutions where admission is charged all such feature attractions should be included in the general price of admission, but it may be preferable, depending on their scale and location, to present them as additional cost features, on offer at the original point of sale when the museum admission is purchased.

3.5.2.1.7 Education Programs

Education programs are usually considered as cost centers, especially if the museum provides guided tours free of charge to school parties as part of its mandate. In such cases, the museum often receives a government subsidy, foundation grant, or corporate sponsorship that is partially or wholly justified by its educational service.

However, educational services can also be revenue centers in themselves. Museums may contract with schools to provide a certain number of guided tours to designated classes or charge school parties a special admissions rate. Sometimes admission is free for school parties but charged when museum staff provide special programs or guided tours. Some museums have time-sharing agreements with school boards or local authorities, whereby school parties have exclusive access during certain hours (certain mornings, for instance) when the museum is not open to the general public; the museum provides guided tours or other educational programs during those hours, and receives a set fee from the school board or educational authority. Teacher training programs may also generate revenue: the Fort Worth Museum of Science and History, for instance, provides both initial and upgrade science classes for primary or secondary school teachers, paid for by state education funds. The same museum has also enjoyed over a half-century of success with its charged museum classes for very young preschool children.

Separate entrances with turnouts for school buses are often provided for school tours so that they may come and go safely without interfering with other visitors. Separate cloakrooms and a school lunchroom are also helpful, with the lunchroom doing double duty as a rentable space for birthday parties on weekends or evenings. Classrooms have become common and may be useful for orientation prior to a visit or for discussion afterward, as long as both museum staff and schoolteachers remember that the museum is the ideal setting for informal, not formal, education, and that the affective learning that the museum can provide can be experienced best in the galleries, not in a classroom. A hands-on learning lab equipped with computer workstations or lab equipment may be a better model for the educational space than a classroom.

Digitally illustrated adult education lectures or films may be a revenue source and are usually more successful in museums if they are offered as series or courses. Such series can also be a means of building membership or recruiting volunteers. An auditorium with digital projection facilities and a sound system is usually sufficient for this level of programming.

Some art museums have studios in which they can teach both fine and applied arts, ranging from informal weekend or evening sessions for families (often booked a year or two in advance) to more structured courses for every level of serious interest in the arts. Artists' demonstrations and artists in residence can be accommodated in the same studios, or the spaces can be made available for rent when not in use for classes.

Travel programs for members, with museum staff as expert guides, can also be revenue generators. The imagination and energy of management and staff are the only limitations to well-conceived educational programs—but they must be effectively target-marketed in order to be successful. In general, marketing to members as a priority serves to encourage visitors to join the museum and is more likely to achieve a break-even point of revenues balanced against costs.

3.5.2.1.8 Publications and Media

The publication of catalogs and books about museum collections and exhibitions has long been a source of revenue for museums, although in many instances print runs were not related to the foreseeable target market, resulting in massive, long-term storage requirements for unsold copies. The production of CDs or DVDs with images from the exhibition or collection today may supplement such publications with more sophisticated media that can reach a worldwide audience at competitive prices.

The development of such media has put a premium on the museum's control of the imagery of its collection—an issue that is particularly important for art museums. Although cash-poor museums are naturally tempted to hand over to others the development of multimedia services in return for immediate financial gain, considerations of control over subsequent usage of the imagery, along with copyright provisions, may lead museum directors to be cautious about leasing rights to digitized images of objects in their collections, while remaining positive about extending their images and information to new and much larger audiences through these media. The answer is a *digital asset management* program that documents and makes available a wide range of images and associated text, drawing on most museums' image banks. Such a program is relevant not only to art museums but to science and history institutions as well; a botanical garden, for instance, is liable to have a huge stock of floral images that may be invaluable as a resource for magazine and book publishers or advertising directors if the museum can provide access to them in an organized way.

Charging for the use of museum sites, buildings, or collections in film, television, or advertising is another revenue source that has multiplied in frequency and value in recent years. Museums need policies that set differential rates for educational films, entertainment, or advertising. These should take into consideration not only rights to the imagery and safeguards concerning ethical uses of it, but also the real costs to the museums of providing access to the filmmakers, most of whom will need to work in the museum when it is closed, often through the night.

3.5.2.1.9 Contracted Services

Museums themselves may undertake contracts to provide research or technical services to other museums, to government agencies, or to the private sector. Some are mandated to provide archaeological services within their geographical areas, while natural history curators may identify pests (or, in Western Australia, snakes) for appropriate regional agencies or municipalities.

Museum conservation departments, in individual institutions or within regional museum services, have attempted to offer conservation services on contract to other museums and to private collectors. These have sometimes been moderately successful, although they have often proven to be more problematic than the optimism of their initial business plans would suggest. The type of equipment, personnel, and practice required for such a regional service is likely to be quite different from what the conservation department normally provides.

One difficulty with all such contracts is that they divert time and attention away from museum priorities toward the imperatives of the revenue-generating contract. Another can be conflict with the private sector, which may complain of unfair competition from a partially (or wholly) subsidised museum staff. Such contracts are therefore best developed in consultation with the private sector, with publicly funded museum management aiming to provide services that do not duplicate private sector capability or impinge on commercial enterprises. It is then more crucial than ever for the museum to conduct a market analysis and draw up a business plan before embarking on the provision of such a service.

Another more fundamental challenge to museum management in the provision of such services under contract is to preserve the spirit of shared scholarship and freedom of access to information that has always been a hallmark of museums. Even more important than the preservation of collections as museums' raison d'être is the provision to the public of information about them. As museum managers strive to develop more revenue sources by tendering for contracts for research or other services, it is important that they ensure that academic freedom of information about the collection is not forfeited in the process.

3.5.2.2 Contributed Revenue

Contributed revenue is given by others in support of the museum's mission. Therefore, despite the current emphasis on earned revenue, contributed revenue remains of the utmost importance, including:

- government funding;
- grants;
- endowments;
- sponsorship; and
- donations.

Having considered the many options for earned revenue in subsections 3.5.2.1.1–9, we now turn to these five sources of contributed revenue, which remain more important on the balance sheets of most museums around the world.

3.5.2.2.1 Government Funding

Governments at all levels contribute to the financial support of museums for a wide variety of reasons, but principally because they provide four main services:

1. Preservation of the collective heritage: Any community of people, whether they constitute a nation, a state, a province, a county, or a municipality, inherits a *natural heritage*—the land, air, and waters they inhabit or use— and a *cultural heritage*—the archaeology and history of their ancestors and those who came before their ancestors in the place or wherever their history has taken them. They are constantly adding to their cultural heritage, as well as affecting their natural heritage. If they are or have become multicultural populations, the collective heritage will be accordingly diverse. Museums are charged with the preservation of the entire collective heritage,

past and present, natural and cultural. Government subsidy is justified primarily by museums' fulfillment of this vital function.

2. Education: Museums are a most effective means of informal education of the public, especially in the values and meaning of the collective heritage, both natural and cultural. Informal education is an important adjunct to formal education institutions, not only because it makes abstract lessons concrete, but even more so because it provides affective rather than merely cognitive learning. Affective learning is far more important in conveying and retaining values than mere cognitive comprehension of them. In countries with limited literacy or multicultural populations, such an affective learning institution can be even more important because it can unite generations with widely differing formal educational backgrounds in the common experience of an exhibition or demonstration.

3. Cultural tourism: Museums are a key part of any area's tourist attractions. Cultural tourism is the most dynamic sector of this vital industry (the world's largest), even in countries whose tourist appeal has relied on the now universally suspect "sun, sea, and sand." Governments must find ways to redirect taxes levied on this industry to make tourism a renewable resource. Providing subsidies to museums is one way of contributing toward the preservation of the natural and cultural heritage, the principal resource for the cultural tourism industry. It may also (as in the Arabian Gulf emirates) facilitate the acquisition or the long-term or short-term loan of important works of art or whole exhibitions that can act as a magnet to cultural tourists.

4. Social cohesion, social capital: A more deep-seated reason for government funding of museums is the contribution these institutions make to the creation of what economists call social capital. This is the intangible but invaluable force of social cohesion that gives people shared learning and enjoyable experiences in stable public institutions—a particularly important function of museums and other public cultural attractions in a fast-changing world often dominated by commercial interests. This is certainly one of the motivations that has led many so-called emerging nations to establish national and other museums. These institutions provide a public forum in which common values may be presented or challenged, common interests pursued, general public knowledge enhanced, or multiple cultures displayed and interpreted on an equal basis.

As governments and people continue to reevaluate the role of government, we may expect that the reasons for supporting museums may change, and the degree of support may also change. In Britain, for example, the Labour government over the past two decades placed a strong and increasing emphasis on *access* to the collections, especially for economic and social groups that have been traditionally underrepresented among museum visitors, thereby stimulating the development of many innovative programs, some more successful than others, aimed at attracting and (with greater difficulty) retaining the interest of these socioeconomic or ethnic groups.

For whatever combination of reasons, government subsidy remains the most important single source of revenue for a large number of museums around the world. It accounts for 90–100 percent of many national, provincial, and state museums' revenue, and for 60–70 percent of all museums' revenue, even in many countries (such as Britain or Canada) where museums have become active in increasing earned revenue. In the United States, however, its importance has been declining: the 2006 Museum Financial Information Survey by the American Association of Museums indicated that support from all government levels together has fallen to a national average of 24 percent, in contrast to the 39 percent reported for the year 1989—a drop of 15 percent over seventeen years. The same source reports that museums' earned income in the United States has remained unchanged from 1989 at 31 percent, while private contributions have made up the difference, rising from 19 percent in 1989 to 35 percent in 2006.

To what extent should governments subsidize museums? The study that the authors conducted with Lord Principal John Nicks, for what was then the U.K. Office of Arts and Libraries, *The Cost of Collecting* (1989), indicated that about 67 percent of all museum expenditure could be directly and indirectly attributed to care of the museums' collections. The figure for American museums is somewhat lower, at about 56 percent. One might take the view, therefore, that government subsidy or a combination of government subsidy and revenue from endowments should amount to approximately 55–70 percent of museum budgets if the collective heritage is to be preserved for future generations. A government with high educational priorities could go further, providing an additional 10–15 percent to ensure that the museum fulfills its educational objectives for the population.

In some jurisdictions, generous government assistance has been instrumental in stimulating higher standards of professionalism among museums. Annual contributions have been made contingent by some governments on the recipient museums' adoption of desired policies or the preparation of long-term plans. In some cases these requirements have been imposed directly by government cultural or heritage departments, in others by agencies established or encouraged by governments to impose registration or accreditation schemes, compliance with which then becomes a criterion in deciding whether to grant subsidies at all, or subsidies above a certain minimal subsistence level. The overall effect of such requirements has been positive for the recipient museums and for the museum profession. The national museums in Spain, for example, were recently required to undertake long-range planning as a condition of continuing to receive government support, with the broadly beneficial effect of stimulating more long-term thinking about the missions and objectives of these institutions.

3.5.2.2.2 Grants

While government line department museums and some "arm's-length" institutions may enjoy government subsidies, independent, nonprofit associations—and many of the arm's-length and government line department museums as well—are more likely to receive government and/or foundation support in the form of *grants*. These are distinguished from subsidies primarily by the fact that they are not an assured allocation but are subject to application by the recipient museums to programs established by government or its appointed agencies. In some countries, lotteries are the sources or administrators of grants. Private foundations also award grants to museums.

Grants may be of two types:

1. Operating grants: These are grant programs that provide contributions to museums annually, so they are similar to subsidies, except that the recipient museums must apply for them and often cannot predict the amount of the annual grant. These are often made subject to their recipients' compliance with professional standards, which may be indicated on the application form. Funds granted for operating purposes may usually be expended on a wide range of activities, or for any running costs.
2. Project grants: These are grant programs that have specific objectives, and therefore make funds available for particular purposes. Although some of these may be museum specific, others may arise from agencies or government departments (or foundations) with very different concerns; among the most common are employment grants. Funds provided under these programs must be expended on the projects for which they have been approved, and separate project accounts are usually required.

In many museums the preparation of grant applications has become a specialized function within the development office, or performed by a contractor. The person responsible for this function needs to meet with the museum personnel who will execute the programs or projects seeking funding before preparing the application, to ensure that all costs—in time, space, personnel, facilities, and materials, as well as money—have been considered. Failing to allow for the cost of administering successful grant applications is one of the more common errors of overenthusiastic museum managers.

Grant projects also need to be carefully correlated with the museum's long-term policies and priorities. Winning a grant from a government employment program is of little value if it conflicts with the museum's personnel policies, or requires far more time for training than is justified by the progress realized on a museum project. Even more important is to ensure that grants are secured because they accord with museum priorities, rather than allowing grant programs to determine the museum's programs.

Some government departments administer grant programs directly, whereas others establish agencies, such as the National Endowment for the Arts, the National Endowment for the Humanities, the National Science Foundation, or the Institute of Museum and Library Services in the United States. Some of these specialized agencies have been instrumental in stimulating higher levels of professionalism among recipient museums.

Private philanthropic foundations are increasingly important sources of grant aid. Some, like the Gulbenkian Foundation, the Getty Foundation, or the Pew Charitable Trusts, have major programs specific to museums, whereas many have more general cultural or educational objectives that museums can fulfill.

A significant trend in both operating grant and project grant programs in recent years has been *evaluation by outcomes*, rather than more narrowly defined functional or project objectives. Not satisfied with merely recording that the museum continues in operation, or that the funded museum learning program served the requisite number of children in so many classes, evaluation by outcomes seeks to determine what difference the funded program made in the world. The application forms for such grants typically require the applicant to articulate social or cultural outcomes in advance, thereby encouraging activities that are more broadly or communally focused, rather than being limited to institutional priorities.

3.5.2.2.3 Endowments

Many museum managers outside the United States have the impression that American museums largely pay for themselves through earned revenues. This is rarely true. A much more important aspect of American museum funding is the tradition of philanthropy through *endowments*. These endowments are not spent directly on museum activities but are invested, with some or all of the interest earned by the investments being devoted to the museum's operating costs. Investment decisions may be made by trustees with expertise in that area or investment counselors may be encouraged to volunteer or may be commissioned. In 2006, average revenue from endowments accounted for just under 10 percent of all American museum operating budgets; botanical gardens did best at 21 percent, with art museums second at 15 percent.

In museums with current or planned endowment funds, raising contributions to the endowment becomes an important aspect of fund-raising in itself.

Museum trustees and members in particular should be encouraged to make donations or bequests to the endowment as the most effective way of helping the museum achieve financial stability in the long term.

The best opportunity to raise contributions to unrestricted endowment funds that may be used for operations arises during capital development campaigns, when endowment requirements can be presented as part of the overall development need. The difficulty in raising endowment funds is that they appear to be too long-term and too diffuse in application, so that potential donors do not feel in control of, or responsible for, the results of their philanthropy. For this reason there are restricted endowment funds with specific aims and uses, such as acquisitions.

Maintaining endowment funds means resisting the temptation to utilize all of the interest earned, or even to bite into the capital, in times of need. The professional endowment fund manager will advise the museum on the appropriate draw. As for utilizing the capital, this is almost always counterproductive, since it strongly discourages future donors to the endowment fund at the same time as it diminishes the capital on which interest can be earned.

3.5.2.2.4 Sponsorship

Sponsorship of exhibitions and other museum programs is one of the most productive ways in which the private sector can be involved in museums. Unfortunately, some advocates of government cutbacks have formed the notion that such sponsorships can somehow supplant grants and subsidies. Even where sponsorships are fully engaged, this is never true, particularly as most corporate sponsors' contributions are contingent on the museum continuing to receive government support.

Nevertheless, private sector sponsorship has taken its place as a significant revenue source, particularly as it can be combined with corporate memberships. Museums should prepare sponsorship policies that articulate the institutional mission and ensure that control over the content and style of exhibitions or other programs is retained by the museum. Company executives are usually relieved to learn of such provisions, since they ensure that the sponsorship does not risk subsequent public criticism for alleged interference. Acknowledgments of sponsors' contributions should include a statement of the museum's responsibility for, and control of, all issues of content and style.

Growing numbers of companies regard contributions to museums as part of their public relations or marketing strategy, rather than as philanthropy. Museums can respond to this orientation (which usually places significantly larger amounts of funding at their disposal) by targeting potential sponsor companies with interests in the content of museum projects, or with a marketing focus on the target market for specific exhibitions or other programs.

Thus companies with products or services directed at children and their parents may be interested in sponsoring a children's gallery or an educational program, while others may be particularly drawn to a program directed at encouraging multicultural participation in the museum.

The museum management should consider the sponsor as a partner and aim to develop mutually beneficial relationships. Sponsorships are most often provided for major special exhibitions that attract a large audience, thereby realizing the greatest "return" on the company's "investment." Not all sponsorships are for large amounts, however; in Canada the Kamloops Art Gallery found it most effective to recruit exhibition sponsors among relatively small local companies, such as accountancy, law, medical, dental, or architectural practices, which could afford relatively small amounts of sponsorship on an occasional basis, and enjoyed being included in the exhibition opening festivities as sufficient reward.

3.5.2.2.5 Donations

Gifts and bequests of artifacts, specimens, or works or art, and related donations of money by relatively wealthy individuals, have historically been responsible for the development of many major museums. For the most part these were made before the donations earned significant tax advantages for the donors; rather, this kind of philanthropy aimed to establish a lasting memorial that would have cultural and educational value for many years to come.

Such donors still exist, and it is very much in the interest of museums to seek their support where it is available. Income tax deductions for donations to museums in the form of acquisitions or cash remain an attraction in some jurisdictions, but have been substantially reduced in others. Another motivation may be to reduce or escape capital gains taxes or estate duties, or to comply with cultural property export and import legislation, which usually restricts sales abroad and makes donations to national institutions more attractive. Museum trustees should include among their number at least one authority on inheritance law, who can give informal advice to prospective donors.

In some countries museums are more successful in attracting donations of goods or services from corporations, rather than asking for money. Such donations in kind may be especially valuable at a time of capital development, whether of new buildings, new facilities, or renewed exhibitions. Computer or audiovisual hardware and software are other frequent donations in kind.

An important consideration for both museum and donor to understand is that donations or bequests of acquisitions convey to the museum the *liability* of caring for the donated material. The donation of a collection, or even of a few works of art, artifacts, specimens, or archival materials, should be accompanied by a cash contribution to the museum's operating funds for the care of the donated material. These funds will be expended on providing the storage areas, display space, security, conservation, documentation, curatorial research, and many other costs associated with the addition of the donation to the museum's collection. The larger the collection donated, the more important such financial support of the museum's running costs becomes.

Proposed donations of acquisitions should be acknowledged with temporary receipts while under consideration. The permanent receipt for an accepted gift or bequest must make clear that the transfer of ownership is total and in perpetuity and is unconditional. Under no circumstances should the museum be persuaded to accept donations with strings attached, such as stipulations that the donation should be placed on permanent display, or that it cannot be loaned to other museums. If such arrangements have been inherited, the museum should move to renegotiate them with the heirs or executors if possible. Such commitments can hamper the museum's scope of operations severely, especially its ability to change displays or to participate in loan exhibitions, and dissolving such constraints is not easy, as the trustees of the Barnes Foundation in Pennsylvania or the Burrell Collection in Glasgow can attest. Refusing donations with such conditions attached takes courage, but accepting them inevitably circumscribes the institution's long-range development.

3.5.2.3 Fund-Raising Campaigns

Fund-raising campaigns are the means of organizing donations. They range from once-in-a-lifetime capital fund-raising drives to annual solicitations, but usually follow a similar pattern.

First is forming a *fund-raising committee*. Raising money is a social enterprise and is best undertaken by a committee of people who can be convinced that it is not only valuable but necessary to raise the required funds because they believe in the institution, project, or programs for which the funds are to be raised. Each member should join the committee by making whatever donation he or she can afford; the trustee or development officer forming the committee should determine in advance the amounts each committee member might donate and invite them to join with a suggestion of a suitable amount.

Committee members who have not contributed appropriately themselves cannot convince others to do so; but those who have already contributed are usually strongly motivated to persuade others to join them. In addition to their willingness to give according to their means, committee members should be selected as representative of the groups who are considered to be the most likely donors—if a certain industry has a special interest in the museum or the exhibition, for instance, then a leading person in that industry should serve on the committee so that he or she can lead the campaign industry-wide.

The most active and most committed members should be considered as possible chairpersons. In addition, a figurehead chair may be named—a well-known person who is willing to add his or her name as an endorsement to the campaign. In Britain these are often members of the royal family, but in many countries they are likely to be well-known figures from the arts, sports, entertainment, or sometimes retired (and therefore nonpartisan) former political leaders.

The committee may also wish to appoint professional fund-raising consultants, and to agree on a campaign budget, which should be at least 10–12 percent of the amount to be raised. Fund-raising consultants can be helpful in providing planning and sound advice, especially about realistic objectives, but unfortunately they cannot do the work of the committee, who must undertake the actual fund-raising themselves.

Second, the *case statement* must be drafted. The first rule of fund-raising is "If you don't ask, you don't get." But the museum must be sure that the use to which the funds will be put is made clear, not only in terms of what will be done with the money, but more importantly, why the museum needs the funds. This is usually articulated in a case statement, in which the museum management makes the case for the project, or for the continuation of the programs to be funded. Drafting a persuasive case statement and publishing it attractively is crucial to a successful fund-raising campaign.

Planning the campaign is the next essential component. Successful fund-raising is three-quarters planning, one-quarter execution. The campaign plan must identify an adequate but realistic *target*, the anticipated groups of *donors*, and attainable amounts to be sought from each group, adding up to the overall target. Remembering that people give money to other people (*not* to projects or causes), the plan should also identify the *fund-raisers*, pairing those who will ask with those who it is hoped will give. The representative of the industry selected to serve on the committee should help to develop a list of leaders in that industry who are likely to donate. Timing is crucial: the campaign plan should schedule the best times to make requests to corporations and private individuals, to be followed by a public campaign. The spring is often considered ideal for individual giving, whereas school holidays are obviously not a good time to approach individuals with families. For corporations, knowing the fiscal year and when the public relations budget is being considered is valuable.

Next, *pacesetting donations* are acquired. Up to 80–90 percent of the target amount is often donated by only 10 percent of donors. The campaign should begin with this relatively quiet phase in which key donors are approached with the case statement, with a view to obtaining pacesetting donations—amounts that can then be cited (anonymously or not, as the donors prefer) when approaching subsequent donors in that group. The other donors may then be persuaded to make their contributions in proportion to the pacesetter. The pacesetting donations should all be sought by personal appeals; the committee can decide whether subsequent appeals may be made by telephone or mail, or should also be made in person. *Naming rights* are often tied to pacesetting donations. Buildings, wings, galleries, or display cases may be named for donors at specific value levels. It is most important that these rights be determined in the fund-raising plan at the outset, with the values required for each level of naming determined in proportion to the total amount needed. Giving away major naming rights early in a campaign for too little is an error that has hurt more than one campaign.

The *public campaign*, a well-published campaign to secure relatively small amounts from a large number of donors (often realizing only 5–10 percent of the total to be raised), complete with fund-raising events, should follow after the pacesetting contributions have been secured, as the rest of the private donations are being made. The value of this part of the campaign is to demonstrate the degree of public support for the museum or the project to be funded.

The *collecting of pledges* is set up. Many campaigns seek *pledges* of amounts to be given over time. Wherever possible, automatic payment methods such as post-dated checks, standing orders, covenants, direct debits, or charge card commitments should be arranged, but however it is organized, it is crucial that the campaign includes a schedule for the collection of the money pledged.

Finally, the *donors are thanked*. It is vital for the museum to acknowledge donors in a suitable way—which might range from throwing a party in celebration of a successful campaign to erecting a plaque in acknowledgment of a major donor. Even small contributions must receive acknowledgment and the museum's thanks in some tangible way.

3.5.3 Controlling Expenditure

The adage "a penny saved is a penny earned" certainly applies to the financial management of museums. Given the challenge of combining the many sources of revenue listed in subsection 3.5.2—or the equally demanding challenge of living within the constraints of a government line department budget—museum managers need to keep close control of their expenditure. David Loye's case study 3.10 earlier in this chapter describes the measures taken to tighten expenditure management at the Canadian Museum of Civilization.

In addition to administering the budget cycle outlined in subsection 3.5.1, the museum's director and the finance officer may facilitate such control by establishing *financial responsibility levels* for each position in the organization chart. Each financially responsible museum officer should have an authorization level, below which each is authorized to commit the museum's resources. Departmental commitments above that amount must be referred to the next higher responsibility level or beyond. Within his or her responsibility level, each officer should be empowered to make requisitions, which should be directed through the finance office. Actual *purchase orders* should be issued only by the finance office, and should be countersigned by both the relevant department head and the finance officer.

Museum *contracts* with suppliers of all kinds—from exhibit fabrication to cleaning or food service—should be administered according to a tendering or bidding policy that meets the standards of the governing body and those of granting authorities from which the museum has received, or hopes to receive, funding. Given these constraints, museum management should, if possible, avoid commitments to automatic selection of the lowest bidder. Very often—in security services or exhibit design, for example—it is crucial that the museum be free to select higher bidders in order to ensure that museum standards are maintained.

Monitoring departmental expenses against the budget throughout the year is now usually carried out by referring to computer printouts that show *variances* from projected expenditures to date. Variance statements should be reviewed with departmental officers monthly, with reports to the chief executive officer on any that exceed a preset level of tolerance—say, 10–15 percent. Very often, such variances may be due to unforeseen opportunities, so they need not necessarily be viewed with alarm; however, a plan for congruence with budget projections should always be in the hands of the director and the finance officer. These often involve balancing underexpenditure in one department, or one section of one department, against overexpenditure in another; again, such changes may represent an entirely positive adjustment of plans as they are recorded and agreed upon by all concerned and fed into the budget cycle.

Almost all museums are required to undertake an annual audit of both revenues and expenditures. The balance sheets that result from such audits usually do not show the true value of the museum's collections, which are often assigned only a nominal value for accounting purposes. There has been considerable resistance to evaluation of collections, because it is felt to be unwise for security and other reasons. Our book, *The Cost of Collecting* (1989), provides a basis for evaluation that is related not to some imagined auction room but to the real worked-up value of collection care dedicated to the objects over the years they have been in the museum's keeping, which may be called the opportunity cost of retaining collections.

Museums in most countries are exempt from many taxes, usually because they are either government agencies or charitable organizations. Many are able to reclaim value-added taxes or sales taxes. In the United States, museums are now taxed on unrelated business income arising from revenue-producing activities that are not directly the result of their core operations as nonprofit or charitable organizations. For example, museum shop proceeds from the sales of items not directly related to the museum collections may be subject to tax.

The operating costs listed in museum budgets and financial reports can usually be classified according to the following the line items:

- salaries and benefits;
- occupancy costs;
- curatorial and conservation costs;
- exhibitions and other public programming costs;
- marketing expenses;
- administrative costs.

Salaries and benefits: Museums are labor-intensive institutions. Salary and benefit packages vary widely, with a few larger institutions offering very attractive compensation levels but most museum staff suffering from below-average salaries and wages relative to other professions. Despite the relatively low wages often paid to each employee, salaries and benefits often amount to 50–60 percent of total expenses, with collecting institutions with curatorial and conservation responsibilities typically requiring a higher percentage than noncollecting science centers or children's museums. Proportions even higher than that—ranging up to or even above 70 percent—are common enough, particularly in some government line department museums in countries where civil service pay levels are subject to annual increments while government budget allocations for museums remain static or are being reduced. Proportions higher than 65 percent may be regarded as unhealthy, since they leave too little money in the rest of the budget for the staff to accomplish its tasks. A target of 55–60 percent might be taken as an attainable goal for many institutions, except in those government line departments. The benefits proportion in many countries accounts for 20–25 percent of total employment costs, although it ranges as high as 40–50 percent in some.

Occupancy costs: By "occupancy costs" we mean expenses incurred by the operation of the museum's site and buildings. These may include rent or taxes (if applicable), utilities, groundskeeping, cleaning, maintenance and repairs, the operation of security systems, and insurance on the building, but not the cost of major renovations, which is a capital expense. Maintaining environmental controls and security to museum standards is expensive, and utility costs have increased substantially with rising oil costs in recent years, so occupancy costs in museums usually account for 15–20 percent of total expenses, unless some functions are being provided by the museum's governing body as part of a centralized government or university campus service.

Curatorial and conservation costs: Most collecting institutions should aim to reserve at least 5 percent—preferably up to 10 percent—of their total budget for direct collection management costs other than salaries. Lesser reserves are often encountered, usually indicating neglect of the museum's most important resource. Yet these direct curatorial and conservation expenses are by no means all the costs of maintaining a collection. They do *not* include acquisitions costs (which are not part of the operating budget), nor the wide range of wages (all the security guards, for instance) made necessary by the collection, nor the indirect administrative and building occupancy costs connected with maintaining a museum-quality environment for the collection. Our 1988–1989 study of the total costs of collection care in one hundred British museums, *The Cost of Collecting* (1989), indicated that when salaries and benefits were allocated to collection-related functions, fully 38 percent of the museum's budgets were indirectly linked to collections care, and that when allowance was made for the indirect costs of administration and building operation that were due to the museum's retention of collections, the total climbed to about 66.5 percent, which, with the median cost of acquisitions added, rose still further to approximately 69 percent of all museum expenditure.

Exhibitions and other public programming costs: Museums serving the public with a lively and well-researched program of exhibitions, education, and other services should aim to reserve at least 10–15 percent of their running costs for the nonsalary costs of such activities. When the proportion is lower than this, the museum is usually failing to serve its visitors. Since some of these public activities may be revenue-generating, it is likely to be in the museum's immediate financial interests, as well as serving its broader concerns with fulfilling its mission, to allocate adequate resources to these ends.

From time to time some museum directors undertake to reduce their institutions' commitments to exhibitions, especially to large and expensive blockbusters, in favor of redirecting their discretionary budgets to collections research, presentation, and care. Such a reallocation is often counseled by curators and conservators, who find their priorities continually warped by the demands of the exhibition schedule. This may be praiseworthy in institutions with collections that merit this attention, but predictions of "the end of the age of blockbusters" have thus far proved to be premature. Incremental changes in the display or interpretation of the permanent collection are seldom sufficient to elicit the broad community interest that an important exhibition can; one viable strategy that Tate Britain pioneered is to transform an annual rehang of the permanent collection into a major exhibition in itself, with an opening and focused marketing. A judicious mix of temporary exhibitions and permanent collection research and care remains the best formula, however difficult it may be to sustain the correct balance between them.

Public programming expenses also include the cost of museum learning programs, often the Cinderella of the budget cycle, used to justify grant applications but often neglected with lower salaries and nonsalary allocations than are really needed to provide a quality service. Special-events budgets are another important component, often requiring expenditure but resulting in a substantial proportion of the museum's attendance on a relatively few days or through a holiday season.

Marketing expenses: Failing to provide adequate funds for marketing is the most common lapse encountered in museum budgets. Many museums spend far less per visitor than a comparable commercial attraction would, with predictable results. The managers of an art exhibition center in Vienna found that they were able to substantially outdraw another Viennese art museum with a retrospective of the same artist, even though the other museum's retrospective had preceded theirs by two years, and therefore might have been thought to have saturated the market for visitors interested in works by that artist; the difference between the two retrospectives was that the later and far more successful one had a significant marketing budget that was used creatively, whereas the earlier and less successful retrospective was given the minimal marketing treatment that is so common in the museum world.

The target for a sound museum marketing budget should be at least 5 percent of the institution's total operating costs. The 2006 Financial Summary published by the American Association of Museums reported that American natural history and anthropology museums spent 6 percent of their operating budgets on marketing, with art museums at 5 percent. Marketing spend per visitor is an even more relevant measure: the same AAM report indicated that the average spent per visitor for all American museums in 2006 was $1.05. Art museums spent far more, at $1.75 per visitor, with natural history and anthropology museums at $1.42; the low marketing budgets of history museums dragged down the average.

Administrative costs: These are the routine operating costs of communications, bookkeeping, auditing and other professional fees; office supplies; and other expenses, for which 5 percent or more of the budget should be reserved.

Figure 3.12 indicates the range of potential distribution of these operating cost components for collecting institutions.

3.5.4 Insurance

Many years ago, after eighteen months during which the authors of this book had served as curators of a major international loan exhibition, we came to the conclusion that the one thing we should have done differently from the outset was to hire an insurance and indemnity clerk—so challenging had those issues proved, from the negotiation of the loans through to their eventual returns!

Although that staff position is not included among the job descriptions provided in the appendix to this volume, curators, registrars, and other professional museum personnel must be familiar with insurance or indemnity. Government line department museums may be wholly or partially exempt

Figure 3.12. Range of Cost Distribution for Collecting Institutions

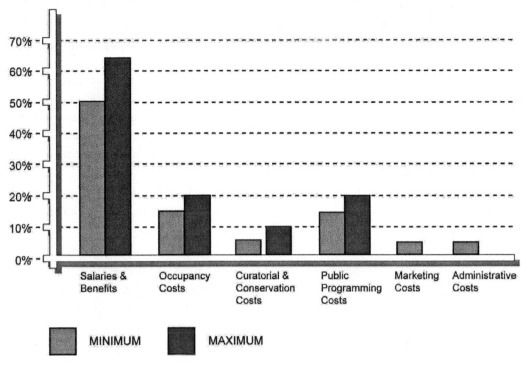

because part or all of their property may be classified as government assets that are not subject to private insurance coverage. But in most museums the registrar is responsible for maintaining insurance on the permanent collection and on incoming and outgoing loans, while the chief of security and the operations officer and building engineer are concerned with insuring the building and equipment, and the finance officer takes care of liability coverage.

Insurance is a means of transferring risks from the museum to the insurer. Subsection 3.4.2.3 defines *risk analysis* as one component of planning for security, and insurance is one form of *risk management*, transferring financial responsibility for the risk to the insurer. Museums generally require insurance of five kinds:

- insurance on the collection;
- insurance on buildings;
- insurance on equipment;
- liability insurance; and
- insurance on loans.

Insurance on the collection: Often called *fine arts insurance*, even for other types of museums, this type of policy is based on a regular *inventory* of the collection and valuations. The inventory should include an up-to-date location file and should be renewed for a specific percentage of the collection each year—one European museum found that its insurer was unwilling to pay for an alleged theft when it was discovered that the inventory of the affected section of the collection had not been checked for decades!

Valuation is another challenge, but may be carried out by distinguishing between low-value items, those of moderate value, and high-value objects:

- values may be assigned on a routine basis for large quantities of similar low-value objects, or for items that are agreed to be below a certain valuation;
- objects of moderate value may be evaluated by the curators; and
- high-value items should be reevaluated regularly, preferably by an authority independent of the museum.

Curators should monitor auction prices and other sale values, and a review of high valuations should be undertaken by the registrar in consultation with the curators every year. Condition reports on all works of higher value can be used to demonstrate their prior condition if objects in the collection should suffer damage. Documentary photographs are essential in case of theft. Reports of thefts should be made not only to local police but also through the various international agencies that reproduce pictures of stolen items. An "*all-risks*" policy is preferable to one that is restricted to "named perils."

Insurance on buildings: Fire insurance is the most common form of protection for museum buildings, but some form of *fire and extended coverage* policy should be considered, to extend to such risks as earthquakes, hurricanes, tornadoes, storms, floods, explosions, sprinkler accidents, vandalism, or civil disturbance. Here again, valuation is a concern, since it is crucial that the insurer should pay not merely for replacement or repair of any building lost or damaged, but for a comparable building of museum quality. (Of course, if the insurer declines on the grounds that the present building is not of museum standard, that is one more argument for upgrading it.) It is also important for the chief of security to ensure that the insurer is kept informed of improvements made in the building, changes in the permanent collection exhibits, or even of relocations of the fire extinguishers.

Insurance on equipment: This may include vehicle insurance; boiler insurance; plate glass insurance; warranties; and other policies protecting the museum against loss, damage, or malfunction of its equipment.

Liability insurance: In most countries, public institutions such as museums assume responsibility for the safety of their users and those persons' property from the moment they open their doors until they close. The museum—and in some jurisdictions, its governing body—may therefore be liable for any damage suffered by its visitors. Public liability and property damage insurance is therefore required. Third-party insurance is needed to cover damages occasioned to or by otherwise unrelated parties to an accident.

The museum's liability also extends to the people who work in the museum: many governments provide worker's compensation for injuries to paid staff while on duty, but the museum will also need employer's liability insurance if volunteers are to be covered as well. Insurance coverage must also be required of all contractors engaged to work in the museum or on its grounds. *Bonding* of those employees responsible for handling money or valuable objects may also be considered. Legal liability coverage should also be carried, to protect the museum in case of legal proceedings, justified or not, taken against the institution.

Director's and officers' liability insurance, often called simply D&O, is a type of liability insurance that museums can secure in order to protect board or trust members so they are in a position to attract and retain high-quality and dedicated trustees, whose anxieties might otherwise cause them to consider resignation due to real or perceived notions of potential personal exposure. It is noteworthy that museums that have D&O insurance report that 90 percent of claims under it are employment-related: alleged discrimination, wrongful dismissal, or harassment are the most common grounds for D&O claims.

Insurance on loans: The registrar should ensure that all outgoing loans are fully covered by insurance, either by extension of the museum's own policies, or by insurance taken out by the borrower (a copy of the policy on the loaned items should be checked and kept on file). Incoming loans may be most efficiently insured by an *all-risks fine arts floater* attached to the insurance on the permanent collection; even if the value of the borrowed exhibition is very high, it will only be a modification of the insured value of the permanent collection, which in most cases is much higher. The floater should provide "*nail-to-nail*" coverage (as it is called, referring to the nails on which pictures hang), extending from the moment it is removed from the lender's gallery or storage area until it returns there. *Condition reports* are imperative each time a borrowed work of art or artifact is packed and unpacked. Insurers may insist on photographs taken at each packing and unpacking of the work on loan.

The cost of insuring large, permanent collections of high value is, in some cases, prohibitive, while the cost of insuring traveling exhibitions of high value has become a major impediment to their organization. In order to protect their major national museums and to maintain the feasibility of nationwide or international exhibitions, various governments have developed programs of *indemnity*, under which the government indemnifies the museum or the lender against loss. The government commits to making good any value damaged or lost, thereby rendering insurance unnecessary. The main challenge of establishing indemnity programs for temporary exhibitions lies in the government, the museum, and the lender arriving at a mutually satisfactory valuation. In the event of dispute, the borrowing museum may be obliged to purchase additional insurance to cover the value above the ceiling set by the government—if an insurer can be found to assume the additional risk.

3.5.5 Financial Planning and Development

Despite their widespread success and growing public, and notwithstanding the list of revenue sources described in subsection 3.5.2, museums almost everywhere are struggling to cope with government cutbacks on cultural funding and demands that they should be more self-reliant and less dependent on subsidy. Although relatively few museums have closed for financial reasons, many are obliged to postpone important tasks and some to close to the public for several hours or days each week.

The financial constraints on museums in the long term can only be increased by the fact that one of their primary activities—collecting—results in constantly growing demands on space and facilities. Hence even financially healthy museums are constantly faced with capital fund requirements for expansion, renovation, or relocation.

Another dimension of the crisis is rooted in museums' very success with the public. Visitors, better informed than ever by travel and television, are constantly raising their expectations of exhibitions, media programs, even museum shops. In an effort to meet rising expectations, museums constantly need fresh development capital, and the requisite additional operating funds.

Trustees and museum directors, therefore, have the responsibility to rise above the constant scramble to meet current operating, capital, and acquisition costs in order to plan the long-term financial future of their institutions. This may be addressed as part of the strategic planning process or when the corporate plan is being reviewed. The principles of such a long-term financial plan may be suggested here as a useful conclusion to this consideration of the financial management of museums:

- The museum's long-term financial plan should aim to secure financial *stability* for the institution. Whenever possible, government, corporate, or university funding should be put on an assured rather than a contingent basis, as a regular allocation rather than being dependent on grants. This may require strenuous representation to government or other funding sources.
- Where appropriate, a government-operated museum should become, and should endeavor to remain, part of the institutional framework of *education*, another area that is subject to government cutbacks, but one that, in the long term, will experience continuity of funding.

- Trustees and senior museum staff should promote the museum as a vital part of the *cultural tourism* industry and lobby to make tourism a renewable resource through taxes on tourism operators or an equivalent arrangement that channels part of the revenue from tourism back to the institutions that are its fundamental resource. Some U.S. cities and states have imposed a "*hotel tax*" of this kind, while others have applied it to such sectors as the car rental industry.

- An *endowment* fund, or some equivalent form of return on investments, should be established. Donors should be persuaded to address the long-term interests of the institution so that contributions and especially bequests may be made to such a fund. Providing for a growing proportion of the museum's needs with the interest earned by such a fund is one way to secure greater financial independence.

- A *visitor engagement program* should extend the museum's appeal to those sectors of the community that are currently underrepresented among museum visitors. Government or other support should be sought to institute such a program and should then lead the museum to a still more widespread base in the community, which in turn can serve as the foundation of further funding. In the long term, this financial sustainability of museums is inextricably linked to providing broad-based meaningful service to the community.

- Since the museum is a knowledge-based institution in the "knowledge economy" of an "information age," the plan should give careful consideration to the museum's ability to gain funding through control of its image and its intellectual capital, including its collections and information about them, as new media for education and entertainment continue to be developed. Beyond a digital assets management program, this points to careful consideration of the best use of the *brand* that the museum has established over the years.

- Whenever the governing body determines that a new or larger building, renovation, or expansion may be needed, or may even be considered essential to the museum's financial future, it is imperative that careful financial planning of the implications of the relocated or expanded facilities should be undertaken in a feasibility study or business plan, in addition to whatever facility planning, architecture, or design is to be done. Capital cost projections should always be accompanied by operating cost and revenue implications in a carefully considered business plan for any changes to the museum's physical plant.

None of these principles in themselves will suffice to ensure long-term financial stability for museums. Together, they may form a basis for the future. In any event, managing the financial future of museums will continue to require diligence, ingenuity, and—above all—courage.

Afterword

This book indicates why museum management is challenging, inspiring, and demanding, and becoming so much more so that some have said the post of museum director is among the most difficult today. The constant search for new and better museum directors in many countries suggests that the job can sometimes be overwhelming. Current efforts to provide improved training for curators who wish to direct are intended to enhance their chances of success and to ensure that the curatorial voice so essential to museums is not marginalized.

This edition has pointed to the significant changes in museums in the early twenty-first century as they become more outwardly focused. Should we be concerned about this institutional transformation of museums from agencies of government to civil society institutions? Should we be worried that in this brave new world of civil society museums all the management, ethical, and technical skills that the profession has fought for over the years will be ignored in favor of vague ideas of "leadership" that sometimes march to the tunes of tourism, sponsorship, and social inclusion above all else? Yes, this is a concern. It is a special concern because at present we as a profession are often failing to train directors, curators, and department managers to be leaders. As a result, we may see more museums being led by lawyers or journalists than by museum professionals.

But it was and remains an equal concern that many talented museum directors, managers, and potential leaders have been and are locked within underfunded government structures without access to the tools either to manage or to lead their museum in a professional way. Instead of thinking of the transformation that museums are undergoing as a "slippery slope," we can see it as an opportunity and urge that museums in the government and corporate sectors be given tools to fulfill new roles in a changing society.

The key tools for these new roles are:

- budgetary control;
- ability to seek outside funding;
- support for engaging more deeply with the community, including the appointment of advisory committees that reflect the demographics of our changing societies; and

- training in teamwork. The old academic model that keeps curators, educators, marketers, and visitor services personnel on separate tracks reflects a government departmental or hierarchical form of organization that is not well suited to filling contemporary social needs. Throughout this book we have stressed the importance of standing committees and especially of task force project teams to accomplish the museum's mission by working together.

For several hundred years now, museums have been developing as one of the most successful social means of communication and learning. They have transformed themselves from private treasure chambers to the scholar's study, and from academies of art or science into government institutions.

Now museums are in the midst of another transition, from the government/corporate sector model to the realm of civil society. This transformation places museums at the heart of social change with tremendous challenges ahead.

It is our hope that this manual demonstrates that management and leadership can and should be exercised by professional staff, trustees, and volunteers at all levels—by security and visitor services staff as well as by directors, curators, educators, and administrators. For the challenges of being visitor responsive and creative, of maintaining the primacy of scholarship and ensuring the preservation and security of the collection, while being of real value to the community and raising funds can only be met by people working together—and that requires leadership and management skills to be activated throughout the entire museum organization.

It is equally our hope that new generations of museum managers will succeed as leaders of these remarkable institutions that communicate meaning and continuity through objects in space and time as a way of creating cultural capital. Museums of the twenty-first century are exploring new levels of meaning, yet continue to find it in their specimens, artifacts, records, and works of art. May their managers realize the full extent of the principles of museum management noted here and extend them to new horizons, serving ever-growing numbers of their public in relevant, stimulating, and inspiring ways.

Appendix
Job Descriptions

No one museum is likely to need all the positions listed here, and there will certainly be still other specialized jobs at some museums. Terminology also varies widely. Nevertheless, we have tried to make the list as inclusive and as representative as possible.

Positions listed here have been assigned a letter and a number for reference. The letters indicate the division in which the post is located:

- D for director's office.
- C for the collection management division.
- P for the public programs division.
- A for administration.
- E for external affairs.

The positions accord with the organization chart in chapter 2. However, some positions could report in either of two departments, and these are noted as such. Smaller and mid-size museums are likely to have the typical three-part organization diagrammed in section 2.3.3, plus a director's office. The fourth division, external affairs, will likely be needed only in larger museums. Qualifications suggested for each position may of course vary according to the location of the museum in question.

Director's Office

D-1   Director

The chief executive officer (CEO) of a museum is usually called a director, but may be a chief curator, curator or director/curator, especially in smaller museums.

Reports to the board, and is responsible for:

- realization of the museum's mission;
- conceptual leadership through specialized knowledge of the museum's mandate;
- recommendation of policies and plans and their revision to the board;

- implementation of policies and plans approved by the board;
- reporting on the implementation of policies and plans to the board;
- planning, organizing, and staffing;
- directing and coordinating day-to-day operations through the staff;
- financial management and funding; and
- liaison with all relevant levels of government, the academic community, and the private sector in the interests of the museum.

Qualifications:

- advanced degree in an area of the museum's specialization;
- extensive experience and proven ability in management and administration in the cultural sector;
- demonstrated knowledge of financial development and the ability to manage ongoing fiscal responsibilities; and
- knowledge of the legal aspects of museum operation and legislation affecting museums.

D-2   Director's Secretary

The director's secretary reports to the chief executive officer (director) and is responsible for:

- reception and inquiries; and
- secretarial support services to the director and the board including transcription of meeting notes, general clerical duties, word processing, and correspondence.

Qualifications:

- secondary school education;
- proficiency in communications media, especially word processing; and
- excellent human relations and personal communications skills.

D-3   Executive Assistant

Many directors of larger museums find it necessary to engage an executive assistant in their office, responsible for:

- administrative support to directorial decisions and programs;
- representing the director within the museum and externally;
- scheduling the director's appointments; and
- other duties as may be assigned by the director.

Qualifications:

- university degree in a discipline relevant to the museum;
- administrative experience in the public or private sector;
- experience with the media; and
- excellent human relations and personal communications skills.

Collection Management Division

C-1 Deputy Director for Collection Management (or Chief Curator)

With either title, this position reports as part of the management committee to the director and is responsible for:

- collection development and management;
- security, preservation, documentation, and interpretation of all collections;
- plans, policies, and procedures relevant to the collections and their care;
- recommendations for acquisition and deaccessioning;
- design and implementation of a collection research program;
- general and object-specific research and the publication of that research in a form accessible to visitors and other users of the museum;
- consultation in the creation of permanent and temporary exhibitions;
- consultation in the creation of public programming;
- cooperative and joint venture research projects and exhibitions;
- supervision of the collection management division and its staff;
- selection of software programs to meet collection management requirements; and
- financial management of the collection management division.

Qualifications:

- advanced degree in an area of the museum's specialization;
- proven ability in management and administration;
- management experience in a museum or related institution;
- specialized knowledge of one area of the collections;
- evidence of scholarly research and writing;
- ability to interpret the collections and communicate knowledge relevant to the collections;
- knowledge of the techniques of selection, evaluation, preservation, restoration, and exhibition of objects; and
- knowledge of the current market, collecting ethics, and current customs regulations in the areas of collecting by this museum.

C-2 Curator

Reports to the deputy director for collection management (or chief curator) and is responsible for:

- research and documentation of the collection in one discipline or area;
- care of the collection in that discipline or area;
- plans, policies, and procedures relevant to that curatorial discipline or area;
- public inquiries and requests for information on the collection in that discipline or area;
- participation in the creation of exhibitions and public programs in that discipline or area;
- preparation of publications resulting from research; and
- acquisition and deaccessioning in the curator's discipline.

Qualifications:

- degree in an area of the museum's specialization or equivalent experience;
- specialized knowledge and demonstrated excellence in one discipline or area of the museum's collection;
- evidence of scholarly research or publication;
- knowledge of the techniques of selection, evaluation, preservation, restoration, and exhibition of objects; and
- knowledge of the current market, collecting ethics, and current customs regulations in the area of specialization.

C-3 Assistant Curator

Reports to the relevant curator; note that this is a distinct position from that of curatorial assistant, which follows. Assistant curator is responsible for:

- research and documentation of the collection in one discipline or area under direction of the relevant curator;
- care of the collection in that discipline or area, as directed by the relevant curator;
- implementation of plans, policies, and procedures in the relevant curatorial discipline or area;
- public inquiries and requests for information on the collection in that discipline or area, as directed by the relevant curator;
- preparation of collections for exhibition as directed by the relevant curator;
- contribution to education programs in the relevant curatorial discipline; and
- implementation of acquisitions and deaccessioning as directed by the relevant curator.

Qualifications:

- degree in an area of the museum's specialization, or equivalent experience; and
- knowledge of the techniques of documentation, preservation and exhibition of objects in the relevant curatorial discipline

C-4   Curatorial Assistant

Reports to the relevant curator or assistant curator and is responsible for:

- safe and secure storage and ongoing care of the assigned discipline or area of the collections;
- accessioning and cataloging materials and condition reporting for that area;
- inquiries and requests for information as directed by the relevant curator; and
- preparation of artifacts, specimens, or works of art for exhibition.

Qualifications:

- university degree in an area of the museum's specialization;
- certificate in museum registration techniques or equivalent experience;
- experience and proven ability to carry out standard cataloging procedures;
- two years' experience in a museum or related organization in the registration area; and
- knowledge of specialized collections areas or disciplines.

C-5   Registrar

Reports to the deputy director for collection management (or chief curator) and is responsible for:

- creating and maintaining orderly systems for the management of collections in keeping with standard museum practice;
- supervising, numbering, cataloging and storing the museum's collections;
- plans, policies, and procedures affecting documentation, storage, or movement of the collection;
- coordinating all aspects of borrowing and lending objects;
- integrating the museum's information data base on its collections with national or international networks;
- providing catalog information on the collection to print or other media; and
- insurance of the collections.

Qualifications:

- degree in an area of the museum's specialization or in liberal arts or museum studies;

- two years in a museum registration department;
- knowledge of standard practice in registration techniques;
- knowledge of conservation and storage practices;
- knowledge of legal matters including contract law and copyright as they relate to collections as well as policies governing rights and reproductions;
- knowledge of records management and data processing systems;
- knowledge of insurance requirements for collections; and
- knowledge of packing and transportation requirements for collections.

C-6   Cataloger (Assistant to the Registrar)

Reports to the registrar and is responsible for:

- support services to the registrar including numbering, cataloging, and storing the collections;
- helping to define procedures for description and indexing and to devise vocabularies;
- inquiries both internal and external, including liaison with curators; and
- implementation of plans, policies, and procedures for documentation, loans, and movement of the collections.

Qualifications:
- certificate in museum registration techniques or equivalent experience;
- experience and proven ability to carry out standard cataloging procedures;
- experience in a museum or related organization in the registration area; and
- knowledge of data entry systems and proficiency in using them.

C-7   Data Entry Clerk

Reports to the registrar and is responsible for:

- entering descriptive and indexing information into the collections management data base; and
- performing periodic database maintenance in the form of vocabulary consistency checks and data validation.

Qualifications:
- certificate in museum registration techniques or equivalent in experience;
- knowledge of database management;
- experience in a collecting institution in the area of collections management; and
- knowledge of data processing systems.

C-8   Photographer

The photographer reports to the registrar and is responsible for:

- documentary images of the collections and details of objects on loan or in the collections for the museum's records;
- producing images of the collections for curatorial research and publications;
- producing images for educational materials and publications, promotions, and public requests for information;
- imaging for all digital and electronic media; and
- maintenance and administration of an image bank of the collections.

Qualifications:

- secondary school graduation and certified technical training in photography;
- studio experience in commercial photography and processing;
- portfolio of past work, especially in documentation of works of art, artifacts, or specimens; and
- proficiency with digitization of imagery and all electronic and audiovisual media.

C-9   Librarian/Knowledge Manager

The librarian reports to the deputy director for collection management (or chief curator). Today the scope of this position may be broadened to include duties related to all aspects of staff or public access to the museum's store of knowledge. The position is responsible for:

- development, management, and operation of the museum library;
- plans, policies, and procedures relevant to the museum library;
- provision of library services to curatorial and all other staff;
- performance of services such as selection, purchase or acquisition, cataloging and classification, circulation and maintenance of print materials and material in all audiovisual and electronic media;
- coordinating visitor access and use of the library (if the museum library is public);
- administering use of museum databases by staff and public;
- liaison with related institutions and information services; and
- provision of a reference and readers' advisory service.

Qualifications:

- advanced degree in library science, with some course work in the area of the museum's specialization;

- experience in a museum or specialized library;
- experience with information retrieval in a research-oriented cultural or arts organization;
- knowledge of the needs and purposes of resources relevant to the museum in all media;
- knowledge of all required support services with a strong emphasis on electronic resources as well as print material; and
- knowledge of storage and retrieval systems for printed materials, audio tapes, and disks and manuscripts.

C-10 Library Technician/Library Assistant

With either title, this position reports to the librarian and is responsible for:

- cataloging, circulation, and maintenance of library materials and services;
- public inquiries, use of multimedia, reference, and reader service; and
- support services related to all aspects of the museum library.

Qualifications:

- secondary school graduation and certified technical training in library science; and
- good communications skills and excellent customer service attitude.

C-11 Archivist

The archivist reports to the deputy director for collection management (or chief curator), and is responsible for:

- research and documentation of the museum archives;
- care of the archival collection in all media;
- plans, policies, and procedures relevant to the museum archives;
- digitization of archival text and images;
- public access to archival resources;
- public inquiries and requests for archival information;
- participation in the creation of archival exhibitions and public programs;
- preparation of catalogs or other publications resulting from archival research in all media;
- acquisition and deaccessioning of archival material in all media; and
- linking museum archives with national or international networks or databases.

Qualifications:

- degree in an area of the museum's specialization or equivalent experience;
- archival training or experience, including experience in all archival media;
- evidence of scholarly research or publication; and
- knowledge of the techniques of selection, evaluation, preservation, restoration, digitization, and exhibition of archival materials of all media.

C-12   Chief Conservator

The chief conservator reports to the deputy director for collection management (or chief curator) and is responsible for:

- preservation of all objects in the collection;
- retarding deterioration of all objects in the collection;
- plans, policies, and procedures relevant to conservation of the collection;
- examination of all acquisitions and loans, and preparation of condition reports on them;
- treatment of works in need of cleaning or restorative conservation;
- maintenance of the optimum conditions possible in the building for preventive conservation aimed at minimizing deterioration of the collection;
- condition reporting on all exhibition materials prior to and immediately after display, whether the property of the museum or on loan;
- research on the methods and materials of the collection; and
- administration of the conservation department.

Qualifications:

- advanced degrees preferably in both one area of the museum's collections and in chemistry or conservation science;
- knowledge of and proficiency in conservation methods relevant to at least one area of the collection, preferably more than one;
- several years' experience as a conservator in a museum; and
- administrative experience.

C-13   Conservation Scientist

The conservation scientist reports to the chief conservator and is responsible for:

- research into the methods and materials of objects in the collection;
- research into environmental conditions to enhance preservation of the collection;

- research into display and presentation methods appropriate to the exhibitions; and
- publication of the results of this research in all media.

Qualifications:

- advanced degrees in one area of the museum's collections or in chemistry or conservation science;
- knowledge of and proficiency in conservation methods relevant to at least one area of the collection, preferably more than one;
- several years' experience as a museum conservator; and
- experience as a research scientist.

C-14   Conservator

The conservator reports to the chief conservator and is responsible for:

- preservation of works of a particular material or medium in the collection;
- examination and treatment of works of that material or medium;
- maintenance of environmental conditions to preserve works of that material or medium; and
- preparation of condition reports on works in the collection, proposed acquisitions, or loans of that material or medium.

Qualifications:

- higher education degree in one area of the museum's collection, and/or in chemistry or conservation science;
- proficiency in conservation techniques for the relevant material or medium;
- experience as a museum conservator.

C-15   Conservation Technician

The conservation technician reports to the relevant conservator, and is responsible for:

- monitoring and recording environmental conditions of the collection;
- treatment of works in the collection under direction of the conservator; and
- preparation of condition reports for works in the collection and on loan.

Qualifications:

- technical college graduation in conservation technology; and
- experience in museum conservation or other scientific laboratories.

Public Programs Division

P-1 Deputy Director for Public Programs

This position reports to the chief executive officer (director), and is responsible for:

- the development and management of exhibitions and audiovisual programming, activities, materials, and events that attract and serve a wide range of audiences including schools;
- plans, policies, and procedures affecting public programs;
- liaison with the school system to increase awareness of the museum as an educational resource;
- liaison with exhibition designers and fabricators, technical program suppliers, and artists;
- meeting revenue and attendance targets as set out in the marketing plan; and
- supervision and performance of staff within the public programs division.

Qualifications:

- advanced degree in an area related to the museum's specialization and/or in museum studies;
- experience in a management position in a cultural attraction;
- proven management ability;
- knowledge of visitor behavior and needs;
- knowledge of the museum's collections;
- knowledge of evaluation methods; and
- entrepreneurial orientation.

P-2 Public Programs Secretary

The public programs secretary reports to the deputy director for public programs and is responsible for:

- reception and inquiries related to public programs;
- administrative support services for the public programs division; and
- coordinating space bookings for visitors and other users of the museum.

Qualifications:

- high school education;
- knowledge of and experience in word processing, scheduling; software and general office procedures; and
- familiarity with the operation of cultural institutions, good communication skills.

P-3   Exhibitions Officer

The exhibitions officer reports to the deputy director for public programs and is responsible for:

- planning and producing in collaboration with the curators a program of exhibitions that meets the museum's exhibition objectives;
- plans, policies, and procedures affecting exhibitions;
- convening and chairing the standing exhibition committee;
- appointing exhibition department personnel to exhibition task forces and other project teams;
- setting design and communication standards;
- planning and implementation of audiovisual and interactive components of exhibits and public programming;
- production and budgeting of exhibitions including proposals, design costing, construction, overall scheduling, maintenance and repairs;
- circulation of traveling exhibitions and achievement of revenue targets associated with these exhibitions;
- evaluation of exhibitions in collaboration with the evaluation officer;
- contact with technical suppliers and creative producers;
- evaluation of all system, product, and service proposals for exhibitions; and
- supervision and performance of exhibition staff.

Qualifications:
- degree or certificate in graphic design, industrial design, commercial art, architecture, interior design, theater design, or studio arts with course work in typography and media use;
- degree in discipline related to one of the areas of concentration of the museum;
- experience and proven ability in exhibition design, preferably in a museum or cultural attraction;
- experience in project management, exhibition fabrication, related construction work;
- demonstrated ability in the use of audiovisual and interactive techniques; knowledge of the museum's collections and standard conservation practice; and
- administrative ability and experience.

P-4   Exhibition Designer

The exhibition designer reports to the exhibitions officer and is responsible for:

- translating curatorial and educational staff ideas into permanent, temporary, or traveling exhibitions through renderings, plans, designs, specifications, drawings, models, lighting, and layout of exhibition materials;
- supervising and participating in fabrication and installation of exhibits, setting schedules and budgets, meeting opening and maintenance deadlines, and keeping within budget;
- dealing with outside contractors and providers of services as required for exhibition production;
- working with the exhibitions officer to integrate and implement technical systems and media operations and to update all warranty requirements; and
- drafting, selecting, and monitoring exhibition design and fabrication contracts.

Qualifications:

- degree or certificate in graphic design, industrial design, commercial art, or in architecture, interior design, theater design, or studio arts with course work in typography and media use;
- experience and proven ability in exhibition design, preferably in a museum or cultural attraction;
- experience in project management, exhibit production, related construction work, model making, or in media;
- demonstrated ability in the use of audiovisual and interactive techniques; and
- knowledge of the nature of the materials to be displayed and standard conservation practice.

P-5   Preparator/Technician

The preparator reports to the exhibitions officer and is responsible for:

- preparation, installation, and removal of all objects and materials in displays;
- preparation and packing of traveling exhibitions;
- preparation of cases and mounts for objects and exhibition materials;
- daily maintenance and operation of all permanent and temporary exhibitions, including audiovisual components;
- updating the designer on details of systems and operations and updating warranty requirements;
- maintenance of electronics, audiovisual, and computer-driven components of exhibits and shows;
- maintenance of lighting systems in exhibits and shows; and
- developing and testing new display techniques for security and conservation.

Qualifications:

- experience in the fabrication and installation of exhibitions;
- knowledge of and ability in carpentry, metal work, plastic forming;
- knowledge of and ability in electronics, audiovisual exhibit applications and computer-driven exhibits and shows; and
- knowledge of lighting systems and applications.

P-6   Graphic Designer

The graphic designer reports to the exhibit designer and is responsible for:

- design and production of graphic elements of exhibits, including signage and labels for all permanent, temporary, and traveling exhibits in keeping with the museum's established design standards;
- design and production of general orientation and circulation signage within and outside the museum; and
- design of virtual (online) exhibitions.

Qualifications:

- degree or certificate in graphic design or commercial art;
- experience in exhibition design, preferably in a museum or cultural attraction;
- experience in exhibit fabrication and installation;
- experience in information technology applications for websites.

P-7 (or A)   Museum Theater Manager

For museums with theaters, the manager reports to the deputy director for public programs. As noted by Amy Kaufman in her case study 3.6 in section 3.3.7, this position could also report to administration as part of the operations division. In either case, the position is responsible for:

- coordinating all performances, activities, and special events in support of the museum's overall programming and revenue goals;
- plans, policies, and procedures affecting the theater;
- liaison with education to schedule school-visit-related performances;
- scheduling, box office operation, ticket sales, front of house operations; and
- operation of the museum theater to maintain acoustic standards and ambience.

Qualifications:

- certificate in arts administration, theater, or performing arts or equivalent in experience;

- experience and proven ability in theater operations and management;
- good supervisory skills;
- knowledge of computerized ticketing systems; and
- entrepreneurial orientation.

P-8   Theater/Audiovisual Technician

This position reports to the theater manager for work in the theater, and to the exhibitions officer for work in the galleries. It is responsible for:

- projection of digital and analogue media in the theater or in multimedia and audiovisual components of the exhibits;
- sound and lighting effects for theatrical or gallery media, and their control systems;
- technical support services for all exhibitions, performances, and productions;
- maintenance and upkeep of museum theater equipment; and
- maintenance and repair of all audiovisual components of the museums exhibits.

Qualifications:

- certificate or other training in electronics; and
- demonstrated ability to maintain and operate sophisticated lighting and sound systems.

P-9 (or A or E)   Director of Communications

This is a position that could report to the deputy director for public programs, integrating all museum communications. In many museums it will report to the deputy director for administration; if there is a deputy director for external affairs, this position could report there. Responsible for:

- planning, design, and production of public programs in all communications media, from publications, graphics, and labels to audiovisual and digital communications;
- operation and maintenance of these programs;
- research and development of applications of imaging and graphic technology to the museum's public programs; and
- evaluation of the museum's publications and media programs in consultation with the evaluation officer.

Qualifications:

- experience in media planning, graphic design, and production;
- familiarity with multimedia programs; and
- knowledge of the collection or of the museum's subject matter.

P-10 (or A)   Director of Information Technology

Alternately or additionally to the foregoing position, an IT director has become a necessity in most museums today. This position could report to the deputy director for public programs, but in many museums will report to the deputy director for administration. Responsible for:

- planning, design, and operation of all information technology systems in the museum;
- cooperation with all departments using the IT systems;
- supervision of webmaster and any other IT personnel on staff or on contract;
- maintenance and upgrade of IT systems and services;
- research and development of new applications and systems; and
- evaluation of the museum's IT systems.

Qualifications:

- proficiency in the installation, operation, and maintenance of IT systems;
- experience in planning, design, and production of IT programs;
- experience with museum applications of IT systems;
- administrative ability; and
- good personal relations skills.

P (or A) -11   Webmaster

Reports to the director of information technology or to a director of communications, and is responsible for:

- planning, design, and production of the museum's website;
- operation and maintenance of the website, including response to interactive programs on the website;
- collaboration with exhibition officers and curatorial or education staff on the planning, design, and production of virtual exhibitions;
- collaboration with marketing and development departments on their web programs;
- research and development of new applications to the website;
- maintenance of website links; and
- evaluation of the website and of virtual exhibitions, in consultation with the evaluation officer.

Qualifications:

- experience in website planning, graphic design and operation;
- familiarity with interactive online programming; and
- experience with virtual exhibitions.

P-12 Education Officer

The education officer (who may be called director of education, or head of education services) reports to the deputy director for public programs and is responsible for:

- planning, managing, and delivery of learning programs in the museum and online;
- managing and developing partnerships with schools to offer curriculum-based programs related to the museum's collection, in the museum and/or in schools and online;
- setting standards for all educational programming;
- ongoing liaison with schools, community groups, and other target audiences to arrange programs of field trips consisting of guided tours and/or demonstrations;
- contributing to the design of exhibitions and other public programming to enhance their educational value;
- programming audio guides to the galleries;
- achievement of school attendance and revenue targets;
- preparation of publications or media-based products to schools;
- approval of promotional copy for the educational programs;
- developing and implementing adult education programs related to the museum's collection; and
- developing training programs for volunteer docents.

Qualifications:

- advanced degree in education and/or in an area related to the museum's specialization, and/or in museum studies;
- experience in the education and/or program area of a museum or cultural attraction;
- ability to design and implement learning programs, including the preparation of exhibitions and publications;
- demonstrated ability in communications and museum education techniques;
- knowledge of the objectives and curricula of the school system;
- knowledge of the museum's collections;
- knowledge of evaluation methods;
- administrative ability; and
- excellent personal relations skills.

P-13 Bookings Clerk

The booking clerk in most museums reports to the education officer, but as Amy Kaufman points out in her case study in section 3.3.7 may also report to the head of visitor services. The bookings clerk is responsible for:

- booking and scheduling school groups and public group tours;
- booking and scheduling paid staff or volunteer docents to meet group tours; and
- liaison with schools, community groups, and tour operators.

Qualifications:

- secondary school graduation;
- knowledge of and demonstrated ability in word processing, data entry, and scheduling software; and
- excellent accuracy and communication skills.

P-14   Studio Manager

For museums with visual arts studios, the studio manager reports to the education officer and is responsible for:

- development, implementation, and evaluation of a program of after-school and weekend classes for all ages in a variety of arts and technical disciplines;
- recruitment and coordination of professional technicians and artists to instruct in this program;
- achievement of attendance and revenue goals established for the program;
- liaison with schools, community groups, and other target audiences;
- preparation of all support materials; and
- preparation of promotional copy.

Qualifications:

- degree or certificate in visual art, or visual art studio experience;
- teacher's certificate;
- experience in a museum or related institution; and
- proven ability to design and implement educational experiences for students and families.

P-15   School Programs Manager

This position reports to the education officer and is responsible for:

- design and delivery of programs for school groups;
- preparation of school kits and resource materials;
- liaison with teachers and schools; and
- coordination of part-time museum teachers;

- training and evaluation of volunteer docents; and
- field trip programs.

Qualifications:

- degree in education or museum studies;
- experience in a museum education department or related institution;
- knowledge of objectives and curricula of the school system;
- knowledge in the area of the museum's collections; and
- knowledge of evaluation methods.

P-16   Adult Education Manager

This position reports to the education officer and is responsible for:

- design and delivery of learning programs for adults;
- coordination of part-time museum teachers; and
- training and evaluation of volunteer docents.

Qualifications:

- degree in education or museum studies;
- experience in a museum education department or related institution;
- knowledge in the area of the museum's collections; and
- knowledge of evaluation methods.

P-17   Educator/Demonstrator/Docent

These positions report to the education officer or to the school programs or adult education managers and are responsible for:

- planning and provision of tours of the museum's galleries for schools and other groups of all ages, for both permanent collection and temporary exhibitions;
- planning and provision of other museum educational programs;
- collaboration with teachers on educational use of the museum; and
- demonstrations in the galleries.

Qualifications:

- undergraduate degree in the museum's subject matter, or in education or museum studies;
- experience as a teacher, docent, or in other educational work;
- excellent communications and requisite language skills; and
- knowledge of the collection.

P-22 (or A or E)   Public Relations Officer

This position has similar reporting options to the marketing manager and is responsible for:

- the public image of the museum;
- relations with all media;
- promotion of all museum products and services;
- community relations; and
- monitoring trends, interests, and issues so the museum can respond to developments in areas affecting it.

Qualifications:

- university degree in public relations, communications, or journalism or equivalent in experience;
- proven experience in public relations in a museum or cultural attraction and in journalism or communications;
- extensive knowledge of the media and of writing, editing, and standard media formats; and
- ability to collaborate effectively with other staff in the implementation of effective public relations programs.

P-23   Evaluation Manager

The evaluation manager reports to the deputy director for public programs and is responsible for:

- measuring and documenting the public's perception of the relevance and enjoyment of the museum's products and services;
- the design and implementation of the museum's evaluation plan;
- design and implementation of visitor and nonvisitor surveys;
- gallery and exhibition evaluation;
- program and special event evaluation; and
- participation in the design of exhibitions, public programming, and other public products and services through normative and summative evaluation.

Qualifications:

- university degree in psychology or psychometry or equivalent in experience;
- knowledge and proven ability in the design, implementation, and interpretation of visitor studies and surveys; and
- experience in evaluation in a museum or other cultural attraction.

P-24   Publications Manager

The publications manager could report to the deputy director for public programs or to a director of communications and is responsible for:

- coordination and supervision of all printed and media materials produced by the museum such as annual reports, books, catalogs, guide books, film and lecture materials, newsletters, research journals, all historical reference works, and photographic and graphic reference works, as well as videos, CDs, DVDs, or other electronic or audiovisual media;
- editing all material and maintaining editorial standards of language and grammatical and stylistic form;
- ensuring all graphic design projects the museum's desired image;
- achievement of revenue targets; and
- distribution of materials in relation to print runs.

Qualifications:

- degree in literature, journalism, public relations, communications, or marketing;
- proven ability and extensive experience in all aspects of publishing, editing, print production, and distribution; and
- experience in working in a museum or related organization.

Administration Division

A-1   Deputy Director for Administration

Reports to the director and is responsible for:

- administration of the museum in accordance with its mission, goals, and objectives;
- establishment of financial objectives, in collaboration with the director and board;
- financial management including budget, accounting, purchasing, human resources, salary and benefits, insurance, taxes, and contracts;
- operation of physical plant and security; and
- visitor services and daily operations.

Qualifications:

- degree in accounting, business administration, or public administration;
- experience in administration;
- experience in a nonprofit cultural organization or related institution;
- knowledge of fund accounting and general fiscal practices including grants administration;

- knowledge of legal aspects of museum operation;
- knowledge of human resource procedures;
- knowledge of insurance requirements; and
- knowledge of office and museum equipment, data processing systems, physical plant management, and security and visitor services.

A-2 Administration Secretary

The administration secretary reports to the deputy director for administration and is responsible for:

- reception and inquiries; and
- administrative support services for the division.

Qualifications:
- secondary school graduation;
- previous experience in an office environment and knowledge of cultural organizations;
- word processing skills; and
- excellent communication skills.

A-3 Finance Officer

The finance officer reports to the deputy director for administration and is responsible for:

- financial management of the museum, including the budget, accounting, purchasing, salary and benefits, and insurance;
- contracts;
- taxes;
- membership, endowment, and fund-raising records;
- investments and interest earning accounts;
- external and internal auditing;
- revenue-generating activities such as the shop and food services; and
- supervision of bookkeeper and finance clerk.

Qualifications:
- degree in business administration or public administration or accounting; experience in administration in a nonprofit organization; and
- knowledge and proven ability in all aspects of accounting and fiscal practices.

A-4 Bookkeeper

The bookkeeper reports to the finance officer and is responsible for:

- maintenance and monitoring of accounts; and
- regular reporting on accounts.

Qualifications:
- certificate in bookkeeping; and
- related experience in a nonprofit organization.

A-5 Finance Clerk

The finance clerk reports to the finance officer and is responsible for:

- support services to the finance officer and the bookkeeper.

Qualifications:
- secondary school graduation; and
- previous experience in the financial administration department of a nonprofit institution.

A-6 Building Manager

This position reports to the deputy director for administration and is responsible for:

- management and operation of the physical plant;
- maintenance of environmental control and security systems in collaboration with the chief conservator and the chief of security;
- management of contracts for maintenance and repair services;
- management of contracts for security services and cleaning, if these are contracted;
- management of rentals of the building for revenue-generating purposes; and
- supervision of maintenance staff.

Qualifications:
- engineering background preferred;
- knowledge of building management and maintenance systems;
- proven ability in the management and operation of a large, multiuse facility; and
- excellent communication and supervisory skills.

A-7   Maintenance Worker

Maintenance workers report to the building manager and are responsible for:

- cleaning of all noncollection items in the galleries;
- cleaning of all other areas of the building;
- removal of garbage;
- replacement of lamps; and
- replacement of supplies to toilets and first aid stations.

Qualifications:

- knowledge of cleaning equipment and techniques to meet museum standards; and
- experience in maintenance of museums or other public facilities.

A-8   Rentals Manager

The rentals manager reports to the building manager and is responsible for:

- promotion and operation of a program to rent the museum's facilities for functions such as meetings, conferences, parties, and receptions;
- inquiries and bookings;
- liaison with caterers and furniture rental companies;
- liaison with tour operators, corporations, and other target client groups; and
- coordination of security and cleaning staff for events.

Qualifications:

- secondary school graduation;
- previous experience in the management of functions in a nonprofit organization;
- entrepreneurial orientation;
- hotel or restaurant experience; and
- knowledge of the museum's potential as well as its limitations as a physical setting for functions.

A-9   Visitor Services Manager

This position reports to the deputy director for administration and is responsible for:

- visitor reception and orientation;
- information in the form of maps of the building or other media;

- visitor inquiries about events and programs;
- operation of amenities such as coat room, toilets, and catering;
- handicapped access and assistance;
- scheduling and supervision of visitor service staff;
- visitor comments and complaints;
- monitoring the overall quality of the visitor experience in collaboration with public program staff; and
- first aid, safety, and emergency planning and provision for staff and visitors.

Qualifications:

- degree in public relations, communications, museum studies, or equivalent in experience;
- proven ability to manage visitor services functions in a cultural attraction or museum setting;
- knowledge of and interest in the museum's field; and
- excellent public relations, communication, and supervisory skills.

A-10 Coat Room Supervisor

This position reports to the visitor services manager and is responsible for:

- daily management and operation of the coat room;
- supervision of staff; and
- first aid and safety for visitors.

Qualifications:

- secondary school graduation or equivalent in experience;
- previous experience in the operation of coat room function; and
- training in first aid.

A-11 Reception/Tickets/Information Desk Clerks

Report to the visitor services manager and are responsible for:

- welcoming visitors;
- providing orientation and other information to visitors; and
- selling tickets (if admission is charged) and admitting visitors.

Qualifications:

- excellent communications skills;
- knowledge of and interest in the museum's field; and
- retail or cashier experience.

A-12   Food Services Manager

Food services are usually contracted, but whether on staff or contract the food services manager reports to the visitor services manager and is responsible for:

- planning and provision of food and refreshments to visitors;
- supervision of kitchen and serving staff;
- meeting food service revenue targets;
- procuring provisions;
- maintaining kitchen and serving equipment; and
- supervision of outside caterers serving rentals.

Qualifications:

- food service experience at a level of quality appropriate to the food services in the museum;
- administrative experience in food service;
- knowledge of dietary and culinary principles; and
- familiarity with equipment appropriate to the museum's level of food services.

A-13   Food Services Staff

Report to the food services manager and are responsible for:

- preparation or serving of food and refreshments to visitors; and
- maintenance of cafe or restaurant and kitchen.

Qualifications:

- experience in kitchens or restaurants of comparable quality to the museum's provision;
- familiarity with cooking or serving equipment and its maintenance; and
- experience in handling cash and making change.

A-14   Chief of Security

Reports to the deputy director for administration and is responsible for:

- security of the collections and the building;
- safety of visitors, staff, and others in the building;
- maintenance of security records and tapes;
- operation and monitoring of closed-circuit television (CCTV); and
- maintenance of intrusion alarm contract and system;

- maintenance of fire detection, alarm, and deterrent systems;
- planning and implementation of response to emergencies of all kinds; and
- supervision and scheduling of security guards.

Qualifications:
- secondary school education;
- experience in security, police, fire protection, or related areas of work;
- administrative experience;
- experience in museums or other public facilities; and
- knowledge of systems in use in the building.

A-15   Security Guards

Report to the chief of security and are responsible for:

- invigilation of galleries;
- surveillance of visitors and all others entering the museum;
- monitoring of closed-circuit television (CCTV) screens;
- admission of visitors, staff, delivery personnel;
- provision of security records; and
- response to emergencies.

Qualifications:
- experience in security, police, fire protection, or related areas of work;
- knowledge of the operation of museum security and surveillance systems; and
- excellent communications skills.

A-16   Human Resources Manager

Reports to the deputy director for administration and is responsible for:

- recruitment, training, and development of an outstanding staff for the museum;
- contributing to the creation of policies concerning the employment and safety of all staff and the terms and conditions that apply;
- developing and managing payment systems in coordination with the finance officer;
- negotiation, hiring, and placement procedures of paid staff;
- liaison with unions and employee associations;
- development and administration of professional training and development policies and procedures;

- developing and managing training and development;
- managing and monitoring health and benefits package;
- programs for all museum staff to stimulate a "learning organization"; and
- assisting managers with regular employment review processes.

Qualifications:

- degree in human resources management or equivalent experience;
- knowledge of health, pensions, tax, and benefits programs;
- previous experience in managing human resources for a nonprofit institution;
- knowledge of human resources data processing systems; and
- excellent interpersonal communications skills.

A-17   Human Resources Clerk

Reports to the human resources manager and is responsible for:

- reception and inquiries regarding personnel matters; and
- support services for the human resources manager including record keeping, correspondence, and circulation of relevant information to employees.

Qualifications:

- secondary school education;
- previous experience in human resources, preferably in a nonprofit institution;
- knowledge of human resources data processing systems;
- word processing skills; and
- good interpersonal communications skills.

A-18 (or E)   Development Officer

The director of development usually reports to the deputy director for administration, but may instead report to a deputy director for external affairs in larger museums where this position is created. Responsible for:

- coordinating and directing the fund-raising activities of the museum, including capital projects, endowments, annual giving, membership drives, sponsorships, and grant applications to government, corporations, and foundations;
- plans and supervises special fund-raising events;
- supervises membership staff; and
- may also supervise retail staff.

Qualifications:

- university degree in business, arts administration, or marketing;
- experience in fund-raising on a scale consistent with the needs of the museum;
- experience in development of a nonprofit institution;
- knowledge of financial management;
- ability to motivate and train trustees and senior museum staff for fund-raising;
- administrative ability; and
- knowledge of and experience in the museum's community.

A-19 (or E) Development Secretary

Reports to the development officer and is responsible for:

- support services to the development officer, including correspondence, scheduling of meetings, and record-keeping.

Qualifications:

- secondary school graduation;
- knowledge of software and data base programs; and
- excellent communications skills.

A-20 Retail Manager

Reports to the deputy director for administration, and is responsible for:

- meeting objectives for sales and revenues;
- promotion and sales of appropriate museum merchandise;
- all aspects of the operation of the shop including record-keeping of sales and expenditures, inventory development and maintenance, monitoring sales and promotions, shop display and organization;
- acquisition of stock, subject to curatorial approval; and
- hiring and supervision of sales staff and volunteers.

Qualifications:

- extensive experience in retail operations of a character related to the intended quality of the museum shop;
- strong entrepreneurial orientation;
- excellent financial management skills;
- knowledge of effective display and promotional techniques; and
- proven supervisory skills.

A-21 Sales Clerks

Report to the retail manager and are responsible for:

- customer sales;
- inventory maintenance; and
- stocking and pricing of merchandise.

Qualifications:

- experience in customer sales;
- ability to handle cash and make change; and
- good communications skills.

A-22 Membership Manager

Reports to the development officer and is responsible for:

- attracting and maintaining the interest and support of target audiences in membership;
- developing and implementing strategies for recruiting members;
- planning, promoting, and coordinating special events, services, and benefits for the members;
- maintenance of records and mailing lists; and
- supervision of membership clerk.

Qualifications:

- secondary school education;
- experience in membership of a nonprofit association;
- knowledge of database records management; and
- excellent interpersonal communications skills.

A-23 Membership Clerk

Reports to the membership manager and is responsible for:

- reception and inquiries regarding membership;
- upkeep of membership records and mailing lists; and
- support services in the coordination of special events.

Qualifications:

- secondary school education;
- ability in word processing and database management; and
- excellent customer relations and communication skills.

External Relations

E-1 Deputy Director for External Relations

This is a senior but optional position that may be considered for larger museums. This position would supervise the directors of communications, marketing, public relations, development, and membership. Although these positions have been shown reporting elsewhere, they would be relocated to this department. The deputy director would report to the director, and would be responsible for:

- the museum's relations with its communities, local to global, including communities of interest;
- coordinating development, marketing, and membership programs to achieve optimal results;
- supervising all museum communications; and
- ensuring that the museum's brand is appropriately managed.

Qualifications:
- university degree in a discipline related to the museum;
- experience in managing the brand of a nonprofit institution;
- proven administrative capability;
- knowledge of and experience in fund-raising, marketing, and public relations; and
- outstanding interpersonal skills.

E-2 External Affairs Secretary

The external affairs secretary reports to the deputy director for external affairs and is responsible for:

- reception and inquiries; and
- administrative support services for the division.

Qualifications:
- secondary school graduation;
- previous experience in an office environment and knowledge of cultural organizations;
- word processing skills; and
- excellent communication skills.

All other reports to the deputy director for external affairs have already been included in other divisions to which they may alternately report.

Glossary

The following is a glossary of commonly used terms in the field of museum management. Most of these terms are more fully described in the text.

acquisition fund: the amount allocated for purchasing objects for the collection, and in some case for the expenses associated with acquisition as well.

acquisitions committee: a group of **trustees** delegated by a museum's **board** to consider issues of **collection policy** and **collection development strategy**, as well as recommendations for additions to the collections (and deaccessioing), which should come only from the relevant curators.

acquisition methods: may include gifts, bequests, purchases, fieldwork, deposits from other museums, and acceptance of acquisitions from government programs or agencies responsible for cultural property protection.

administration: coordination of museum functions in order to realize the museum's **mission**.

advisory board (or visiting committee): a nongoverning group usually appointed to represent the public interest and empowered only to recommend policy, usually to the governing authority of **line department** museums.

aesthetic display: a mode of exhibition of works of art, specimens, or artifacts arranged to stimulate contemplation of museum objects for their own sake.

architect of record: a local architect licensed to practice in that jurisdiction, who may be responsible for continuing the building or renovation process through detailed design.

arm's length: the metaphorical distance between a museum and the political authority allocating or granting funds to it.

attendance, revenue, and expense projections: a forecast of all sources of income and all categories of expenditures.

automation: the process of transferring manual records (e.g., collection records) to computerized form.

best practice study: comparative analysis of outstanding successes in specific programs or activities in other institutions.

bid documents: formal issue of detailed technical scope of work for a competitive contract award for construction or fabrication.

board (or trust): a fiduciary body to whom the public interest in the museum may be committed to be administered with the same diligence, honesty, and discretion as prudent people would exercise in managing their own affairs.

brief: instructions for the architect or designer from the client or user pertaining to the requirements for space, facilities, or exhibitions.

budget: a plan with money attached; monetary values allocated as the resources needed to attain the **objectives** which are the quantified short-term applications to the budget year of the museum's longer-range qualitative **goals**.

budget by department: the most common method of projecting revenue and expenditures, whereby each department is asked to review its past year's allocations, adjust for current objectives and tasks, and recommend next year's figures.

budget by function: a useful method of review of allocations in terms of the fundamental museum functions—collecting, documentation, preservation, research, display, interpretation, administration.

budget by objectives: a useful review process in which fluctuations in the current year's proposed allocations are evaluated in relation to the **objectives** identified in the museum's **corporate plan** and the outcomes they are intended to achieve.

budget by program: projection of revenue and expenditures in terms of activities or services to be provided in accordance with the priority given to that activity in the current year's plans.

building code: standards for built space as defined by government authority in a given jurisdiction.

building committee: a group appointed by the museum's **board** to oversee and control a construction or renovation project.

building imagery modeling (BIM): computer application combining many or all structural, mechanical, electrical, plumbing, and other designs for a planned construction or renovation.

building management (or automation) system (BMS or BAS): a computerized system of controlling and monitoring atmospheric conditions throughout a building.

building team: a group of professionals—architect, engineers, landscape architects, contractors, construction manager, and other technical specialists—who meet with the **project manager** and endeavor to meet the requirements of the **functional brief** with technical drawings and specifications, and with the actual construction of the building.

business plan: a document that projects the viability of a project or of operations under certain conditions or assumptions, which in the museum context may include a collections analysis; a public programming plan; statements of mission, mandate, and purpose; recommendations as to institutional status and structure; space and facilities requirements; staffing requirements; market analysis; marketing and operational recommendations; projections of capital and operating expenditures and revenues; and an implementation schedule.

capital budget (or funds): financial resources retained for planned development of the museum's site or buildings, such as renovation, relocation, new construction, or exhibition renewal.

capital cost projection: the amount needed to upgrade or build the requisite space, to provide furnishings and equipment, or to build the planned exhibits.

capital costs: the onetime costs of acquiring a site and building or renovating a facility or exhibit.

case statement: a document that articulates the rationale for donating funds for a particular project or for the continuation of the programs to be funded.

cataloging: curatorial recording of works of art, artifacts, or specimens (more extensive than **registration**), aiming to record a full sense of each object's significance in relation to other objects in the collection, in other collections, and in the world at large.

change order: a contract document issued by the client to the contractor, authorizing an alteration in the original design or specifications of a building or exhibition under construction or installation.

code of ethics: a set of principles affecting **trustees** and staff of museums in relation to the museum they serve, intended to avoid conflicts of interest and to respect relevant international conventions and national, state, provincial, or local laws pertinent to artifacts, specimens, or works of art.

collection analysis: quantitative and qualitative study of the contents of a museum collection in meaningful groups or classifications, and of the spatial and facilities requirements of the collection, including projection and provision for its future growth over a stated time period and for the security, documentation, and preservation of the collection.

collection development strategy: projection of both qualitative and quantitative growth of the collection.

collection policy (or collection management policy): the museum's fundamental document governing the scope and limitations of its intended collection, together with standards for its acquisition, documentation, preservation, security, and management.

collective bargaining agreement: a set of principles, policies, and practices affecting the working conditions of personnel in museums where the staff are unionized, approved by both the union and the museum.

commissioning: provision of the completed building (or exhibition) to the client by the contractor and architect (or designer).

comparables analysis: Examination of successes and failures of museums of comparable size and scope.

competitive bidding: comparison of tenders submitted by contractors for work specified; the tender selected usually being the lowest in other sectors, but not always in the museum field due to the need for museum standards of quality.

condition report: a document prepared by a conservator to record the state of a work of art, artifact, or specimen at the time of the report.

connoisseurship: the intimate knowledge of a collection rooted in an acquired ability to perceive, to make distinctions, and above all, to make judgments, about the works of art, artifacts, or specimens in the collection.

conservation: maximizing the endurance or minimizing the deterioration of an object through time, with as little change to the object as possible.

conservation policy: a document establishing the museum's long-range qualitative standards for both preventive conservation and conservation treatment.

conservation treatment plan: a detailed proposal for intervention in the condition of a work of art, artifact, or specimen aimed at enhancing its preservation through reversible procedures.

contemplative mode: type of presentation most commonly used in art galleries (but also found in other museums) in which works of art, artifacts, or specimens are presented in an aesthetic mode enhancing the visitors' affective experience or aesthetic appreciation of them.

contemporary collecting: acquisition of artifacts or works of art of today with a view to their future appreciation as the heritage of later generations.

contextual, thematic, or didactic display: a mode of presentation in which artifacts, specimens, or works of art are placed in context so that their significance may be better understood, often in relation to an interpretative theme.

contracting: agreements with individuals or companies to undertake specific functions for the museum (e.g., security, cleaning, catering) as an alternative to employing permanent staff.

contractor: individual or company who undertakes to fulfill a contract to build or renovate a structure.

contributed revenue: funds allocated, granted, or donated by individuals, governments or agencies to the museum in support of its **mission,** including government subsidy, grant-aid, endowments, sponsorship, and donations.

control: a function of management, monitoring budgets, and scheduling to ensure that resources of time and money are utilized in accordance with allocations.

corporate plan (or business plan): a document focussing all museum functions towards fulfillment of the museum's **mission** and **goals** within a specific planning period and financial framework.

cost-effectiveness: a measure of the qualitative and quantitative extent to which the museum's expenditures achieve the intended result.

criticality: correlation of the probability of a security risk and the degree of its impact (vulnerability), used to determine priorities among security requirements.

cultural tourism: travel away from home to experience the arts, heritage, or lifestyle of people and places.

deaccessioning: removing works of art, artifacts, or specimens from a collection.

defense: a countermeasure identified in the museum's **security policy** that should be detailed in the **emergency procedures manual** for the appropriate response by staff in the event of a threat.

delay: a countermeasure identified in the museum's **security policy** to retard progress of a threat.

design/build: a contract combining design responsibilities with the construction of the object of design.

design concept: the initial drawings of a building or exhibition, which are generally based on a brief.

design development: the stage in exhibition or building design in which the design concept is elaborated into detailed drawings, sometimes called information drawings (see also **schematic design**).

design team: the group of practicing professionals who plan the disposition of spaces, materials, and facilities of a museum building or exhibition based on the approved **brief** or **program**.

design day: a day of good (but not peak) attendance for which space and facilities are to be provided.

design year: the year for which a long-range plan, such as a master plan or a collection development strategy, is to provide—usually about ten to twenty years in the future.

detection: countermeasures identified in the museum's **security policy** to determine whether and when threats occur, including surveillance by warders or guards, intrusion alarms, smoke detectors, display case alarms, and closed-circuit television.

deterrence: a countermeasure identified in the museum's **security policy** to reduce the likelihood of a threat.

display collection: a group of artifacts, specimens, or works of art acquired primarily for exhibition and interpretation purposes with the intention of their indefinite preservation.

documentation: preparation and maintenance of a permanent record of the history and description of collections and all transactions related to them.

documentation procedures manual: explicit instructions for registrars, catalogers, and data entry clerks to register and/or catalog the collection.

donation: a gift or bequest of artifacts, specimens, or works of art and/or of funds in support of the museum's **mission**.

donation in kind: provision of goods (other than collections) and/or services in support of the museum's **mission**.

education plan: a document projecting the **goals** and **objectives** of the museum's education services, together with the means of attaining them.

effectiveness: a measure of the qualitative and quantitative extent to which the museum's efforts of all kinds achieve the intended result.

efficiency: a measure of effectiveness in proportion to the effort required to achieve it—in person-hours, money, space, or in the use of facilities or equipment.

emergency procedures manual: a staff handbook of actions to be taken in the event of threats, accident, illness, flood, fire, earthquake, hurricane, tornado, or other disruptions of museum buildings or services.

emergency team: a group of museum employees empowered to coordinate emergency procedures.

employee development programs: assisting workers to acquire new capabilities so that they may qualify for other positions.

endowment fund: donations or bequests that are invested, with all or only a portion of the interest earned being spent, either on operations (in the case of unrestricted funds) or for specific purposes such as acquisitions, exhibitions, or lectures series (restricted funds).

environmental mode: type of presentation in which a room setting or large scale exhibit is used to re-create or evoke the atmosphere of the time and place in which the museum objects were used or developed.

environmental scan: the initial step in a strategic planning process, aimed at beginning with an understanding of changes in the external environment affecting the museum or gallery directly and indirectly, such as economic, demographic, community, market, and museological issues, taking into consideration local, regional, national, and international trends and developments.

evaluation: qualitative and quantitative measurement of museum programs relative to their objectives.

exhibition committee: sometimes a group of **trustees** delegated to consider **exhibion policy**; but more often a specific staff committee or task force that combines the talents of all those responsible for the many aspects of an exhibition program.

exhibition plan: a statement of the theme, objectives, and means of expression of a proposed exhibition, which may be accompanied by a projected layout and budget (see also **interpretative plan**).

exhibition policy: a statement of the objectives of the exhibition program, the philosophy of presentation, and the number, frequency, size, and scope of temporary as well as permanent collection exhibitions.

extension: programs that museums offer outside the museum building or site.

external assessment: as part of a strategic planning process, an effort to see the museum as others see it and to learn from this external perspective by such means as visitor surveys; community surveys; workshops; focus groups; and interviews with knowledgeable persons in the field, community leaders, donors, sponsors, and funders as well as frequent museum-users and—notably—nonusers.

facilities plan or strategy: a document deducing the space and facilities required for the collections in storage and on display, for the public programs and amenities, and for the needed support facilities and work spaces for staff.

facilities programming: a broad planning activity usually undertaken by a specialist consultant to determine the facilities required by an institution undergoing new construction, physical expansion, or alteration, including the design and performance criteria of those facilities.

feasibility study: a determination of the viability of a proposed or existing institution, or of the further development of an institution, including financial feasibility, marketing prospects, funding sources, visitation and revenue projections, structural suitability of an existing building, viability of various proposed sites, and other factors, undertaken by specialist consultants independent of the project itself, with a view to making explicit the conditions under which a proposed project may be viable, usually not in terms of a profit-making or even a break-even budget, but in proportion to the requirement for subsidy, endowment, or other sources of contributed income.

fire compartmentalization: the practice of dividing large spaces (such as a museum storage area) into smaller areas by means of fire walls, in order to contain the spread of fire.

fire rating: standardized projection of the time period that a building material or construction can withstand fire without collapsing or allowing the fire to pass through.

fire wall: a division between rooms that is resistant to fire for the length of time specified in its fire rating.

first-person interpretation: method of interpretation in which costumed actors play their parts in period and answer visitors' questions from within the time and space parameters of the historic setting.

formative evaluation: measuring the effectiveness of an exhibition while the exhibition is taking shape (or form) so that the exhibition will communicate accurately and effectively with its visitors.

foundation: philanthropic organization with educational, research, or social service objectives that can be a source of contributed revenue for museums.

fumigation: elimination of insect pests from museum objects.

functional brief (or program): a systematic document written in the users' language, describing the functions required of a building and its systems and facilities, its circulation patterns, and adjacency and access requirements, including a room-by-room identification of every technical variable (light, humidity, filtration, and the like) affecting each room in the building.

functions: the essential activities of a museum—collecting, documentation, conservation, research, display, interpretation, and the administration of these six core activities.

fund-raising: programs or activities designed to stimulate contributed revenue.

funding strategy: meets both the **capital fund** and **operating fund** requirements from public, private, and self-generated sources.

goals: the long-range qualitative standards or levels of program fulfillment or achievement toward which the museum is striving, usually articulated in a **master plan** or **corporate plan**.

governance: the ultimate legal and financial responsibility for a museum.

governing board: the group of **trustees** appointed to assume responsibility for governance of the museum; reviewing and determining policy and long-range plans; and usually engaging, evaluating, and eventually terminating the museum's director.

grant project: government or foundation funding program with specific objectives.

grievance procedure: method of handling staff complaints about working conditions or treatment of personnel, usually defined in a **collective bargaining agreement**.

halon fire extinguisher: a method of control of fire by means of expulsion of halon gas from hand-held extinguishers, now being phased out due to environmental considerations.

halon system: a method of control of fire by means of expulsion of halon gas from overhead, now illegal in many jurisdictions and being phased out everywhere due to environmental considerations.

hands-on mode: type of presentation or approach whereby exhibits encourage visitors to learn by doing, especially popular in children's museums and science centers but also used elsewhere.

hazardous materials store: a storage cabinet constructed of nonflammable and fire retardant materials and under key control to qualified users only, for storing hazardous materials used in the museum, such as some conservation laboratory supplies.

hierarchy: any organizational structure in which lower levels of responsibility and authority report to higher levels, resulting in a pyramidal structure culminating in the director.

high-security store: a level of security for museum stores, typically with all-interior masonry walls, ceilings, and floors, and with steel doors and frames with a minimum six-pin tumbler lock and key control, usually required for works of art, weapons, furs, and other objects of high value.

high security: a degree of security required for exhibitions of highly valuable items with special provisions, possibly including constant surveillance during open hours.

human resources policy: a set of guidelines addressing issues such as statutory regulations, salary, benefits, expense provisions, probationary period, hours of work and overtime, statutory holidays, vacation, sick leave, maternity or paternity leave and leave of absence, training and professional development, intellectual property provisions, grievance and harassment procedures, performance review, and termination conditions.

hygrothermograph: a device for monitoring and recording fluctuations in relative humidity.

hypertext: a link between one computer document and other related documents elsewhere in a collection, facilitating staff or visitor access to related museum documentation.

implementation: deployment of time, money, and staff to accomplish the museum's **goals** and **objectives** according to agreed priorities, assigning responsibility and reallocating or acquiring new resources.

implementation schedule: a calendar of the steps needed to develop the museum from its present situation to the one outlined in the master plan.

indemnity: a process in lieu of insurance of objects on loan for museum exhibitions, under which the government secures the museum or the lender against any loss.

information management: activities and programs facilitating the effective production, coordination, storage, retrieval, and dissemination of spoken and written text and images in all formats and from internal or external sources, leading to the more efficient functioning of the museum.

information model: a graphic illustration of the current tasks and consequent flow of text and image data and desired improvements in these patterns.

information policy: a commitment by museum management to standards of documentation of and public access to records about and interpretation of the collection, addressing issues of intellectual property and the museum's participation in databases or other means of dissemination of museum records, including images.

information system plan: an analysis of all data-related functions, both text and imagery, with recommendations for their efficient integration, compatibility, and future growth.

institutional context: issues related to the museum's relationship with other institutions and agencies, such as all levels of government, educational institutions, other museums, specialist groups, the tourist industry, and potential donors or sponsors in the private sector.

institutional plan: a strategic planning document that examines and makes recommendations for both the museum's internal organization (its governance structure, and its **mission**, **mandate**, and **statement of purpose**), and its external relations with its institutional context (government, educational institutions, other museums, private sector, tourism, and so on).

interactive mode: a means of expression in museum exhibitions that involves the visitor in active physical and/or intellectual dialogue with the exhibition.

interactivity: physical or intellectual interaction between the public and museum exhibits.

internal assessment: a step in the strategic planning process consisting of a review of the institution's programs and operations using available documentation and discussions with museum management, staff, volunteers, members, and **trustees** to develop an analysis of a museum's strengths, weaknesses, opportunities, and threats (a "SWOT" analysis).

Internet: a global network of data networks and an informal computer service that links groups of computers from government, university, and private or public service organizations and individuals all over the world.

interpretation: communication of the museum with its public about the meaning of its collections.

interpretative plan (or exhibition brief): a strategy that articulates the objectives of the museum in interpretation, the quality of the visitor experience intended, and a component-by-component description of the exhibition that lists the communication objectives of each component and the potential means of expression to achieve these objectives, along with diagrams of visitor flow patterns and concept sketches to give the "feel" of the exhibition (see also **exhibit plan**).

job description: a succinct statement of the responsibilities of and qualifications for a post and the reporting relationship (see appendix).

key issues: in the strategic planning process, the fundamental questions that the museum must address in order to become a more effective and successful institution.

leadership: the ability to inspire people with a sense of the museum's **mission** in order to achieve its **goals**.

liability: legal and financial responsibility for one's own or other's actions, especially for the actions of an institution such as a museum.

life-cycle costing: projecting long-range capital and operating costs of a building through to its eventual replacement.

line department museum: museum administered as an integral division or agency of a government ministry, university, or corporation, and funded primarily through allocations from the budget of the governing organization.

lux: metric unit for measuring the intensity of light (10.76 lux = 1 footcandle).

lux level: the amount of visible light to which a museum object is being exposed; most accurately calculated as lux hours per annum, being the lux level at any given time multiplied by the number of hours the lights with that lux level are turned on the object.

management: facilitating decision making in an organization so that it can achieve its **goals**.

mandate: the range of material culture for which a museum assumes responsibility, which may be stated in terms of an academic discipline, geographical range, chronological range, or specialization, and may be qualified in relation to other institutions.

market: the actual and potential public for a museum.

market analysis: the process by which existing and potential audiences for a facility or program may be understood and projected.

market segmentation: analysis of the potential visitors to a museum into groups sufficiently homogeneous that the institution can effectively plan programs to meet the needs of each segment and prioritize its development of staff, facilities, and budget accordingly.

marketing: all ways and means to provide museum services to visitors by stimulating and increasing attendance, length of stay, visitor satisfaction, expenditures, and return visits, not merely through advertising but through customer services and activities that will meet the museum's **objectives** and motivate visitors to return.

marketing strategy: ways in which the museum enhances its communication with and service to its target audiences with the objective of boosting attendance and visitor spending, thereby building a closer relationship with its audiences leading to return visits, increased membership, and donations.

master plan: organization of museum functions and resources toward the achievement of a desired level of effectiveness, often reviewing all aspects of the institution and projecting requirements for additional space, staffing, or finances, as well as means of attaining them.

matrix: an organizational structure in which functions are arranged as axes of interaction.

microenvironment: a climate-controlled and secure space for the display or storage of artifacts or specimens within a sealed case or frame, used in buildings where such control is not feasible in entire rooms.

mission: an objective, brief, and hopefully inspiring assertion of a museum's long-range reason for existence, which serves as the foundation of all **policy** development.

multimedia: use of multiple methods of communication in one coordinated exhibit apparatus to appeal to multiple senses, usually employing computer and/or electronic technology.

museum: a nonprofit permanent establishment open to the public and administered in the public interest, for the purpose of conserving and preserving, studying, interpreting, assembling, and exhibiting to the public for its instruction and enjoyment objects and specimens of educational and cultural value, including artistic, scientific (whether animate or inanimate), historical, and technological material.

museum planner: a museum professional specializing in the planning of museum space, facilities, functions, services, operations, and/or administration.

museum planning: the study and practice of facilitating the preservation and interpretation of material culture by ordering all those components that comprise a museum into a constructed or renovated whole that can achieve its functions with optimal efficiency.

museum project team: the working group of museum personnel in a museum renovation or construction project whose task is to ensure that the museum's requirements are clearly stated in a **functional brief or program**, and that those requirements are met by the architects, engineers, and contractors.

museums service: an organization of museums and/or a government agency to serve a group of museums.

naming rights: acknowledgment given to donors often tied to pacesetting donations. Buildings, wings, galleries, or display cases may be named for donors at specific value levels.

nomenclature: a structured and controlled list of terms organized in a classification system to provide the basis for indexing and cataloging collections.

nonpublic collection zone: areas of a museum in which environmental controls and security are provided for the preservation of the collection, but with a level of finish adequate for staff use only (Zone C).

nonpublic noncollection zone: areas of a museum requiring environmental controls adequate for staff comfort only and levels of finish appropriate to staff use only (Zone D).

nonprofit (or charitable) organization: an institution registered with its government under letters of patent or a charitable tax number allowing it to provide tax-deductible receipts for donations and to receive other benefits allowed by government policy in each jurisdiction.

object theater: a mode of presentation to visitors in which artifacts, specimens, replicas, or other apparatus may be featured, usually by means of spotlights or other illumination, with a voice-over script and projected imagery interpreting them by relating a thematic story line in which they appear.

objectives: short-range, quantified levels of achievement specified in plans and budgets as measures of fufillment of longer-range qualitative **goals**.

operating budget: a projection of allocations for the museum's **operating costs**, usually prepared annually.

operating (or running) costs: ongoing expenses of a museum, including salaries and benefits, building occupancy costs, maintenance, security, curatorial and conservation expenses, administration, marketing, and the cost of public programming.

operating grant: a grant-aid program that provides contributions to the **operating costs** of museums.

organizational chart: a diagram of an institution's management structure.

orientation: information provided to visitors as to where they are, what services are available and where, in what languages service is provided, what there is to see and do, and how to find it.

outreach: museum activities that are designed to appeal (or "reach out") to new or nontraditional audiences, whether offered in the museum or at another location.

pacesetting donation: a gift that can be cited (anonymously or not, as the donor prefers) when approaching other potential donors.

partnerships: cooperation with other museums, institutions, agencies, and attractions by sharing resources.

performance review: evaluation of an employee's effectiveness and efficiency in the accomplishment of museum functions in relation to the museum's **goals** and **objectives**.

perimeter alarm: an intrusion alarm that should be installed at all entrances and on all windows, including any skylights or other roof access points, preferably with direct telephone connection via dedicated lines to a police station or security company.

personnel policy: a statement of the museum's expectations and a commitment within the museum's means to its staff in relation to working conditions.

picture (or art) rental: a service to visitors of providing works of art for monthly hire to homes or offices, sometimes restricted to museum members only.

planned giving: donations and bequests scheduled to meet the needs of the donor and his or her estate as well as those of the museum.

policy: a statement of the museum's commitment to its **mission, mandate,** and **statement of purposes** in relation to a particular museum function (such as a **collection policy, conservation policy, security policy, exhibition policy, research policy, interpretation policy,** and the like), and to the achievement of specific levels of quality in fulfilling this commitment.

preparator: a museum worker whose task is the preparation of works of art, artifacts, or specimens for display or loan, and the installation and dismounting of these museum exhibits.

preventive conservation: the applied science of providing an environment that minimizes the deterioration of works of art, artifacts, or specimens.

private ownership museums: those owned and operated by individuals, foundations, or companies either for a profit or as private charities.

procedures: the systematic means of accomplishing museum functions in such a way as to achieve the museum's **objectives.**

procedures manual: a method of codifying and communicating the systematic means of conducting museum functions and related tasks in order to realize the level of quality desiderated in the museum's **policies.**

production for sale: manufacture in traditional methods by museum demonstrators, often on industrial heritage properties, of products that are offered for sale, either directly to visitors or by distribution to others.

program budget: estimated cost of an activity reflecting the performance and quality criteria indicated for that activity.

project manager: an individual or company, independent of or on the museum staff whose function is to bring under a single coordinating authority all those involved in a project's implementation, in order to ensure that the project **objectives** are achieved and that it is completed on time, within budget, to an agreed level of quality, and with minimal disruption to other functions.

public collection zone: areas of a museum with environmental controls and security designed for the preservation of the collection and with a level of finish and durability appropriate to public use (Zone B).

public fund-raising campaign: the well-publicized aspect of a fundraising campaign that is usually directed at securing relatively small amounts from a large number of donors, often amounting to only 5–10 percent of the total to be raised, but demonstrating to other funding sources the degree of public support for the museum or the project to be funded.

public noncollection zone: area of a museum in which environmental controls need to achieve human comfort levels only, but in which levels of finish and durability must be appropriate for public use.

public program plan: a strategy for all activities that the museum wishes to undertake or has been undertaking to serve its visitors and other users, ranging from exhibitions through interpretation of its collection to education; publications; extension services; outreach; and such public amenities as toilets, shops, or catering, projected in relation to the museum's target markets.

public private partnership (PPP): an agreement between a public service institution such as a museum or government organization and a private sector entity, which could be a for-profit corporation or a private nonprofit institution, to undertake a project or development together for mutual benefit.

public trust: responsibility (in some jurisdictions a legal responsibility) for the collective material heritage of others, which is assumed by the governing body of the museum, to care for that heritage not only for the present generation, but for their descendants in perpetuity with the same prudence that one would be expected to exercise if the property were one's own.

quantity surveyor: a professional consultant specializing in the estimation of quantitative requirements to achieve qualitative goals, and therefore projecting capital cost and occupancy cost estimates for buildings, systems, facilities, and functions.

redundancy: the capability of building systems to sustain operation despite malfunction or power outage.

registration: the process of numbering artifacts, specimens, or works of art in a museum collection, and recording a range of data about each of them—such as name and function of the object, its artist or maker, source and provenance, place and date of origin, materials, and so on.

relative humidity (RH): the ratio, expressed as a percentage, of the absolute humidity of sampled air to that of air saturated with water at the same temperature.

representative collection: museum objects selected to represent ideas, concepts, or themes, or to be indicative of a time period or geographical area.

request for proposals: formal document asking companies or individuals to present their understanding of, approach to, and methodology for a defined scope of work, usually but not always asking for a cost projection as well.

request for qualifications: formal document asking companies or individuals to present their qualifications and experience records relative to a defined scope of work.

research: academic or applied investigations in disciplines relevant to a museum's collection or public programs.

research plan: proposal to undertake academic or applied investigations in a discipline relevant to part or all of a museum's collection or its public programs, including a budget and time estimate for its execution.

research policy: a statement of the museum's commitment to academic or applied investigations relevant to its collections and public programs; the levels of quality and priorities sought; and its realistic undertaking within budget limitations to provide the personnel, time, library, travel budget, and other resources required.

reserve collection: those works of art, artifacts, or specimens that are either pending assignment to **display** or **study collections**, are duplicate or secondary examples assigned to hands-on educational programs, or are objects pending deaccessioning.

reserves: funds retained for contingencies or for future development projects.

restoration: returning a building or artifact as far as possible or as far as desired to an earlier condition or appearance, sometimes (but not always) its original state, through repair, renovation, reconditioning, or other intervention.

restoration policy: a statement of the museum's philosophical intent in restoring works of art, artifacts, or specimens specifying standards of quality and levels of responsibility, including requirements for reversible processes and clear directives in regard to manifesting lacunae or wear in the original objects.

restoration procedures manual: a step-by-step document for the execution of the museum's **restoration policy**, including a statement of the responsibility of curators or conservators, the role of paid or volunteer workers, and requirement for both written and photographic documentation of all processes.

retreat: part of a strategic planning process consisting of extended meetings at which **trustees** and senior staff withdraw for a day or more to consider long-range directions and key issues and challenges both within the institution and in its global environment.

risk: possibility of occurrence of an event that may adversely affect the normal functions of an institution, which may be measured for a museum by assigning values to the **criticality** of a loss and the museum's vulnerability to it, and multiplying the criticality index by the vulnerability index.

risk analysis: calculation of the priority of security needs in terms of the possibility of all threats, the **criticality** of those threats, and the vulnerability of the institution to them.

risk management strategy: a plan that identifies threats to the collection and the measures that the museum takes to meet them.

room settings: a mode of presentation in which artifacts, works of art, or specimens are grouped as they would have been found in their original setting.

schedule: a plan with a calendar attached.

schematic design: the stage of planning a building or exhibition that follows on the **design concept** phase by developing drawings that indicate the contours and character of the building or exhibition according to the general requirements of the **functional brief or program** or **interpretative plan**, usually including floor plans and three-dimensional views (or presentation drawings) of each building or exhibition component (see also **design development**).

security: the entire range of activities concerned with the protection of the public, staff, and others in the museum, and especially the protection of the collections, from all threats to them.

security policy: a commitment of the museum to safekeeping of its assets, including a risk analysis, description and distribution of levels of security, health and safety precautions, security equipment (present and recommended), routine and emergency procedures, and insurance coverage and valuation.

security screws: threaded metal connectors intended to fasten the stretcher (not the frame) of a painting to a gallery wall by means of a metal "fishplate," operable only by screwdrivers specially fitted to turn in the heads, which are more complex than the usual slots or squares.

security station: a post where warders (or guards) may operate and observe closed-circuit TV systems, monitor alarms, and regulate entry and exit to the building.

self-generated revenue: funds earned by the museum's operations, including admissions, retail sales, catering, memberships, rentals, films, performances, special events, educational programs, publications, media, and contracted services.

set point: the condition to be attained and maintained by environmental control equipment, such as humidifiers or dehumidifiers.

simulator: apparatus for providing visitors with an experience of motion, usually presented in a thematic context when used in museums.

site selection: determination of the optimal location for a museum based on weighted evaluation of such factors as availability, access, audience development potential, cost of acquisition and development, funding opportunities, security considerations, building type, size and layout, parking, visibility, and compatibility of neighboring facilities.

smoke detectors: the preferred means of fire detection for museums, except in kitchens where heat detectors should be used.

snag list: a record of outstanding errors or shortcomings to be remedied by a contractor or fabricator.

specifications: detailed statement of work to be done by each contractor, materials to be used, standards to be met, procedures to be followed, matters of jurisdiction between contractors, procedures to resolve jurisdictional disputes, procedures for change orders, and so on, relating to an exhibition or a building project.

sponsorship: contributions of funds or donations in kind by corporations or individuals toward a specific project such as an exhibition or other program.

sprinklers: devices installed in the ceiling that respond to fire with a deluge of water.

staffing plan: a projection of requirements for personnel in order to operate the desired level of public programs with the collection resource identified.

statement of purpose: a concise identification of the functions of a museum in relation to the objects defined in its **mandate**.

storyboards: scene-by-scene illustrations of what the viewer will see on the screen or stage.

story line: consecutive theme of an exhibition or other museum program, sometimes but not necessarily narrative (see also **theme**).

strategic directions: in the strategic planning process, meaningful and memorable guidelines indicating the institution's approach or philosophy in resolving the **key issues** affecting that museum.

strategic plan: determination of the optimal future for an organization and the changes required to achieve that future.

study collection: a collection acquired for purposes of comparative or analytical research, usually intended for indefinite preservation.

summative evaluation: an assessment of the visitor experience of an exhibition or other museum program that considers the outcome in the context of the original **interpretative plan** to determine whether or not the exhibition actually communicated what it planned to communicate, and if so, how effectively this was accomplished.

sustainable tourism: hosting of foreign or domestic visitors, or providing programs for them, in such a way that their environmental footprint is reduced, or their impact is compensated, so that the attractions and other resources involved can be replenished.

systematic collection: artifacts or specimens selected to exemplify an entire range of significant types or variants within that collection category.

systematic mode: presentation of specimens or artifacts in which the comprehensiveness of the display and the information provided is intended to demonstrate all type variations.

target markets: those segments of the museum's actual or potential public that are identified as a priority on which the museum's programs should focus in order to increase and enhance levels of visitation.

task force: a group of individuals, usually from several departments, who cooperate to achieve a common aim, such as an exhibition.

technical program: the plans, drawings, and specifications of the architect and engineers that should meet the requirements of the **functional brief or program.**

tender (bid): a proposal to undertake work on contract.

tender documents: the detailed designs and specifications that are issued to competing contractors and that form the basis of the consequent contract with those who are awarded the contracts to undertake the construction, renovation, fabrication, installation, or other work necessary to complete a museum building or exhibition (see **bid documents**).

tendering: the process of issuing requests for tenders or bids on work to be contracted, evaluating the bids, negotiating, and awarding the contract.

terms of reference: a statement of mandate and requirements for a committee, a planning process, a program or a project.

thematic (or contextual) display: a mode of exhibition of works of art, specimens, or artifacts arranged to illustrate a **theme**, subject or **story line** in order to facilitate comprehension of their significance in relation to that theme, often employing graphic or other interpretative devices to place the objects in context for the visitor.

theme: connective statement or relationship among works of art, artifacts, or specimens that is articulated in an **exhibition plan** or **interpretative plan** as the core content that an exhibition or other museum program is intended to communicate.

time-sharing agreement: a partnership between a museum and a school administration whereby school parties have exclusive access during certain hours when the museum is not otherwise open, and the museum provides guided tours or other educational programs, in return for a set fee from the school district or a subsidy allocation from the relevant level of government.

training and development strategy: a plan agreed between the museum and the individual employee related both to the individual's needs for learning how to do his or her job to the requisite level of quality and his or her program of upgrading skills and capabilities for future advancement.

total design: the term that has been used to refer to ensuring that all aspects of a museum or an exhibition are designed to encourage access by all visitors, whatever their limitations. The museum's interpretative policy should include its commitment to these principles.

training programs: instruction for employees in how to do their job.

transit store (or temporary exhibition storage): an area in which works of art, artifacts, or specimens loaned to the museum for temporary exhibitions are to be held, with levels of security approximating those of the permanent collection store, since it is likely to be visited by couriers accompanying loans from other museums and must meet insurance and indemnity requirements.

trust: See **board**.

trustee: member of a **board** or trust in either a governing or advisory role.

trustees' manual: publication providing members of the museum's governing or advisory **board** with all relevant **mission, mandate,** and **policy** statements and the Board Constitution, as well as a history of the institution, current plans, staff organization charts, budgets and financial reports, board roles and responsibilities, and an outline of the committee structure.

turnkey contract: see **design/build**.

ultraviolet (UV) light: rays beyond the visible spectrum of light that are the chief cause of color fading and chemical changes due to exposure to light.

value engineering: reconsidering plans or design for a construction or renovation project in order to reduce capital costs.

vapor barrier: an impermeable barrier to prevent movement of water vapor into a building.

virtual reality: a simulated environment, usually computer-generated, intended to provide the visitor with meaningful and exciting experiences with which he or she may interact.

visible storage: provision of public access to part or all of a complete museum collection by means of systematic presentation of artifacts, specimens, or works of art as in closed storage, but presented in a public gallery, normally on shelves or in drawers behind or under glass, with publicly accessible catalogs providing interpretation either by means of laminated flip cards of entire catalog entries, or computer screens where similarly detailed information is available.

visitor analysis: both quantitative and qualitative analysis of the museum's present visitors, usually undertaken to determine visitor perceptions of and needs in the museum.

visitor responsiveness: the quality of visitor experience in all aspects of the museum's programs.

visitor services: activities directed at accommodating the visitor, including admissions, orientation, way-finding, retail and food services, toilets, rest areas, and customer care policies that affect the quality of the visitor experience and communicate the museum's attitude to its public.

volunteer: an unpaid employee whose rewards are in the form of personal development and social recognition for work done.

volunteer agreement (or contract): a signed commitment of the volunteer to the museum, and of the museum to the volunteer, making reference to all working conditions and schedules.

volunteer manual: a document that links the museum's mission and mandate to the museum's volunteer policy and to practical details pertaining to the daily work of volunteers, including all museum **policies** and **procedures** relevant to the volunteers' area of work.

volunteer policy: the museum's commitment to the recruitment, training, deployment, evaluation, and social rewards of unpaid museum workers.

vulnerability: the extent to which a work of art, artifact, specimen, or an entire museum collection is at risk.

warders (or guards): museum workers with the responsibility for security of the collection and safety of all persons in the museum.

work plan: a statement of **objectives** and resources together with a budget and a schedule for achieving particular tasks.

World Wide Web: a system for the organization of information on the Internet, using hypertext links, facilitating movement from one multimedia website to another.

zero-based budgeting: a method of projecting revenue and expenditures that requires museum managers to justify each allocation in relation to the programs it makes possible without reference to historical levels of service provision.

Index

institutions: educational, 68–69, 137; museums as learning/social, 13, 49; political, 64–65. *See also* arm's length institutions

insurance, 254; on buildings, 256; on collection, 255–56; on equipment, 256; fine arts, 255; liability, 256–57; on loans, 257

intellectual property, 76

interactive mode, 308

internal assessment, 308

International Conservation Network (ICN), 109

International Council of Museums (ICOM), 68; Code of Professional Ethics of, 26–27

International Council on Conservation (ICC), 68

Internet, 308

internships, 47

interpretation, 308; communication through, 130–31; management of, 136

job descriptions, 39–40, 309; of administration secretary, 286; of adult education managers, 281; of archivists, 270–71; of assistant curator, 266–67; of audiovisual technicians, 277; of bookings clerks, 279–80; of bookkeepers, 287; of building mangers, 287–88; of cataloger, 268; of CEO, 263–64; of chief of security, 290–91; of coat room supervisor, 289; of conservation scientists, 271–72; of conservation technicians, 272–73; of conservator, 272; of curator, 266; of curatorial assistant, 267; of data entry clerks, 268; of deputy director for administration, 285–86; of deputy director for external relations, 295; of deputy director for public programs, 265–66, 273; of development officers, 292–93; of development secretary, 293; of director of communications, 277–78; of director of information technology, 278; of director's secretary, 264; of education officers, 279; of educators, 281–82; of evaluation managers, 284–85; of executive assistant, 264–65; of exhibition designers, 274–75; of exhibitions officers, 274; of external affairs secretary, 295–96; of finance clerks, 287; of finance officer, 286–87; of food services manager, 290; of graphic designers, 276; of human resources manager, 291–92; of librarian, 269–70; of library technicians, 270; of maintenance workers, 288; of marketing managers, 283–84; of membership clerks, 294–95; of membership managers, 294; of museum theater manager, 276–77; of outreach manager, 282; of photographer, 269; of preparators, 275–76; of publications managers, 285; of public relations officers, 284; of reception/tickets/information desk clerks, 289–90; of registrar, 267–68; of rentals managers, 288; of retail managers, 293–94; of sales clerks, 294; of school programs manager, 280–81; of secretaries, 273–74; of security guards, 291; of studio managers, 280; of visitor services managers, 288–89; of volunteer coordinator, 282–83; of webmaster, 278

job titles, 30–40

labels, 132–33

lamps, 201

language(s): of functional briefs, 186–87; universal design and, 135

leadership, 309; toward goals, 8–10; for good management, 9, *9*

learning: adult/family programs for, 138–39; affective, 242; in museums, 13, 49, 136–37; outreach, 138; self-directed, 138–39

Le Laboratoire, 112

lenders, 196

liability, 309; of board members, 26; donated material and, 247–48; insurance, 256–57

librarian, 269–70

library: assistants, 45, 270; technician, 270

life-cycle costing, 200, 309

light: collections and, 104–5. *See also* ultraviolet light

line department museums, 309; board of, 15; earned revenues of, 14–15; examples of, 14; funding of, 14; mode of governance of, 14–15

listening, 75

loading dock, 197

loans: insurance on, 257; museum policy on, 89

location tracking methods, 99–100

Lord, Barry, 68, 136

Luce Foundation Center for American Art, 179–80, *180*

lunchroom, 233–34

lux: as defined, 309; level, 309

maintenance: budget for, 201–2; of museum buildings, 200–202; preventive, 202; workers, 288

public collection zone, 192, 314
public noncollection zone, 192, 314
public private partnership (PPP), 314
public programs: costs for, 253–54; deputy
    directors for, 273; division organization,
    34; evaluation, 175; management,
    109–40, *120*, 153–59, 163–66; as mis-
    leading, 83; plan, 59, 314; secretary,
    273–74
public relations officers, 284
publicity: word-of-mouth, 142. *See also*
    social networking

qualifications, request for, 316
quantity surveyor, 314

reception clerks, 289
redundancy, 314; capacity, 197; planning
    and, 197
registrar, 267–68
registration, 315
Registration Procedures Manual, 99
relative humidity (RH), 103, 195, 315; man-
    aging, 199
relocations, 60
renovations, 66
rentals: manager, 288; of museum space,
    235–36; picture/art, 230, 271, 313; serv-
    ices, 164–65; volume of, 236
repair: access for, 201; budget for, 201–2; of
    museum buildings, 200–202
*Report of the Commission on the Future of the
    Smithsonian Institution*, 96
reports: condition, 106, 300; qualitative
    analysis provided by, 63; regular, 62–63
representative collection, 315
request for proposals, 315
request for qualifications, 315
research: conservation, 108–9; curatorial,
    83–85; as defined, 153, 315; museum
    programs and, 83; plan, 84, 108, 155,
    315; policy, 83–84, 315
research assistants, 45
reserve collection, 87–88, 315
reserves, 315
restaurants. *See* food services
restoration: as defined, 315; of museum
    objects, 107–8; policy, 107–8, 316; proce-
    dures manual, 107, 316; technicians, 45
retail manager, 293–94
retail sales: clerks, 45; pricing for, 229; types
    of, 230–31
retail services, 163–64

retail shop: location of, 229–30; publica-
    tions/media in, 230
retailing services, 15
retreat(s), 316; in strategic planning process,
    58
revenue: admissions, 223; contributed, 241,
    302; earned, 222; generation, 217–21; of
    line department museums, 14–15; self-
    generated, 265, 317
RH. *See* relative humidity
rights: naming, 311. *See also* copyright
risk(s): analysis, 203–4, 316; defining, 316;
    evaluating, 204–5; management strategy,
    316; planning and, 55–56
rodents, 105
room settings, 316

SAAM. *See* Smithsonian American Art
    Museum
salaries, 252
sales clerks, 294
scan, environmental, 304
schedule, 316; monitoring, 10
schematic design, 126–27, 316
school groups: educational programs for,
    238–39; guides for, 138; lunch-room for,
    233–34; provision for, 137–38
school programs manager, 280–81
secretary: administration, 286; development,
    293; director's, 264; external affairs,
    295–96; public programs, 273–74
security, 163; building fabric and, 207–8;
    chief, 203, 290–91; of collections, 90; cost
    of, 236; as defined, 317; guards, 208–10,
    291; high, 140, 206, 307; levels of, 206–7,
    210–11; limited, 206; of museum
    grounds, 207; planning, 202–12; screws,
    210, 317; staff, 198; station, 208, 317;
    storage and, 141, 206, 307; unions for
    staff in, 43. *See also* alarms; security policy
security policy, 317; countermeasures identi-
    fied in, 205–6; delay and, 139, 302; deter-
    rence in, 139, 303; levels of security
    defined in, 206–7; risk analysis in, 203–4
self-directed learning, 138–39
self-generated revenue, 317
service(s): contracted, 240–41; educational,
    238–39; food, 165–66; museum, 22, 311;
    rental, 164–65; visitor, 62, 159, 166, 248,
    321. *See also* retail services
set point, 317
shipping and receiving bay, 197
simulators, 237, 317

27; manual for, 46, 321; promotion by, 259; role of, 25, 320

ultraviolet (UV) light, 105, 320
unions: difficulty with, 44; role of, 43–44; as supportive forces, 43
universal design, 135
UV light. *See* ultraviolet (UV) light

vacuums, 200–1
valuation, 256
value engineering, 321
vandalism, 204
vapor barrier, 321
vaults, 206
Victoria and Albert Museum, 55–57, 98
virtual reality, 321
visitors: analysis, 175, 321; characteristic of museum, 153; operations and experience of, 160–62; orientation, 131–32; research, 154–55; responsiveness, 109, 163, 321; services, 62, 159, 166, 321; services manager, 288–89; surveying, 15

volunteer(s): agreement, 46, 321; coordinator, 45–46, 282–83; individual development of, 45–46, 258; interviewing potential, 46; manual for, 46, 66, 321; for nonprofit organizations, 18; operating program for, 44–47; policy, 321; recruitment of, 46; role of, 44–47, 321; as school visit guides, 138; social recognition of, 44
vulnerability, 322

The Walters Art Museum, 225
warders, 322
webmaster, 278
websites, 142–43; social networking, 144
World Wide Web, 140, 323; trend in use of, 141–42

You Tube, 141–42; Guggenheim's use of, 145–46

zero-based budgeting, 322
zones, 191–92, 311, 314; normative space distributed by, *193*